Challenges to Democracy in the 21st Century

Series Editor
Hanspeter Kriesi
Department of Political and Social Science
European University Institute
San Domenico Di Fiesole, Firenze, Italy

Democracy faces substantial challenges as we move into the 21st Century. The West faces malaise; multi-level governance structures pose democratic challenges; and the path of democratization rarely runs smoothly. This series examines democracy across the full range of these contemporary conditions. It publishes innovative research on established democracies, democratizing polities and democracy in multi-level governance structures. The series seeks to break down artificial divisions between different disciplines, by simultaneously drawing on political communication, comparative politics, international relations, political theory, and political economy.

More information about this series at
http://www.palgrave.com/gp/series/14889

Regula Hänggli

The Origin
of Dialogue
in the News Media

Regula Hänggli
Department of Mass Media
and Communication Research
University of Fribourg
Fribourg, Switzerland

Challenges to Democracy in the 21st Century
ISBN 978-3-030-26581-6   ISBN 978-3-030-26582-3   (eBook)
https://doi.org/10.1007/978-3-030-26582-3

Cover credit: Paulo Gomez/Alamy Stock Vector

This Palgrave Macmillan imprint is published by the registered company Springer Nature
Switzerland AG
The registered company address is: Gewerbestrasse 11, 6330 Cham, Switzerland

Acknowledgements

This book emerged within the framework of the Swiss research program on democracy—the National Center of Competence in Research (NCCR) Democracy—which has used interdisciplinary research to investigate the Challenges to Democracy in the twenty-first century. Thus, I would like to thank the Swiss National Science Foundation and the University of Zurich, that jointly financed the NCCR Democracy program. My deep gratitude goes first to Hanspeter Kriesi for his generous support, and his enormous energy and drive, which paved the way for this work. It also goes to Laurent Bernhard for letting me be part of this journey, for meaningful (phone) discussions, and for many humorous moments. I would like to thank the former Swiss Federal Chancellor, Oswald Sigg, and the former Secretary-General of the parliament, Christoph Lanz, for the support they have given to our study. I would also like to thank Urs Dahinden, Jörg Matthes, Christian Schemer, and Werner Wirth for their contributions in the data collection and beyond. I am also very grateful to all the politicians, campaign managers, public officials, journalists, newspaper editors, and all respondents of the survey samples who were willing to devote their valuable time to answer our questions. The cooperation of all these people has allowed us to put together a truly exceptional data set, without which I would not have been able to describe the origin of dialogue in the news media, and its role in the opinion formation process.

I owe particular gratitude to Dennis Chong for invaluable publishing guidance, a very careful reading of the entire manuscript and for his thoughtful comments prompting considerable revision, while James Druckman has offered many precious comments and targeted pointers toward further literature. Furthermore, the book benefited from comments I received from anonymous reviewers, from exchanges at international conferences, from audiences at the universities of Amsterdam, Antwerp and Mannheim, at Aarhus University, the EUI in Florence, and at Northwestern University. I have profited from feedback from many colleagues, including André Bächtiger, Toby Bolsen, Amber Boydstun, Robert Entman, Jennifer Jerit, Gabriel Lenz, Wolf Linder, Steven Livingston, Arthur Lupia, Benjamin Page, Michael Schenk, and Rune Slothuus.

In countless ways, my academic and personal connections with Lene Aarøe, Peter Van Aelst, Camilla Bjarnøe, Sandra Bolsen, Matthias Gerth, Nathalie Giger, Christopher Green-Pedersen, Silja Häusermann, David Hopmann, Eva Buff Keller, Otfried Jarren, Yph Lelkes, Sophie Lecheler, Olga Litvyak, Ann Marshall, Peter Mortensen, Anne-Catherine de Perrot, Andreas Schuck, Peter Selb, Joost van Spanje, Marco Steenbergen, Rune Stubager, Knut de Swert, Penny Sheets Thibaut, Anke Tresch, Rens Vliegenthart, Claes de Vreese, Stefaan Walgrave, and Richard van der Wurff, and many more valuable encounters made this book even stronger. I wish to thank Sarah Mannion and Martin Simmonds for proofreading.

My heartfelt thanks goes to my family and friends. To Lisbeth, Urs, Silvan, Brigitte, Barbara, and Csongor, who bring together a healthy mixture of love, interest in my work, entrepreneurial thinking, and a sense of reality. To the Locher family for their love and confidence in me. To Charlotte, Roland (Deceased), Robin, Corinne, and Livia for their help and example of a sustainable lifestyle. Thanks to Nicole, Ben, Sara, Maja, and Sophia for making me feel I was not alone in balancing motherhood and profession, for exchanges about my book, and for friendship. To Lis for an expressive drawing (see conclusion). And last but not least, my deep gratitude goes to my beloved husband Jonas for having been at my side in all the phases of this book and discussing it with me time and time again, and to our beloved children for being here and giving me a sense of life far beyond the writing of books.

Baden   Regula Hänggli
June 2019

PRAISE FOR *THE ORIGIN OF DIALOGUE IN THE NEWS MEDIA*

"Hänggli investigates a fundamental topic: how elite rhetoric, through the presence or absence of dialogue, shapes citizens' understanding of the policy options before them. This book is novel both for its comprehensive theoretical treatment of the framing process as well its rich content analyses of Swiss direct-democratic campaigns."
—Jennifer Jerit, *Stony Brook University, USA*

"This is a refreshingly innovative conceptual and empirical contribution to the vast literature on political communications. Analyzing Swiss referendums, Hänggli shows how campaign dialogue is framed by the competing norms and interests of politicians, parties, and the media. Readers will gain valuable insights about the conditions promoting discussion, learning, and debate that are essential to the democratic process."
—Dennis Chong, *University of Southern California and Northwestern University, USA*

CONTENTS

Part III   Conclusion

LIST OF FIGURES

LIST OF TABLES

PART I

Introduction and Methodology

CHAPTER 1

Dialogue in the News Media

The people are powerless if they cannot choose between *alternatives*. Imagine that you—as an ordinary citizen and member of the public—are asked to participate in the decision-making process of, let us say, the asylum policy. What policy will you design? Unless you have expertise in the field, or have the time or motivation to become informed about this issue, you might feel that you are the wrong person to design such a policy. Schattschneider's statement makes this point: "Above everything, *the people are powerless if the political enterprise is not competitive.* It is the competition of political organizations that provides the people with the opportunity to make a choice. Without this opportunity, popular sovereignty amounts to nothing [...] *Democracy is a competitive political system in which competing leaders and organizations define the alternatives of public policy in such a way that the public can participate in the decision making process*" (Schattschneider 1988 [1960]: 137–138, emphasis in original).

He states that competing leaders define the alternatives, which allow the ordinary citizen to participate. I agree and understand the alternatives to mean both the options *and* their interpretations. Thus, imagine that the parliament (which consists of two chambers, the National Council similar to the US House of Representatives and the State Council similar to the US Senate) has prepared a new asylum law and you can decide whether or not you will accept it. As an ordinary citizen, it is easier to participate in this situation. In actual fact, in Switzerland,

© The Author(s) 2020
R. Hänggli, *The Origin of Dialogue in the News Media*,
Challenges to Democracy in the 21st Century,
https://doi.org/10.1007/978-3-030-26582-3_1

this happened and the people were able to vote on a new asylum law. This example from the real world serves to illustrate what I mean by options and interpretations. The options are either to accept or reject the new law, while interpretations we will look at below.

The new law contained these most important aspects: It stipulated that asylum requests from refugees who have already been given refugee status or some other form of protection by another state will not be dealt with. The new law also prohibited social assistance for refugees whose requests have been legally rejected. Moreover, it introduced more restrictive rules for considering the question of refugees without proper identification; it adopted a so-called airport procedure allowing for rapid decisions at the refugees' point of entry, and it enabled the possibility of exchanging information with the refugees' home countries. The new law also brought an improvement for asylum seekers with a provisional admission. They are allowed to work and to receive a residence permit for their families after three years. The interpretations of the leaders are part of the alternatives. Political leaders offered these interpretations (I shall call them frames, see below): Proponents of the new law argued that Switzerland needs instruments to fight the abuse of its asylum legislation (abuse), and that the new law provides a more efficient implementation of the asylum legislation (efficacy). Opponents claimed that the new asylum law is contrary to the humanitarian tradition of Switzerland (human. trad.), and that the provision of the new law undermines the rule of law (rule-of-law). Their interpretations make clear that the *new* law is more restrictive than the previous one. In the vote on the new asylum law, similarly to related previous votes in 1987 and 1999, the proposal for a new asylum law was accepted by two-thirds (67.7%) of the Swiss people (compared to 67.3% in 1987 and 70.6% in 1999). The first asylum law dates back to 1981 and was considered liberal. Previously, asylum matters were part of the law on foreigners. Over the years, the asylum law was gradually tightened. In this book, alternatives and their interpretations are of key importance and I will keep a constant eye on competing interpretations. I will raise the question: *Under what conditions do we see competing interpretations (= dialogue)?* As Schattschneider points out, the process of defining the alternatives is *competitive*. Political elites deploy arguments and attempt to steer thinking toward their point of view in order to gain an edge in partisan contests.

The alternatives need to be presented in the *news media*. Since, in our diverse society, the media play a vital role in conveying information from the political scene to the public, citizens get an important share of their information from the news media. In other words, democracy today is largely mediated democracy. People not only learn about the options and their interpretation directly from politicians (be it in person or impersonal contact like a speech on TV). They also learn about the alternatives *indirectly* through the media. They read about them in a newspaper report, or listen to a discussion about or summary of a political issue being presented in the news on the radio and TV. As a consequence, the alternatives (i.e., the yes or no choice and its interpretation) should also be found *in the news media.*

Thus, I investigate: *Under what conditions do we see dialogue (= competing interpretations) in the news media? What are the driving mechanisms?* To complete the picture, I will end with the question: *What is the role of dialogue in the Public Opinion formation process?*

TOOLS FOR THE STUDY: FRAMES AND DIALOGUE

This book investigates the origin of dialogue in the news media by *using frames.* A frame is defined as an interpretation of an issue, or a perspective on the topic. It is a central organizing idea that emphasizes certain aspects of a perceived reality (Entman 1993: 52) and "provide[s] coherence to a designated set of idea elements" (Ferree et al. 2002: 105). It is like a "spotlight" that attracts our attention to certain aspects of an issue and directs it away from other aspects (Gamson 2004: 245). By selectively emphasizing/evaluating certain facets of a perceived reality and by making them salient in a communicating text, frames also "promote a particular problem definition, causal interpretation, moral evaluation, and/or treatment recommendation for the item described" (Entman 1993: 52).[1] The framing approach is well suited for modeling a process with different actors involved. It has the great strength of enabling the behavior of elites, decisions of journalists, and choices of citizens to be

---

[1] In terms of Entman's frame definition, substantive frames focus mainly on problem definition. The other elements mentioned by Entman would be called reasoning devices by Gamson and Modigliani (1989: 3) and explain what should be done about the problem. Framing devices, as opposed to frames, are condensing symbols that suggest the frame in shorthand (Gamson and Modigliani 1989: 3). They include metaphors, illustrative examples (from which lessons are drawn), catchphrases, descriptions, and visual images (icons). What Iyengar (1991) calls "episodic" frames, I would call a framing device.

linked. Contending elites compete to establish the meaning and inter-pretation of issues in the news media or in the public. Journalists edit the information, add to it, and offer help for opinion formation, and citizens who engage with an issue must grapple with opposing frames and decide what their individual cognitive understanding is of a given situation. In this way, frames serve as the *conceptual bridge* (Scheufele 1999) between organizing ideas in presented news (for instance, the aspects of an issue emphasized in elite discourse) and comprehended news (for instance, the aspect of an issue a citizen thinks is the most important). In this sense, frames are interpretative structures embedded in political discourse and, at the same time, also live inside the minds of individuals.

Let me illustrate the definition of a frame. With respect to the direct-democratic vote on the asylum law, the argument that the new asylum law is contrary to the humanitarian tradition belongs to the "humanitarian tradition" frame (human. trad.). All similar arguments, i.e., arguments that focus on this aspect, are also categorized under this frame. This is shown in Table 1.1. The arguments are grouped and coded based on their position, i.e., whether they are pro or con arguments. All of these arguments are categorized as "humanitarian tradition" frame irrespec-tive of their position, i.e., independent of whether an argument is for or against the new law. The same procedure is used for all arguments. If not otherwise stated, I use argument as a synonym for frame. In this sense, I mean the group of similar arguments belonging to one frame.

The struggle between alternatives can be more or less *dialogical*. Dialogue occurs when competing leaders and organizations talk directly about each other's interpretations or discuss the same interpretations of an issue, rather than rerouting (or displacing) the discussion to focus on alternative interpretations. The opposite of dialogue is the *absence* of opposing viewpoints and a *monologue* about one's own viewpoints, as is the case in (one-sided) propaganda. *Dialogue* looks at *all main* interpre-tations in a campaign and investigates how far the two camps converge on them. I will use convergence as a synonym for dialogue. Dialogue includes the idea of competing interpretations and looks at the exchange and convergence around these. Let me illustrate my understanding of dia-logue based on the asylum law in Table 1.2. There are four important different interpretations: humanitarian tradition, rule-of-law, abuse, and efficacy. Opponents of the new law came up with the first two, while proponents offered the second two. In situation 1, there is a maximum degree of dialogue (Dialogue = 100). Opponents (contra camp) and pro-ponents (pro camp) of the new law discuss each other's interpretations to

Table 1.1 Illustration of frame definition: the humanitarian tradition frame in the asylum law

Humanitarian tradition frame			
Pro arguments	Frame	Con arguments	Frame
Humanitarian tradition *in general*		Humanitarian tradition *in general*	
Human dignity, conformity with human rights, no human rights violation		Human dignity/human rights/principle of humanity in danger	
Law corresponds to Swiss tradition	Human. trad.: defensive use	Law is un-Swiss/contradicts Swiss tradition	Human. trad.: offensive use
Conformity with children's rights convention		Children's rights in danger/UN children's rights convention (also separation of children and parents in detention)	
Improvement of social and cultural quality		Improvement of social and cultural quality	
Conformity with religious norms		Religious norms in danger	
		The basic rights of asylum seekers must be protected	
Other *specific* ethical/humanitarian pro argument		Other *specific* ethical/humanitarian argument	

the same extent. In order to measure dialogue, I use a measure developed by Sigelman and Buell (2004) and Kaplan et al. (2006). This dialogue measure works with the absolute differences between the two camps in the share of attention each camp devoted to a certain frame, divides the sum by 2 in order to calibrate the measure to the range between 0 and 100, and subtracts that sum from 100 in order to convert the measure to one of similarity rather than dissimilarity (see Appendix for formula). Monologue appears in situation 2 (Dialogue = 0). Here, proponents concentrate exclusively on the abuse interpretation, opponents focus exclusively on a different interpretation (humanitarian tradition), and both sides ignore third interpretations (efficacy, rule-of-law). Obviously, no

Table 1.2 Three situations with different degrees of dialogue

	Situation 1: fully dialogical		Situation 2: fully monological		Situation 3: asylum law (news media)	
	Contra camp	Pro camp	Contra camp	Pro camp	Contra camp	Pro camp
Human. trad.	25	25	100	0	48	25
Rule-of-law	25	25	0	0	15	8
Abuse	25	25	0	100	26	46
Efficacy	25	25	0	0	12	21
Total (%)	100	100	100	100	101	100
Dialogue	100		0		70	

dialogue occurs, and each side talks about its own interpretations here. Situation 3 is what actually occurred in the news media regarding the asylum law. It is highly dialogical (Dialogue $= 70$, resulting from $100 - ((\,|\,48 - 25\,| + |\,15 - 8\,| + |\,26 - 46\,| + |\,12 - 21\,|\,)/2)$. In this situation, each camp mostly presents its own interpretations, but engages also with the interpretations offered by the other camp. The observed clustering of scores around 70 indicates that, on average, the attention profiles of the competing sides were seven-tenths of the way toward perfect convergence. In this instance, only about 30% of the proponents' attention would have had to be reallocated to bring about a perfect match with the opponents, or vice versa.

As mentioned, my understanding of dialogue is inspired by Sigelman and Buell (2004) and Kaplan et al. (2006). According to their understanding, dialogue means convergence on the same issue(s). Their studies are at the issue level. In my study, the issue is given and we look at the exchange of arguments about this issue between two camps. Thus, dialogue investigates the *argument* level. In this regard, my definition comes close to the understanding put forward by Simon (2002: 22, 107), who defined (sustained) dialogue as responding to the opponent's claims and also discussing the minority opinion of an issue. It also comes close to the understanding used by Jerit (2008, 2009). She defines dialogue as issue engagement (focusing on the same consideration) or direct rebuttal (a statement making the opposite prediction).

The value of 70 is very high. Simon (2002), who analyzed US Senate Campaigns, reports relatively low levels of dialogue. He finds that dialogue occurs in less than 20% of discussions in a race. Kaplan et al. (2006) also observe a relatively low value of 25 (standard deviation 35) in US Senate Campaigns. By contrast, Sigelman and Buell (2004) report a relatively high mean value of 75 in US presidential campaigns. Franz (2014: 17) concludes that convergence rates often are higher in presidential campaigns than in Senate campaigns. Nevertheless, our value is higher because Sigelman and Buell and Kaplan et al. look at the extent to which two sides talk about the same issue without looking at the *content* about that issue. Simon's analysis (and mine as well) includes the *content* about one issue, i.e., the extent to which one reads about both perspectives (pro and con). In our cases, we would have a value of 100 in the way Sigelman and Buell and Kaplan et al. measured dialogue because every statement is about the same issue. Thus, we go beyond the issue level and look at the extent of political discussion and debate about a topic.

Of course, dialogue has many more connotations and denotations, which extend beyond competing camps talking about each other's arguments or discussing the same aspects of an issue. A concept related to dialogue is deliberation. Deliberation—it is argued—requires mutual civility and respect for the opinions of others, as conditions that enable and support the exchange and justification of arguments (Bächtiger et al. 2010; De Vries et al. 2010; Habermas 1996; Wessler 2008; Zhang et al. 2013). My standards here are somewhat lower. The actors are not expected to ultimately agree on arguments, to act respectfully, or to justify their argumentation. My approach is also less demanding than the approach of Bennett et al. (2004), who use the concept of "responsiveness", i.e., mutual reactions from the opposing political actors. Their concept entails not only that a political actor uses the opponents' arguments but also that he *identifies* the source of the opponents' message. For our purposes, it is crucial that the audience learns about the position of a political actor on each message and that a set of messages from both camps are discussed in the news media. It is less important that the actors refer to each other.

The Importance of Dialogue in the News Media

Dialogue in the news media matters for a number of reasons. First, dialogue is relevant for the opinion formation process. The presence of competing arguments increases the likelihood that citizens will choose the alternative that is consistent with their values and predispositions

(Zaller 1992; Sniderman and Theriault 2004; Chong and Druckman 2007a). In addition, individuals are more motivated to engage in conscious evaluation when they are exposed to opposing considerations addressing the same aspect of an issue (Chong and Druckman 2007b). Furthermore, competition fosters political judgment (Chong and Druckman 2007c: 639, 651): It can moderate ideological extremes; it prompts people to consider which argument is the most applicable and to make their judgments based on the persuasiveness of a message (not merely on its frequency of repetition). More specifically, Benz and Stutzer (2004) show that direct democracy in Switzerland and the EU makes voters better informed. Colombo (2016: 147; 2018) supports the argument that direct-democratic campaigns (with their dialogical character) have a positive effect on public opinion with findings from the real world of Swiss direct-democratic campaigns: "[T]he provision of information during the campaign, by media and elite actors, is crucial". There was no measure of dialogue at her disposal but she shows that an intense campaign (with arguments from both sides) increases the quality of decision-making process. In addition, she can show that 70% of the interviewees were able to justify their decision with at least one argument. Post-vote opinion polls also show that arguments play a decisive role, with the main arguments of the analyzed campaigns also being the important ones used to justify the voters' decisions (Hirter and Linder 2008; Milic and Scheuss 2006; Engeli et al. 2008). Indeed, Wirth et al. (2011: 202) showed that in the direct-democratic campaigns analyzed here, arguments "play a decisive role in determining the voting outcome".

Second, dialogue can help to ensure that democracy works well. This point is relevant for scholars who recommend a realistic model of democracy. In such a perspective, in order for democracy to function well citizens must be able to become informed (e.g., Schudson 1998, 2000). Citizens "monitor" or "scan" the political and social environment and are ready to take action if it is needed. In line with the statement above by Schattschneider (1988 [1960]), the idea is that clear position-taking by politicians and clashes between their views are prerequisites for an informed democratic choice.

Third, dialogue is relevant for democratic theory, which conceives citizens' preferences to be formed *endogenously* to the political process (=within the political process) (Chong and Druckman 2011; Disch 2011). In particular, we need to know more about the ability of elites to shape the news (Druckman et al. 2013). In this view, citizens' preferences are not formed exogenously (as many have thus far assumed), but are rather formed based on the content of news. Thus, elites' strategies of communications, conditions that moderate elite influence, and generally the factors that influence the presence of alternatives in the news media are relevant for gaining a better understanding of the public–elite interactions.

Fourth, dialogue in the news provides a counterbalance to possible "filter bubbles" (Pariser 2011), "echo chambers" (Sunstein 2001), or "cyber apartheid" (Putnam 2000). These concepts refer to the risk of fragmentation, allowing people to sort themselves into homogeneous groups, which often results in them receiving news tailored to their own interests and prejudices, amplifying their preexisting view. Dialogue in the news media is a counterbalance in the sense that people are confronted with unsought, unanticipated, and even unwanted ideas, and dissenting people.

Fifth, dialogue in the news media not only counterbalances "echo chambers" in social media; it can also work as a corrective to interpersonal communication where citizens mainly talk to like-minded people. It increases tolerance among people and awareness of the rationale behind one's own and oppositional views (Mutz 2006). Mutz (2006) showed for personal discussion networks that the most interested and politically knowledgeable citizens are the least likely to be exposed to oppositional viewpoints in personal discussion networks. Thus, it is essential that these citizens are exposed to oppositional viewpoints in the news media.

Sixth, we know surprisingly little about the strategic use of dialogue in debates, even though dialogue can be a clever strategy, as Jerit (2008) illustrated. She found considerable evidence of dialogue for the 1993–1994 healthcare reform debate and showed that dialogue can be effective, particularly for the pro camp. Thus, political actors have reasons to engage in dialogue, and convergence on a message can be a successful strategy.

Seventh, majorities formed on the basis of public dialogue tend to be more legitimate than simple majorities (Simon 2002; Fishkin 1991, 1992; Chambers 2009; Disch 2011) because a decision based on the preceding debate in the public is more likely to represent the authentic will of the public. Furthermore, if minorities can contribute to the discussion and influence the decision in their favor, dialogue can reduce inequality and empower minorities or the have-nots.

Eighth, examining dialogue in the news media is also relevant in terms of the health of democracy. Understanding the level of dialogue in the news speaks directly to concerns that the increased profit orientation, the entertainment-oriented presentation of information, or the conglomeration of news media owners is unhealthy for democracy and jeopardizes the offer of alternatives.

Ninth, dialogue increases the likelihood that diverse ideas are present. The presence of diverse ideas is the basis for high innovation rates, collective intelligence, and societal resilience (Helbing 2016; Page 2008). In other words, dialogue increases the likelihood that good solutions to societal problems are found.

The Main Thesis of the Book

The main thesis of the book is that dialogue in the news media occurs as a result of choices taken by the involved actors, i.e., the elites and journalists. In this sense, dialogue is a desirable but not necessarily intended outcome. Besides the actors' choices, certain campaign characteristics are the key driving mechanisms. To work out the mechanisms that drive dialogue in the media, I use a procedural model. In Chapter 2, I will introduce this theoretical framework of the study (frame building model) and suggest that the level of dialogue is dependent on the political actors' constructing choices, on their promoting choices, and on journalists' choices. The model of frame building yields six core hypotheses:

1. Dialogue in the news media occurs because political actors strategically choose to discuss each other's interpretation and because they concentrate on substance to a good extent. Campaign characteristics additionally influence the level of dialogue. Issue complexity and imbalance in financial resources handicaps dialogue, whereas issue familiarity and expected closeness of vote outcome increases dialogue (Chapter 4).
2. A good level of dialogue can be explained by the anticipatory effect of media on the part of political actors. In order to test this hypothesis, I will distinguish between mediated (media input, i.e., press releases and documents written for media conferences, and letters to the editor), unmediated (political advertisements and direct mail) and internal (info for members) channels. In the mediated channels, campaigners must cater to the needs and values of

journalists. If the political actors anticipate the media logic, they behave differently in the mediated channels. Thus, I expect to find a higher level of dialogue here (Chapter 4).

3. Dialogue stays high because of a constant effort by the political actors to attract news coverage and a constant behavior of political actors over time (Chapter 5). In order to attract news coverage during the whole campaign period, the campaigners produce routine staged events actively and reactively. If they become reactive, they react to events in their own camp, to the opponent, to the media, and to facts. In all their activities, the political actors want the audience to learn about their position and thus repeat their messages over time. Therefore, they stay on message, and as a result, I find no concentration on a smaller number of interpretations in the mediated channels over time.

4. By deciding on their choices, journalists also contribute to the dialogue in the news (Chapter 6). In particular, journalists balance out the messages of each camp in all the three campaigns we will look at. In this way, they ensure that both camps can bring in their interpretations and enforce a journalistic norm of presenting their audience with competing positions. The journalists mainly stay within the range of views presented by the political actors and discreetly bring in their own interpretations. This promotes dialogue because the concentration on main frames allows dialogue to take place. Journalists can challenge views, can interview key players, and confront them with counter-frames. With regard to differences between media types, we find less dialogue in free news media.

5. In direct-democratic campaigns, there is a relatively clear order in the flow of information (Chapter 7). The political actors prepare the main interpretations in the media releases and have the lead in the debate. The journalists can focus on confronting perspectives and on challenging views. This division of work might also contribute to dialogue. Furthermore, it is also relatively clear that direct-democratic campaigns are important. This means that political actors and journalists make an effort and engage in the discussion. In addition, the involved actors know when campaigns take place and when they are covered. It is routine action and they can concentrate on the discussion. Both aspects might also be supportive for dialogue.

6. Direct-democratic campaigns are relevant for the opinion formation process (Chapter 8). The arguments from both sides
in the news media help the voter to vote in line with his or her
preferences.

EMPIRICAL EVIDENCE

In Chapter 2, I will introduce my theoretical framework of the study, the
frame-building model. It suggests that the level of dialogue is dependent
on the political actors' choices in the construction and promotion phase
and on journalists' choices in the edition phase. The remaining part of
the book is empirical in nature.

Chapter 3 introduces the design of the study (incl. Swiss direct
democracy, relevant policy domain, relevant cases, main frames, and
campaign selection) and data. In order to analyze the three relevant processes in frame building in direct-democratic campaigns—frame construction and frame promotion by the political actors, and the frame
edition by the journalists—I rely on a rich data set and use different types
of data.[2] The content analysis is most important. In all three campaigns,
I conducted a content analysis of media input (=press releases and documents written for media conferences), political advertisements, letters to
the editor, and of the media's news reporting. Additionally, direct mails
and information for members were coded in one campaign (asylum law).
All material was coded in the same manner, with three levels of analysis—the level of the article, the political actor or journalist, and the argument (for details, see Appendix). To explore the framing strategies of
the *political actors*, I occasionally also rely on data collected in interviews
with these actors. The relevant organizations were identified on the basis
of various sources: the parliamentary debates, the campaign for the collection of signatures, voting recommendations, the press, and Web sites
more generally. I used cross-checks with the persons we interviewed in
order to complete the set of relevant actors.

In Chapter 4, I will look at how political actors craft their messages for press releases and media conferences (=media input). By

[2]A group of researchers from mass communication and political science collected
these data together. This research belongs to a national center of competence in research
(<http://www.nccr-democracy.uzh.ch/>, March 2019), which has been financed by the
Swiss National Science Foundation (for the design of the study, see Hänggli et al. 2012a).

constructing their message, I will argue that political actors decide strategically on at least three framing choices ("Substantive Emphasis Choice", "Oppositional Emphasis Choice", and "Contest Emphasis Choice"). Chapter 5 will investigate the frame *promotion* process. In this process, I suggest that the political actors are concerned about how they can spread their message the furthest and maximize the impact of their campaign. The promotion effort can include both the variations of the strategic framing choices in the different communication channels and over time. The media input is the baseline channel because, as I will argue in Chapter 5, it is the most important channel in frame building. The variation in different communication channels also tells us the extent to which the political actors adapt their strategies to the media logic. Moreover, by promoting their message, the political actors think about how they can continuously garner media attention and bring their message into the media *during* the whole campaign. Instruments of direct democracy are well developed in Switzerland (Kriesi and Trechsel 2008: 49) and all actors involved know exactly how it works. Thus, it is routine action, and commonly resources restrict the political actors from substantially changing their strategy during a campaign. By discussing the variation of the framing choices over time, I will argue that promotion practices used in direct-democratic campaigns are used such that a frame finds media attention during the whole campaign.

The contribution of journalists is analyzed separately in the final process of frame building, called the frame *edition* process (Chapter 6). I consider the journalists and the media as an active element in society. In such a way, journalists have to select, process, and interpret stimuli from the environment (Schulz 1989: 142). I will look at the choices made by journalists and suggest four choices which journalists decide upon ("Balancing Choice", "Range of Views Choice", "Story Choice" and "Interpretation Choice"). I find dialogue to be the result of all of these choices.

In Chapter 7, I will look at the *flow of frames*. In a first step, I will argue that the frame-building process is highly asymmetrical. Frames promoted by political actors in their media input influence media frames more strongly than vice versa. In a second step, I will investigate the importance of the media input for frame building in comparison with the influence of other channels. Then, I will look at *how much* media attention direct-democratic campaigns receive and *when* they are covered (effort and timing routines). Finally, I will investigate framing effects

(Chapter 8) and the *strengths of frames in communication*. I will compare the new measure of a strong frame in communication to the commonly used measure of a strong frame in thought. I will also explore the relative importance of the framing-based (=systematic) path of opinion formation process in comparison with the partisan heuristic path.

IMPLICATIONS

The insights of this book are relevant to all situations in which we would like to have competing messages and dialogue in the media, such as when citizens need to form their own opinion or need to participate in ordinary political processes (e.g., following or influencing parliamentary debates), or in elections. The first argument is that dialogue in the news media is more likely if the debate becomes similar to a debate of direct democracy, i.e., if the discussion is restricted to one issue (or a few issues), if the topic is salient, if political actors from two sides are involved, and if the duration is limited. These insights are not new, but can be deduced from the existing literature (Kaplan et al. 2006; Simon 2002). The focus chosen in this book allows controlling for these factors and going beyond existing insights. I can identify more mechanisms that further stimulate dialogue. The second argument is that dialogue is more likely if the issue is simple and familiar, if the financial resources are balanced, and if the race is expected to be close. Third, dialogue is more likely if communication is mediated. Fourth, dialogue is sustained if political actors stay on message. Finally, dialogue is more likely if journalists balance out the efforts of the political actors.

Since the book builds on studies for which the role of the elite is central (e.g., work on the indexing hypothesis, failure of the press), the findings are applicable to public debates or campaigns that involve a leading role of the elite, or in which the control by the elite is crucial. We can learn from this study that dialogue can occur with the participation of such a powerful actor as the government. However, in line with the indexing hypothesis, we also see that the range of views is more or less set by the range of views of the powerful actors.

Furthermore, the insights of this book show the importance of free and independent media, their norms, and their implications (anticipation effect of these norms on political actors) for dialogue. We have to take care of these norms and implications. They are helpful for the whole opinion formation process. It also speaks to concerns regarding the health of democracy or to people who conclude that the media are in crisis. Journalists contribute to the process of news-building in a later step. Consequently, a possible profit orientation or entertainment orientation, or the conglomeration of news media owners, is not primarily a problem for the range of arguments (except the debate is about media policy, or other topics in which media organizations have own interests) in these debates. In addition, the results are important for framing studies. "To turn the concept [framing] into a viable research avenue, future research should specify the conditions under which frames emerge" (De Vreese 2005: 60). In this regard, Ferree et al. (2002: 296) state that "the relative roles of parties and movements in taking leadership roles in framing issues in the media is an important and understudied aspect". By focusing exclusively on framing and the effects of framing on public opinion or on voters, the whole question of how frames originate is sidestepped. Finally, this study speaks to studies on political representation. It supports the normative argument that political representation is intrinsic to democratic government (Disch 2011). In the cases of our study, the set of alternatives is defined by political actors and journalists. Thus, it is unlikely that citizens' preferences are endogenous. Citizens rather form preferences based on these alternatives present in the news media and further spread by interpersonal communication.

References

Bächtiger, A., Niemeyer, S., Neblo, M., Steenbergen, M., & Steiner, J. (2010). Symposium: Toward More Realistic Models of Deliberative Democracy Disentangling Diversity in Deliberative Democracy—Competing Theories, Their Blind Spots and Complementarities. *The Journal of Political Philosophy, 18*(1), 32–63.

Bennett, W. L., Pickard, V. W., Iozzi, D. P., Schroeder, C. L., Lagos, T., & Caswell, E. C. (2004). Managing the Public Sphere: Journalistic Construction of the Great Globalization Debate. *International Communication Association, 54*(3), 437–455.

Benz, M., & Stutzer, A. (2004): Are Voters Better Informed When They Have a Larger Say in Politics? Evidence for the European Union and Switzerland. *Public Choice, 119*(1), 31–59.

Chambers, S. (2009): Rhetoric and the Public Sphere: Has Deliberative Democracy Abandoned Mass Democracy? *Political Theory, 37*(3), 323–350.

Chong, D., & Druckman, J. N. (2007a). Framing Public Opinion in Competitive Democracies. *American Political Science Review, 101*(4), 637–656.

Chong, D., & Druckman, J. N. (2007b). A Theory of Framing and Opinion Formation in Competitive Elite Environments. *Journal of Communication, 57*(1), 99–118.

Chong, D., & Druckman, J. N. (2007c). Framing Theory. *Annual Review of Political Science, 10,* 103–126.

Chong, D., & Druckman, J. N. (2011). Public-Elite Interactions: Puzzles in Search of Researchers. In R. Y. Shapiro & L. R. Jacobs (Eds.), *The Oxford Handbook of the American Public Opinion and the Media*. Oxford: Oxford University Press.

Colombo, C. (2016). *Partisan, Not Ignorant—Citizens' Use of Arguments and Justifications in Direct Democracy* (PhD thesis). European University Institute, Florence.

Colombo, C. (2018). Justifications and Citizen Competence in Direct Democracy: A Multilevel Analysis. *British Journal of Political Science, 48*(3), 787–806.

De Vreese, C. (2005). News Framing: Theory and Typology. *Information Design Journal + Document Design, 13*(1), 51–62.

De Vries, R., Stanczyk, A., Wall, I. F., Uhlmann, R., Damschroder, L. J., & Kim, S. Y. (2010). Assessing the Quality of Democratic Deliberation: A Case Study of Public Deliberation on the Ethics of Surrogate Consent for Research. *Social Science and Medicine, 70*(12), 1896–1903.

Disch, L. (2011). Toward a Mobilization Conception of Democratic Representation. *American Political Science Review, 105*(1), 100–114.

Druckman, J. N., Peterson, E., & Slothuus, R. (2013). How Elite Partisan Polarization Affects Public Opinion Formation. *American Political Science Review, 107*(1), 57–79.

Engeli, I., Anouk, L., & Nai, A. (2008). Analysis of the Federal Votes of June 1, 2008 (Analyse der eidgenössischen Abstimmungen vom 1. Juni 2008). *Vox Analysis.*

Entman, R. M. (1993). Framing: Toward Clarification of a Fractured Paradigm. *Journal of Communication, 43,* 51–58.

Ferree, M Marx, Gamson, W. A., Gerhards, J., & Rucht, D. (2002). *Shaping Abortion Discourse Democracy and the Public Sphere in Germany and the United States*. Cambridge: Cambridge University Press.

Fishkin, J. S. (1991). *Democracy and Deliberation: New Directions for Democratic Reform.* New Haven: Yale University Press.

Fishkin, J. S. (1992). *The Dialogue of Justice: Toward a Self-Reflective Society.* New Haven: Yale University Press.

Franz, M. M. (2014). Interest Group Issue Appeals: Evidence of Issue Convergence in Senate and Presidential Elections, 2008–2014. *Forum, 12*(4), 685–712.

Gamson, W. A. (2004). Bystanders, Public Opinion, and the Media. In D. A. Snow, S. A. Soule, & H. Kriesi (Eds.), *The Blackwell Companion to Social Movements* (pp. 242–261). Oxford: Blackwell.

Gamson, W. A., & Modigliani, A. (1989). Media Discourse and Public Opinion on Nuclear Power: A Constructionist Approach. *The American Journal of Sociology, 95*(1), 1–37.

Habermas, J. (1996). *Between Facts and Norms: Contributions to a Discourse Theory of Law and Democracy.* New Baskerville: MIT Press.

Hänggli, R., Schemer, C., & Rademacher, P. (2012a). Toward a Methodological Integration in the Study of Political Campaign Communication. In H. Kriesi (Ed.), *Political Communication in Direct Democratic Campaigns: Enlightening or Manipulating?* (pp. 39–53). Hampshire: Palgrave Macmillan.

Helbing, D. (2016). Why We Need Democracy 2.0 and Capitalism 2.0 to Survive. *Jusletter IT, 2016,* 65–74.

Hirter, H., & Linder, W. (2008). Analysis of the Federal Votes of February 24, 2008 (Analyse der eidgenössischen Abstimmungen vom 24. Februar 2008). *Vox Analysis.* Berne: University of Berne.

Iyengar, S. (1991). *Is Anyone Responsible? How Television Frames Political Issues.* Chicago: The University of Chicago Press.

Jerit, J. (2008). Issue Framing and Engagement: Rhetorical Strategy in Public Policy Debates. *Political Behaviour, 30,* 1–24.

Jerit, J. (2009). How Predictive Appeals Shape Policy Opinions. *American Journal of Political Science, 53*(2), 411–426.

Kaplan, N., Park, D. K., & Ridout, T. N. (2006). Dialogue in American Campaigns? An Examination of Issue Convergence in Candidate Television Advertising. *American Journal of Political Science, 50*(3), 724–736.

Kriesi, H., & Trechsel, A. H. (2008). *The Politics of Switzerland.* Cambridge: Cambridge University Press.

Milic, T., & Scheuss, U. (2006). Analysis of the Federal Votes of September 24, 2006 (Analyse der eidgenössischen Abstimmungen vom 24. September 2006). *Vox Analysis.* Zurich: University of Zurich.

Mutz, D. (2006). *Hearing the Other Side: Deliberative Versus Participatory Democracy.* New York: Cambridge University Press.

Page, S. E. (2008): *The Difference: How the Power of Diversity Creates Better Groups, Firms, Schools, and Societies.* Princeton, NJ: Princeton University Press.

Pariser, Eli. (2011). *The Filter Bubble: What the Internet Is Hiding from You.* New York: Penguin Press.

Putnam, R. (2000). *Bowling Alone: On the Internet's Social Capital.* New York: Simon & Schuster.

Schattschneider, E. E. (1988 [1960]). *The Semisovereign People: Realist's View of Democracy in America.* South Melbourne: Wadsworth Thomson Learning.

Scheufele, D. A. (1999). Framing as a Theory of Media Effects. *Journal of Communication, 49*(1), 103–122.

Schudson, M. (1998). *The Good Citizen: A History of American Civic Life.* Cambridge: Harvard University Press.

Schudson, M. (2000, Spring). Overcoming Voter Isolation: Citizenship Beyond the Polls. *The Responsive Community, 38*–45.

Schulz, W. (1989). Massenmedien und Realität. *Kölner Zeitschrift für Soziologie und Sozialpsychologie, Sonderheft, 30,* 135–149.

Sigelman, L., & Buell, E. H. (2004). Avoidance or Engagement? Issue Convergence in U.S. Presidential Campaigns, 1960–2000. *American Journal of Political Science, 48*(4), 650–661.

Simon, A. (2002). *The Winning Message: Candidate Behavior, Campaign Discourse, and Democracy.* New York: Cambridge University Press.

Sniderman, P. M., & Theriault, S. M. (2004). The Structure of Political Argument and the Logic of Issue Framing. In P. M. Sniderman & S. M. Theriault (Eds.), *Studies in Public Opinion: Attitudes, Nonattitudes, Measurement Error and Change* (pp. 133–165). Princeton, NJ: Princeton University Press.

Sunstein, C. R. (2001). *Republic.com.* Princeton, NJ: Princeton University Press.

Wessler, H. (2008). Investigating Deliberativeness Comparatively. *Political Communication, 25*(1), 1–22.

Wirth, W., Matthes, J., & Schemer, C. (2011). When Campaign Messages Meet Ideology: The Role of Arguments for Voting Behaviour. In H. Kriesi (Ed.), *Political Communication in Direct Democratic Campaigns: Enlightening or Manipulating?* (pp. 188–204). New York: Palgrave Macmillan.

Zaller, J. R. (2005 [1992]). *The Nature and Origin of Public Opinion.* Cambridge: Cambridge University Press.

Zhang, W., Cao, X., & Tram, M. N. (2013). The Structural Features and the Deliberative Quality of Online Discussions. *Telematics and Informatics, 30*(2), 74–86.

CHAPTER 2

Origin of Dialogue:
A Model of Frame Building

GENERAL APPROACH

My general approach for conceptualizing the relationship between political actors and the media is an actor-centered political process model, as introduced by Wolfsfeld (1997). Thus, I conceive the political actors as the first source of influence in frame building, in contrast to Scheufele (1999, 2000), who seems to adopt a more journalistic-centered view. Following Wolfsfeld's (1997) lead, I believe that the best way to understand the role of the news media is to view it as part of a larger contest among political antagonists for control of the public agenda and the public's interpretation of specific policy issues. Given the crucial role of the news media in reaching out to the citizens, the struggle for attention and for the meaning of political issues becomes a struggle for control of the news agenda and for the framing of the news. The relationship between political actors and the news media is one of mutual dependence: Political actors need the media to reach the public, while the media need the input of the political actors for their news production. As Wolfsfeld (1997: 13) puts it, their relationship is one of "competitive symbiosis", "in which each side of the relationship attempts to exploit the other while expending a minimum amount of costs". Or, as Gans (1979: 116) pointed out in an often-cited quote: "The relationship between sources and journalists resembles a dance, for sources seek access to journalists, and journalists seek access to sources".

© The Author(s) 2020
R. Hänggli, *The Origin of Dialogue in the News Media*,
Challenges to Democracy in the 21st Century,
https://doi.org/10.1007/978-3-030-26582-3_2

But, significantly, Gans went on to stress that this relationship was likely to be an asymmetrical one, too: "Although it takes two to tango, either sources or journalists can lead, but more often than not, sources do the leading". Wolfsfeld's (1997: 3) key hypothesis makes the same point: The political process is likely to be the driving force in this relationship. The reasons he provides for this hypothesis are numerous, but, most importantly, he suggests that the news media are much more likely to react to political events than to initiate them.

Related Work

The term frame building is borrowed from the concept of "agenda building", which was introduced by Cobb and Elder (1971: 905) and is concerned with "how issues are created and why some controversies or incipient issues come to command the attention and concern of decision makers, while others fail" (see also Scheufele 2000: 303f.). Whereas agenda building (e.g., Brandenburg 2002) is concerned with the issue level, frame building looks at the different dimensions or aspects of the same issue. In communication science, frame building is also called "second-level agenda building" (e.g., Kiousis et al. 2006) and focuses on the salience of issue-specific attributes in the media. Most studies have addressed the production and selection of news (e.g., Gans 1979; Shoemaker and Reese 1996; Tuchman 1978), whereas there has been less investigation of news media frames as a dependent variable. Nevertheless, there are some qualitative approaches to this aspect of framing. Edelman (1993) concludes that authorities and pressure groups use their societal influence to establish certain frames, while the indexing approach (Bennett 1990; Bennett et al. 2007; Mermin 1999) documents the relationship between elite dissent and frame contestation and basically argues that the media tend to "index" the range of elite views. Studying framing processes in an integrated way is almost absent from current literature. Claes de Vreese's book *Framing Europe* (2003) is one of the few exceptions. He also uses a "process model" of framing. The current model is more elaborated and sophisticated than his model, paying particular attention to both the behavior of political actors and the news media. Entman's (2004) "cascade model" investigates whether frame contestation (=in the media) arises by looking at strategy, elite power, motivation, and cultural congruity. In comparison with the indexing model, the cascading model looks at a broader range of influencing factors. My work comes closest to Entman's model, but differs from his with regard to the following points: First, my frame-building model analyzes frame contestation in the media and works out the mechanisms that lead to frame contestation. In other words, it does not look at *whether* frame contestation occurs but rather *how* it occurs. Thus, it focuses on the right-hand side of Entman's spectrum between frame dominance and frame parity. Frame contestation/parity has been shown empirically to play a critical role in political opinion formation processes, capable of increasing the chances of a genuine instead of a manufactured will (Schumpeter 1976 [1942]: 263), reducing the chances of manipulated public opinion (Zaller) or decreasing framing effects (Sniderman and Theriault 2004; Chong and Druckman 2007a). It "describes the condition that free press theories prefer: two (or more) interpretations receiving something like equal play" (Entman 2003: 418). Even though we are aware of the importance of frame contestation, it is surprising how little we know about the mechanisms that foster it. My work makes a contribution here. Entman himself argues that we should try to increase frame contestation within elites, and this book shows a way in which we can advance this goal. Second, my work assumes elite competition (=competition between political actors). In line with Schattschneider's definition of democracy, elite competition is at the core of my frame-building model, whereas it is not necessary for the cascade model. Third, my research applies the cascade hypothesis to a European context and to the study of domestic policies. The cascade model is used most often for analyses about public debates on foreign policy. This appears to me to be a rather atypical case: Debates on foreign policy bear the highest risk of a dominant frame situation because government monopolizes information, which impedes opposition. Such one-sided situations seem to be rare in everyday politics. More often, there is a competitor (the second camp or the opposition) who can challenge the first camp or the government. Fourth, my work not only looks at frame contestation, but also includes dialogue. In contrast to contestation, dialogue requires a discussion on certain frames and involves positions on frames (pro/contra the issue). Fifth, it is more concrete than Entman's work and refines theory: Most importantly, it looks in greater detail at the strategic choices and the frame-building process, including politicians' employment of different types of frames, the significance of different types of communication channels (mediated or unmediated) and journalists' use of frames. Finally, I can call upon on a unique set of data, which allows me to follow the whole production process (and, crucially, also examine media input) and its effects.

MODEL OF FRAME BUILDING

Under contemporary conditions, the chain of communication from the political actors to the voters is—essentially—a multi-step process, which includes the flow of frames from the political actors to the journalists, and from the journalists to the voters. The process including the steps from the political actors to the journalists is called frame building. It is illustrated in Fig. 2.1.

Frame building (Scheufele 1999) uses media frames as a dependent variable and investigates the processes and factors that influence the creation or changes of frames applied by journalists (frames in news media or media frames). Media frames refer to the arguments, words, or images that journalists use when relaying information about an issue to an audience. They are defined as working routines for journalists, which "organize the world both for journalists who report it and, in some important degree, for us who rely on their reports"[1] (Gitlin 2003 [1980]: 7). A media frame "organizes everyday reality" (Tuchman 1978: 193) by providing "meaning to an unfolding strip of events" (Gamson and Modigliani 1987: 143, 1989).

Figure 2.1 suggests that media frames originate in three processes. First, political actors *construct* the message, and second, they *promote* it. Political actors are collective actors involved in the campaign, such as political parties, authorities, economic interest groups, citizens' interest groups, or ad hoc committees. The frames which result from the construction and promotion processes are called the *frames in media input*, i.e., the frames found in documents written for the media such as press releases or documents from media conferences. Third, journalists contribute to frame building in the *edition* process. Although the journalists of different media outlets or the journalists and editor from the same outlet sometimes differ in their reporting and commentary on an issue, more striking is their broad similarity in reporting. As a consequence, I define the news media actors as more or less homogenous, while noting significant variation where it occurs. I will explain each of the processes in greater detail below. Since the *media frames* result from the construction, promotion, and edition processes, frame building should actually be called media frame building. However, since I apply the term exclusively for the investigation of how media frames originate,

[1] See also Hall (1973).

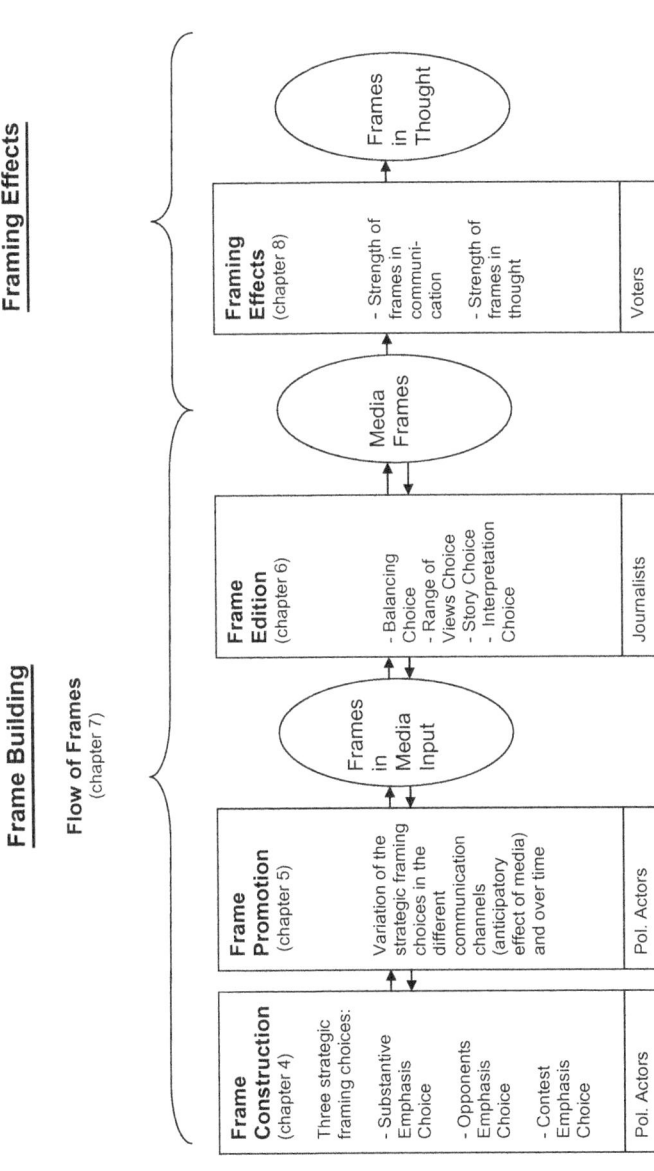

Fig. 2.1 Frame building (construction, promotion, and edition processes) and framing effects in direct-democratic campaigns

it is unambiguous and I will thus employ the commonly used term of frame building.

For this study, I define the frames in the news media together with the frames in the media input as the frames in communication. A *frame in communication* is "the key consideration emphasized in a speech act" (Chong and Druckman 2007c: 106) or written communication. A media frame is a particular frame in communication, which is characterized by the fact that the information is provided by the media. Frames in communication are more comprehensive: They can also include information presented by other actors, such as campaigners, politicians, or friends, including frames in media input. The graph in Fig. 2.1 also shows backward-directed arrows. There are three important feedback mechanisms in the form of anticipated reaction of the journalists by the political actors (anticipatory effects of media). First, political actors behave differently in different media channels. In the documents written for the media, they discuss their opponents' frames, whereas they focus more on their own frames in the other channels. Second, the actors do not organize too many media conferences. They know that if they invite journalists too often, journalists will no longer attend. These two aspects will be addressed in Chapter 5. On the other hand, weak political actors join forces with more powerful ones in order to enter news media coverage. This aspect will be mentioned in Chapter 6. The flow of argument in the process is analyzed separately (Chapter 7).

The whole process of frame building would be irrelevant if the media frames remained without influence on the citizens. In order to gauge the impact of frame building in direct-democratic campaigns, I also evaluate the effects of the media frames. In Fig. 2.1, they are illustrated on the right-hand side of the graph. Framing effects[2] have been defined as effects from frames in communication on frames in thought (Druckman 2001). *Frames in thought* (or individual frames or audience frames [Entman 1993: 53]) are "internal structures of the mind" (Kinder and

---

[2] Chong and Druckman (2007c) question the utility of the distinctions between framing, priming, and agenda-setting. I agree. However, even if the distinction of these concepts should be shown as helpful, the approach adopted here of framing analysis seems to be highly suitable. First of all, it is essential to study contexts in which we find combinations of frames because in actual public policy debates, people are generally exposed to different perspectives on an issue (e.g., Sniderman and Theriault 2004; Nelson 2004; Brewer and Gross 2005; Chong and Druckman 2007a; Jerit 2009). Framing studies have explored the role of multiple competing frames, whereas priming and agenda-setting have paid little

Sanders 1990: 74). For instance, a voter who reads a specific frame in the media might add some personal experience, forge links not made explicitly in the text, or use another individual cognitive device to make sense of the political news. In other words, a frame in thought is the individual's cognitive understanding of a given situation (Goffman 1974). By contrast, a *frame in communication* is "the key consideration emphasized in a speech act" (Chong and Druckman 2007c: 106).

Frame Construction (Substantive Emphasis Choice, Oppositional Emphasis Choice, and Contest Emphasis Choice)

In order to win a campaign, political actors frame the issue at stake strategically and "campaign on behalf of competing ways of understanding what is at issue" (Sniderman and Theriault 2004: 158). By competing and framing the issue strategically, political actors face at least three strategic framing choices (Fig. 2.1). First, they are expected to search for a frame they think has the capacity to become a strong substantive frame. They might additionally provide a second or third mainframe, to which they can switch if their core frame is not resonating well. At the same time, and in line with marketing knowledge, they do not want to overload the processing capacity of the people and of the media (Shoemaker and Reese 1996: 104) and therefore might not promote too many frames. If they do so, it will not be in their hands anymore as to which one comes through. The number of frames with which they will ultimately campaign is an empirical question. I call this choice the "Substantive Emphasis Choice". A strong frame is a frame that provokes a defensive reaction by the opponents and/or that resonates in the media. This conceptualization of strength is based on Koopmans' idea that resonant messages (i.e., messages which provoke reactions) travel

attention to competitive situations (Chong and Druckman 2007b: 101). Second, framing analysis not only refers to the salience of an issue attribute, but also it expands beyond the analysis of salience and tackles the way in which actors understand a political issue and attempt to influence the public's interpretation of it. "By appropriately framing an issue, political actors attempt to construct the meaning of the reality in question in a sense that supports their own point of view" (Kriesi 2010: 8). Third, from a supply-based point of view, I am concerned with the speakers' (or senders') view, which is well suited to the framing approach (Selb 2003: 22), whereas agenda-setting and priming are more concerned with the receivers' perspective.

further (Koopmans 2004: 374). It means that a frame discussed by the opponent is a strong frame. Of course, it is possible that political actors choose to ignore the message of their competitors because it cannot be rebutted. However, the political actors have strong incentives to try to rebut a frame. They know that the impact on opinion formation is higher if a frame is one-sided and not counter-argued (see more about this discussion in Chapter 4). The relative strength of the frame is issue- and context-specific and difficult to determine in general. Chong and Druckman (2007b: 100) argue that we have little knowledge about what determines the strength of a frame. They suggest that it depends on two sets of factors: The credibility of its source, and its congruence with central cultural themes. These two factors probably also drive the strength of a frame in communication (Table 2.1).

Table 2.1 Constructing the frame—the three strategic framing choices (Chapter 4)

Strategic framing choices	The political actors...	Central concepts
Substantive emphasis choice	...search for a frame they think has the capacity to become a strong substantive frame	Strong frame in communication: a frame that provokes a defensive reaction by the opponents and/or that resonates in the media
Oppositional emphasis choice	...decide on the amount of attention they want to pay to the opponents' substantive frame(s) as compared to their own frames and whether they want to use their opponents' frames offensively or defensively	Trespassing: offensive use of opponents' frames Counter-framing: defensive use of opponents' frames
Contest emphasis choice	...decide on how much priority they want to give to their own substantive frame(s) as compared to the campaign contest	Substantive frames: a frame with a focus on the substantive content of the debate—on policy Contest frames: a frame which does not address the issue(s) at stake, but focuses on the actors involved or on the contest per se—on politics

Second, political actors have to decide on the amount of attention they want to pay to the opponents' substantive frame(s) as compared to their own frames and whether they want to use their opponents' frames offensively or defensively ("Oppositional Emphasis Choice"). The offensive use of the opponents' frames corresponds to what Sides (2006) has called "*trespassing*": Political actors may use strong images, issues, or issue attributes of their opponents in order to appear responsive to the general public. In other words, if a certain position on a frame is well supported and accepted by the general public, political actors trespass. In all other situations and probably more widespread, however, is the defensive use of the opponents' frames: Political actors may feel forced to react to the successful frames of their opponents, to adopt *counter-frames* to offer rebuttals, and to counter-attack their adversaries. In this sense, a counter-frame contains three defining elements as mentioned by Chong and Druckman (2013: 2): A counter-frame claims a position on the issue that is contrary to an existing frame (i.e., it is "counter"), the existing frame affects opinions on the issue, and it comes later in time than the initial frame. The latter point is less important in our study because of the campaign logic: Once a direct-democratic campaign starts, the frames and their counter-frames are prepared and they are presented more or less contemporaneously.

Third, political actors have to decide on how much priority they want to give to their own substantive frame(s) as compared to the campaign contest ("Contest Emphasis Choice"). In this respect, I propose to distinguish between two types of frames—contest frames and substantive frames.[3] The peculiarity of the former is that they do not address the issue(s) at stake, but focus on the actors involved or on the contest per se—on politics—while the latter focus on the substantive contents of the debate—on policy. Examples of the former include "strategic frames" (analyzing the rationale and strategy underlying the candidate's rhetoric and positions, e.g., the unions launched this initiative because

---

[3] De Vreese (2005) makes a distinction between "issue-specific" and "generic" frames. This distinction suffers from the difficulty that it mixes up thematic and contest frames in both the generic and the issue-specific categories. I agree with Chong and Druckman (2007c: 107), who find it difficult to specify a frame as generic or general. However, I do not follow Chong and Druckman (2007c) and Entman (2004) when they suggest using a different label than frame (like "script") for a "feature in the communication such as a conflict". Finally, Entman (2004: 5f.) explores two classes of frames, substantive and procedural. My distinction is similar, also in terms of meaning.

they want to exert pressure on the parliament to change something), "horse race frames" (framing the campaign not as a contest of ideas or policy platforms, but as a race between two teams, each bent on getting more votes and support than the other, e.g., a wide alliance of parties, associations, and unions support the initiative), "conflict frames" (emphasizing conflict between individuals, groups, or institutions, e.g., the minister Widmer-Schlumpf holds a different opinion to her own party. Nevertheless, she stands up for her position because it is her own, it is an objective position and can well be justified), or "personalized frames" (emphasizing personal characteristics of the actors involved or attacking another person, e.g., the yes committee consists of do-gooders who cannot objectively evaluate the situation). Thus, the main criterion is that contest frames do not mention the issue and are about politics (see also Appendix "Coding Procedures for Arguments"). Theoretically, there could be dialogue on contest frames. However, this is irrelevant for my book and I do not investigate it. Contest dialogue does not legitimize decisions and does not inform citizens about the issue at stake. Substantive frames, by contrast, are variable in scope: They can either be issue-specific or transcend a single issue (Gamson et al. 1992: 385; Matthes 2009). The abuse frame is an example that transcends a single issue and could be used for several topics. For instance, political actors might claim that asylum seekers or disabled persons abuse the system. The first case concerns the asylum law, whereas the second is about disability benefits. The distinction between substantive and contest frames is relevant since it helps us to ascertain how much substance and dialogue we find in a debate. In light of increasingly media-centered politics, it is important to investigate the degree of substance in a debate. For deliberative theorists, the public debate that precedes the democratic decision, its inclusiveness, and its deliberative quality are essential for the quality of a democracy (e.g., Habermas 1996).

The three framing choices are by no means exhaustive. In strategic framing, just as in any kind of strategic action, there are, as Jasper (2006: 171) points out, "few rules... but many choices". However, I do suggest that all actors involved in strategic framing are implicitly or explicitly confronted with at least these three choices.

In this frame construction phase (Chapter 4)—as introduced in Chapter 1—dialogue occurs because political actors strategically choose to discuss each other's interpretation (they counter-frame) and because they concentrate on substantive frames to a good extent. Campaign characteristics additionally influence the level of dialogue. Issue complexity and imbalance in financial resources handicaps dialogue whereas issue familiarity and expected closeness of vote outcome increases dialogue.

Frame Promotion

Political actors vary their choices depending on the communication channel. The study of social movements has demonstrated the usefulness of the concept of the *action* repertoire of challengers, because social movements in a given context tend to use more or less standardized repertoires of action (Tilly 1978, 1986, 1995). In an analogous way, Kriesi et al. (2009) propose the concept of the *communication* repertoire to characterize the channels that are used in direct-democratic campaigns. Campaigners have learnt how to use a well-defined set of communication routines, which they apply in a standardized way. Such routines may be legally prescribed, but more often they are the result of informal rules that have been established over the years. While fairly institutionalized, such routines are also subject to change as new channels become available thanks to technological development, or as new actors enter the fray, who experiment with new techniques and who, if successful, are imitated by their competitors. I use a slightly different typology than Kriesi et al. (2009) because I am not interested in the way in which they reach the public but rather in how they communicate differently depending on the target group.

In general, campaigners first vary their framing choices depending on whether they are targeting the general public and citizens or their own members. With regard to communication with the general public, they secondly vary their framing choices depending on whether the channel is mediated or unmediated. In the *mediated* channels, they promote messages which have to pass the selection by journalists. As a consequence, they try to provide newsworthy messages (Shoemaker and Reese 1996). The news values theory states that news values determine how much prominence a message or frame is given by a media outlet. In the original theory (Galtung and Ruge 1965), news decisions are traced back to specific properties of events and actors—so-called news factors—that make them newsworthy and increase their chances of making the news. Such news factors include, among other things, importance of the message (measured according to its impact: how many lives it affects), conflict or controversy, resonance with well-understood story themes, the involvement of personalization, proximity of an event, or the status and relevance of an actor (Galtung and Ruge 1965; Schulz 1976; Price and Tewksbury 1997). These characteristics of the news can be seen as endemic to newsgathering, stemming in one way or another from time pressures faced by journalists and from the challenge of relaying complex information in highly condensed formats (Tuchman 1978). In addition, campaigners anticipate the media logic and adapt their communication strategy accordingly (Cook 1989; Entman 1989; Jacobs and Shapiro 2000; Jerit 2008). The anticipation of the media role leads the political actors to address the opposing view more in the mediated channels (e.g., more dialogue in input and in letters to the editor). They assume that the media want to have a balance of views, and they wish to ensure that they are in the media with the best possible counter-argument. For this reason, they provide the counter-argument themselves.

The campaigners can rely on two mediated channels to reach out to the public: First, and most importantly, political actors try to get news media coverage by producing *media input*. The organization of media conferences and the editing of news releases are among the most common forms of media input in Swiss direct-democratic campaigns. News coverage is also referred to as free media (Iyengar and McGrady 2007: 9), even though it is not always cost-free. Sometimes, public relations or advertising professionals are hired in order to maximize the visibility of a campaign in the media. Second, campaigners also organize the writing of *letters to the editor*.

Unmediated channels guarantee campaigns control over the content and form of the message. They are a way to get the message to the public unfiltered by media gatekeepers (Shoemaker and Reese 1996: 174). In Norris et al.'s terms, unmediated channels offer the political actors the opportunity to use their "ideal" message, with "ideal" meaning that the political actors are in "sole control of the content" (Norris et al. 1999: 62). "There is a significant trade-off, however: advertising is unmediated, but it is also a much less credible messenger than news reports are" (Iyengar and McGrady 2007: 137). By comparing the media input with the unmediated channels, we can evaluate the ways in which the political actors anticipate the media logic. Campaigners can be provided with an unmediated route to the minds of voters through two channels: First, they can pay for political ads in the media, sponsored ads (e.g., online on Facebook), posters in the public sphere or videos which they spread online through social media. I will refer to this as the *political ads* channel. It is the largest expenditure

Table 2.2 Communication channels in Swiss direct-democratic campaigns (Chapter 5)

Target	Members	Citizens or general public			
Characteristic	*Internal*	*Unmediated*		*Mediated*	
Channel	Info for members	Direct mail	Political ads	Letters to the editor	Media input
Examples	Newsletter Magazine for members E-mail	Direct mail Flyer Demonstration Leaflet Tweet Post	Newspaper ad Sponsored ad Poster Online video	Letters to the editor	Media release Media conference

incurred by campaigns. This channel is also called paid media (Iyengar and McGrady 2007: 9). Note that paid political advertising is prohibited on television and radio in Switzerland. Second, political actors can also target citizens directly. For this form of political communication, direct mail, flyers, tweets, or Facebook posts are particularly suitable.[4] I call this the *direct mail* channel.

Finally, political actors can address their members instead of addressing the general public or the citizens. They can target their members using such means as their own newspapers and magazines, newsletters, or e-mail actions. I call this the *info for members* channel. This channel also enables the campaigners to use their "ideal" or unmediated message. However, in this channel, the campaigners primarily want to tie their members to their organization and inform them. Thus, as summarized in Table 2.2, I will investigate one internal channel, two unmediated channels (direct mail and political ads), and two mediated channels (letters to the editor and media input).

---

[4]There was no use of tweets, social media posts, or online videos in these campaigns—they happened too early for this to be a factor. Indeed, until now social media has only been of minor importance in Swiss direct-democratic campaigns. The targeted, individualized placement of political online advertisements is not yet a big issue in Switzerland (*Source* https://www.swissinfo.ch/ger/direktedemokratie/digitale-demokratie_-das-ist-ein-angriff-auf-die-schweizer-demokratie--/43325134, March 2019). Switzerland is small and language-wise divided. There are only few scaling effects. If political actors use social media, they use it as an additional channel to spread their messages (Klinger 2013).

I consider media input as the most important communication channel in direct-democratic campaigns. First, it is the channel which highly influences free media coverage because journalists rely on it in a routine way (Sigal 1973; Shoemaker and Reese 1996). In addition, direct-democratic campaigns generally enjoy high news coverage, making the other channels a minor trickle in the cumulative message stream. Letters to the editor can also garner free publicity. Since these two free media channels entail considerably less cost than the paid media channel, all organizations should strive for newsworthy media input and letters to the editor.

By promoting their message, political actors also have to find a way in which to garner media attention *during the whole campaign*. By promoting their message, political actors can use inductions and adaptations (Bentele et al. 1997: 240). In their "Intereffikation" model, Bentele et al. (1997) investigate the relationship between journalists and political actors and describe it as a complex relation of mutually existing influence and reciprocal dependency of relatively autonomous systems. Inductions are intended, directed communication suggestions or communication impulses which—if noticed or absorbed—become communication influences. Adaptations are communicative actions which are geared to the social facts of the respective other side, often to optimize the communication success of one's own side (Bentele 2005: 211).

In this promotion phase of the frame-building process (Chapter 5), we will see that a good level of dialogue can be explained by the anticipatory effect of media on the part of the political actors. In the mediated channels, campaigners must cater to the needs and values of journalists. The political actors anticipate the media logic. Accordingly, I find a different behavior in the mediated channels. In addition, dialogue also emerges from a constant behavior of political actors over time. For the elites, to "keep going" is most important. First, in Swiss direct-democratic campaigns, elites have limited resources. There are two to four national votes a year and parties are financially weak. It is a challenge for them to construct the frame, and only very rarely do they have the resources (money and persons) to change the message over time. Second, the promotion of the same interpretations over time gives the audience time to learn about them. The political actors want the audience to learn about their position and thus repeat their messages over time. Therefore, they stay on message, and as a result, I find no concentration on a smaller number of interpretations in the mediated channels over time. If campaigners act dynamically, it can be actively or reactively. If they become reactive, it can manifest itself in four different ways: reaction to events in one's own camp, to the opponent, to the media, and to facts.

Frame Edition: Contribution by Journalists

The communication between the political actors and the voters is typically not direct, but rather edited by the journalists. Research has demonstrated that the public does form its impressions about the political world from the news media (Graber 2001; Zaller 2003). Even though the journalists generally respect the lead of the political actors with regard to the content of the debate, the journalists decide on the degree to which they want to balance out the messages ("Balancing Choice"), whose messages they want to cover ("Range of Views Choice"), the weight they will give to available messages ("Story Choice"), or whether they will investigate official claims or provide interpretations ("Interpretation Choice"). Journalists contribute to the dialogue in the news through their decisions on these choices (Chapter 6).

Flow of Frames

In Swiss direct-democratic campaigns, the political actors take the lead by framing the issue strategically. The three strategic framing choices (causal order) and the promotion activities, particularly in the media input (channel), are intended to influence the creation or changes of frames applied by journalists. The journalists generally respect the lead of the powerful political actors and contribute to the debate by clarifying the opposing positions (which Bennett et al. 2004 call "recognition") and by eliciting mutual reactions from the opposing political actors (which they call "responsiveness"). The flow of frames is also dependent on how much news media report about direct-democratic campaigns and when they start to provide information prior to a vote (effort and timing). By analyzing the flow of frames, I show that there is a reasonably clear order in the flow, in effort and timing. These factors might also be supportive of dialogue.

Role of Dialogue for Public Opinion Formation: Framing Effects

How relevant is dialogue in the news media? Frame dialogue is only important when frames evolving from the construction, promotion, and edition processes have an effect on opinion formation. It is also in the aim of political actors to finally reach a framing effect, i.e., an effect from a frame in communication on a frame in thought (Druckman 2001). Thus, I end the empirical analysis by investigating framing effects[5] in Chapter 8. The most commonly encountered framing effects in political contexts are *emphasis* framing effects (or issue or value framing effects) (Druckman 2001). A speaker involved in emphasis framing offers alternative frames, which focus on different aspects of the same policy problem. An emphasis framing effect occurs when he or she alters the salience and perceived strength of an accessible consideration about this issue (Iyengar and Kinder 1987; Zaller 2005 [1992]; Druckman 2001) and influences citizens' preferences or attitudes (e.g., O'Keefe 2002; Druckman and Holmes 2004; Chong and Druckman 2007c). A second class of framing effects involves the use of different, but logically equivalent, frames to alter individuals' preferences: *Equivalency framing effects* (or valence or message framing effects) typically occur when a frame casts the same information in a positive or negative light (Druckman 2001: 228). For the study at hand, equivalency framing effects are irrelevant. With framing effects, I exclusively refer to emphasis framing effects.

The influential theory by Zaller (2005 [1992]) regarding the nature and origin of mass opinion showed that the elites play a major role for

[5] Studies about framing effects have built on studies about agenda-setting and priming. Agenda-setting was first examined empirically by McCombs and Shaw (1972) and was guided by the famous conclusion of an early study that "the press may not be successful much of the time in telling people what to think, but it is stunningly successful in telling its readers what to think about" (Cohen 1963; also see Kinder 2003: 361ff.). Priming has been defined as salient issues or news stories which influence "the standards by which governments, presidents, policies and candidates for public office are judged" (Iyengar and Kinder 1987: 63). For Scheufele (2000: 306), priming (dependent variable) is the outcome of agenda-setting (independent variable). Framing studies then expanded beyond the interest of agenda-setting and priming studies in what people talk or think about, and began to investigate also *how* they think and talk about political issues (Pan and Kosicki 1993: 70). Scheufele (2000) distinguishes between frame setting and individual-level effects. For him, frame setting is the impact from the media frames on the frames in thought, whereas the individual-level effect is the impact from the frames in thought on the individual behaviors or attitudes. Since I am ultimately interested in the voters' attitudes toward the issue and not only in their frames in thoughts, I define the second step in my study as framing *effects* and not as frame *setting*. In addition, it seems unnecessary to distinguish between these two processes.

the construction of individual opinion. However, the conventional view on the effect of mass communication on public opinion is highly skeptical about the extent of possible effects. Although the classic "minimal effect" verdict no longer constitutes the received wisdom, the conventional view is nevertheless that the effects of frames on public opinion are rather limited and contingent (Kinder 1998, 2003). Most strikingly, for citizens who discuss politics informally with others, the framing effects seem to disappear. In an experimental setting, Druckman and Nelson (2003) found that counter-framing and heterogeneous discussions limit framing effects by prompting deliberative processing and offering reformulations of the problems. However, when distinguishing the *quality* of a frame, framing effects seem to be less limited. Jerit (2009: 423) finds that "predictive appeals can have a significant effect on public opinion". Chong and Druckman (2007a: 651) show that "strong frames have a significant effect in both competitive and non-competitive contexts". There is still much to learn about how different framing strategies influence public opinion (e.g., Druckman and Nelson 2003; Chong and Druckman 2007a; Jerit 2009), particularly in real-world settings.

The definition of a strong frame introduced above applies to the frames in communication (=frames in media input and news media). Thus, a strong frame in communication is a frame which provokes a defensive reaction by the opponents and/or resonates in the media. Credibility of source and cultural congruence of frame content have proved to be important in influencing strength (Chong and Druckman 2007b: 100). By contrast, a strong frame in thought is defined as persuasive or applicable (Druckman 2009: 25). The precondition for a frame in thought to become strong (=applicable) is that it is accessible (=one is exposed to this frame) and available (=understandable) (Druckman 2009) (Table 2.3).

The overall result of this chapter is that the frames present in the news media dialogue are indeed very relevant for the vote decision. The more important the topic for a person, the less polarized the context, and the less complex the topic, the more a person relies on the frame-based path.

Table 2.3 Strength of the frames in communication and in thought (Chapter 8)

	Frames in communication (=frames in media input + media frames)	Frames in thought
Strong frame	A strong frame in communication is a frame that provokes a defensive reaction by the opponents and/or that resonates in the media	A strong frame in thought is a frame that is applicable (=persuadable)
Precondition	– Credible source – Cultural congruence	– Accessibility (one is exposed to a frame) – Availability (the frame is understandable)

Generalizability of the Study

First of all, the generalizability of the findings is restricted because of the *small number of cases*. However, since frame building in Swiss direct-democratic campaigns is routine action which usually follows the same pattern, the three cases still provide an insight into the *typical* frame-building process. Therefore, the theoretical framework provided in this study and the main findings should be representative for Swiss direct-democratic campaigns in general. With regard to the differences *between* Swiss direct-democratic campaigns, the results vary depending above all on issue complexity, familiarity, and intensity. Further research is needed in order to appraise the generalizability of the issue-specific findings.

Second, the *campaign specificity* limits the generalizability of my findings. In order to strengthen their generalizability, I present three types of campaign and outline in which regard the theoretical framework and my results might depend on the type of campaign. Firstly, direct-democratic campaigns imply *the involvement of two competing camps* (=structuration of actors), which guarantees competing substantive frames. Secondly, direct-democratic campaigns are of *limited duration* (=closure) with a clear beginning and a clear end. They imply, thirdly, an *issue-specific choice* (=focus). Based on these three criteria, direct-democratic campaigns can be distinguished from election campaigns and public debates (Table 2.4), and the model of frame building and the main findings should also be

Table 2.4 Different types of campaigns

	Campaign type		
	Direct-democratic campaigns	Election campaigns	Public debates
Structuration of actors	2 opposing camps	2 or more opposing candidates	Open, dominating actor is possible
Closure	Closure by final vote	Closure by final vote	Open end
Focus	Issue-specific	No given focus	Issue-specific

representative for political communication in which two camps are involved and which is led by the elites, such as debates about salient issues that take place in the national parliament. Similarly to direct-democratic campaigns, *election campaigns*[6] are also characterized by the involvement of competing actors. In majoritarian electoral systems, election campaigns typically give rise to the confrontation between two main opposing camps, whereas in proportional electoral systems, more camps are involved. In addition, election campaigns also include a closed end, but do not have an issue-specific focus. *Public debates* share the advantage of direct-democratic campaigns in that they are issue-specific. They are "the sum of all public communications related to a particular issue" (Helbling et al. 2009: 5). The debates about privacy or security issues in social networks, transparency of advertising in web search results, same-sex marriages, or about the Iraq war, are examples of such debates. In contrast to direct-democratic campaigns, public debates are not necessarily prestructured into a binary logic and no final vote takes place.

Third, we studied frame building only in one single *country*. With regard to differences between countries, I suggest that at least two aspects are relevant (see also Kriesi et al. 2019: 48). Firstly, the *degree of control exercised by the elites* (Smith 1976; Bowler and Donovan 2006: 665; Budge 1996: 90) is important. Swiss direct-democratic campaigns are organized and tightly controlled by the political elites. Both the executive branch and parliament have an important role to play in the preparation of the proposals submitted to voters. The control of the whole process by the government and the parliamentary majority

---

[6] More precisely, I am thinking of *national* election campaigns.

implies the formation of two specific coalitions, the government camp versus the issue-specific opposition. Political campaigns in most other European countries are also organized by the elites (De Vreese 2004: 50; Bowler and Donovan 2006). By contrast, in the USA the government has less control over the direct-democratic process. The US populist and progressive reformers of the late nineteenth century introduced direct-democratic procedures in order, above all, to restrict the power of political parties and their political machines, which controlled the state parliaments at the time (Cronin 1989: 50–57; Smith and Tolbert 2001: 740, 2004: 112ff.; Bowler and Donovan 2006). Even today, in the USA the popular initiative is used primarily by social movements and interest groups to circumvent the state parliaments controlled by the parties. This is possible because the popular initiatives are submitted to popular vote without the intervention of the state governments and their parliaments. Secondly, the *political communication culture* is relevant. Pfetsch (2003) suggests that the communication culture is characterized by two dimensions: the distance between journalists and political actors and the orientation of political communication. Distance is related to different professional and social norms. For instance, in the US journalists refer more to professional norms such as vocational professionalism, objectivity and impartiality of information, balanced content and diversity, and transparency, whereas German actors give priority to social norms such as ethically correct behavior, openness, and honesty. As a consequence, we find a greater distance between journalists and political actors in the USA than in Germany. The orientation of political communication is dependent on the relative importance of media and political logic. If the media logic (Mazzoleni 1987) prevails, then journalists are relatively independent. The media can set the agenda of an election debate, and news values, selection criteria, and media attention are important in the news production. The actors try to garner as much media attention as possible and to achieve positive news coverage. If the political logic dominates, power-political aspects are at the fore. The political actors aim to strengthen their organization, to legitimize their position, or to increase support and trust for their own policy positions. Based on the two dimensions, we arrive at four different types of political communication culture (Table 2.5).

The media-oriented political communication culture is characterized by the distance between political and media actors and dominance of media logic (example: USA). In the PR-oriented political communication,

Table 2.5   Political communication culture and its two dimensions

Distance between political actors and journalists	Orientation of political communication	
	Dominant media logic	Dominant political logic
Strong/great distance	Media-oriented political communication culture	Strategic political communication culture
	Example: USA	Examples: Germany, Switzerland, and Denmark
Weak/small distance	PR-oriented political communication culture	Party-political communication culture
	Example: Italy	Example: France

culture, political, and media actors are close but the production of news is media-oriented (example: Italy). When we find a great distance between politicians and journalists and the political logic is dominant, I call this strategic political communication culture (examples: Germany, Switzerland, and Denmark). The party-political communication culture is identified by a weak distance and the dominance of the party logic (example: France).

REFERENCES

Bennett, W. L. (1990). Toward a Theory of Press-State Relations. *Journal of Communication, 40*(2), 103–125.

Bennett, W. L., Lawrence, R., & Livingston, S. (2007). *When the Press Fails: Political Power and the News Media from Iraq to Katrina.* Chicago: University Press.

Bennett, W. L., Pickard, V. W., Iozzi, D. P., Schroeder, C. L., Lagos, T., & Caswell, E. C. (2004). Managing the Public Sphere: Journalistic Construction of the Great Globalization Debate. *International Communication Association, 54*(3), 437–455.

Bentele, G. (2005). Intereffikationsmodell. In G. Bentele, R. Fröhlich, & P. Szyszka (Eds.), *Handbuch der Public Relations: Wissenschaftliche Grundlagen und berufliches Handeln* (pp. 209–222). Wiesbaden: VS Verlag für Sozialwissenschaften.

Bentele, G., Liebert, T., & Seeling, S. (1997). Von der Determination zur Intereffikation. Ein integriertes Modell zum Verhältnis von Public Relations und Journalismus. In G. Bentele & M. Haller (Eds.), *Aktuelle Entstehung von Öffentlichkeit. Akteure-Strukturen-Veränderungen* (pp. 225–250). Konstanz: UVK.

Brandenburg, H. (2002). Who Follows Whom? The Impact of Parties on Media Agenda Formation in the 1997 British General Election Campaign. *The International Journal of Press/Politics, 7*(34), 34–54.

Brewer, P. R., & Gross, K. (2005). Values, Framing, and Citizens' Thoughts About Policy Issues: Effects on Content and Quality. *Political Psychology, 26,* 929–948.

Bowler, S., & Donovan, T. (2006). Direct Democracy and Political Parties in America. *Party Politics, 12*(5), 649–669.

Budge, I. (1996). *The New Challenge of Direct Democracy.* Cambridge: Polity Press.

Cook, T. (1989). *Making Laws and Making News. Media Strategies in the U.S. House of Representatives.* Washington, DC: Brookings Institution.

Chong, D., & Druckman, J. N. (2007a). Framing Public Opinion in Competitive Democracies. *American Political Science Review, 101*(4), 637–656.

Chong, D., & Druckman, J. N. (2007b). A Theory of Framing and Opinion Formation in Competitive Elite Environments. *Journal of Communication, 57*(1), 99–118.

Chong, D., & Druckman, J. N. (2007c). Framing Theory. *Annual Review of Political Science, 10,* 103–126.

Chong, D., & Druckman, J. N. (2013). Counterframing Effects. *The Journal of Politics, 75,* 1–16.

Cobb, R. W., & Elder, C. D. (1971). *Participation in American Politics: The Dynamics of Agenda-Building.* Baltimore: Johns Hopkins University Press.

Cohen, B. C. (1963). *The Press and Foreign Policy.* Princeton: University Press.

Cronin, T. E. (1989). *Direct Democracy: The Politics of Initiative, Referendum, and Recall.* Cambridge, MA: Harvard University Press.

De Vreese, C. H. (2004). The Effects of Frames in Political Television News on Issue Interpretation and Frame Salience. *Journalism & Mass Communication Quarterly, 81*(1), 36–52.

De Vreese, C. (2005). News Framing: Theory and Typology. *Information Design Journal + Document Design, 13*(1), 51–62.

Druckman, J. N. (2001). The Implications of Framing Effects for Citizen Competence. *Political Behavior, 23,* 225–256.

Druckman, J. N. (2009). What's It All About? Framing in Political Science. In G. Keren (Ed.), *Perspectives on Framing.* New York: Psychology Press.

Druckman, J. N., & Holmes, J. W. (2004). Does Presidential Rhetoric Matter? Priming and Presidential Approval. *Presidential Studies Quarterly, 34,* 755–778.

Druckman, J. N., & Nelson, K. R. (2003). Framing and Deliberation: How Citizens' Conversations Limit Elite Influence. *American Journal of Political Science, 47*(4), 729–745.

Edelman, M. J. (1993). Contestable Categories and Public Opinion. *Political Communication, 10,* 231–242.

Entman, R. M. (1989). *Democracy Without Citizens: Media and the Decay of American Politics.* New York: Oxford University Press.

Entman, R. M. (1993). Framing: Toward Clarification of a Fractured Paradigm. *Journal of Communication, 43,* 51–58.

Entman, R. M. (2003). Cascading Activation: Contesting the White House's Frame After 9/11. *Political Communication, 20,* 415–432.

Entman, R. M. (2004). *Projections of Power Framing News, Public Opinion, and U.S. Foreign Policy.* Chicago, IL: University of Chicago Press.

Galtung, J., & Ruge, M. H. (1965). The Structure of Foreign News. *Journal of Peace Research, 2*(1), 64–91.

Gamson, W. A., Croteau, D., Hones, W., & Sasson, T. (1992). Media Images and the Social Construction of Reality. *Annual Review of Sociology, 18,* 373–393.

Gamson, W. A., & Modigliani, A. (1987). The Changing Culture of Affirmative Action. In R. D. Braungart (Ed.), *Research in Political Sociology* (pp. 137–177). Greenwich: JAI.

Gamson, W. A., & Modigliani, A. (1989). Media Discourse and Public Opinion on Nuclear Power: A Constructionist Approach. *The American Journal of Sociology, 95*(1), 1–37.

Gans, H. J. (1979). *Deciding What's News: A Study of CBS Evening News, NBC Nightly News, Newsweek, and Time.* New York: Pantheon Books.

Gitlin, T. (2003 [1980]). *The Whole World Is Watching: Mass Media in the Making and Unmaking of the New Left.* Berkeley: University of California Press.

Goffman, E. (1974). *Frame Analysis.* Cambridge: Harvard University Press.

Graber, D. A. (2001). *Processing Politics: Learning from Television in the Internet Age.* Chicago: University of Chicago Press.

Habermas, J. (1996). *Between Facts and Norms: Contributions to a Discourse Theory of Law and Democracy.* New Baskerville: MIT Press.

Hall, Stuart. (1973). *Encoding and Decoding in the Television Discourse.* Birmingham: Centre of Contemporary Cultural Studies, University of Birmingham.

Helbling, M., Höglinger, D., & Wüest, B. (2009). Public Debates Over Globalization. In H. Kriesi, E. Grande, M. Dolezal, M. Helbling, S. Hutter, D. Höglinger, & B. Wüest (Eds.), *Restructuring Political Conflict in the Age of Globalization.* Zurich: Unpublished Manuscript.

Iyengar, S., & Kinder, D. R. (1987). *News That Matters: Television and American Opinion.* Chicago: University of Chicago Press.

Iyengar, S., & McGrady, J. A. (2007). *Media Politics: A Citizen's Guide.* New York: W. W. Norton.

Jacobs, L. R., & Shapiro, R. Y. (2000). *Politicians Don't Pander.* Chicago: University of Chicago Press.

Jasper, J. M. (2006). *Getting Your Way: Strategic Dilemmas in the Real World* (Vol. 9). Chicago: University of Chicago Press.

Jerit, J. (2008). Issue Framing and Engagement: Rhetorical Strategy in Public Policy Debates. *Political Behaviour, 30*, 1–24.

Jerit, J. (2009). How Predictive Appeals Shape Policy Opinions. *American Journal of Political Science, 53*(2), 411–426.

Kinder, D. R. (1998). Communication and Opinion. *Annual Review of Political Science, 1*, 167–197.

Kinder, D. R. (2003). Communication and Politics in the Age of Information. In D. O. Sears, L. Huddy, & R. Jervis (Eds.), *Oxford Handbook of Political Psychology* (pp. 357–393). Oxford: Oxford University Press.

Klinger, U. (2013). Mastering the Art of Social Media. *Information, Communication & Society, 16*(5), 717–736.

Kinder, D. R., & Sanders, L. M. (1990). Mimicking Political Debate with Survey Questions: The Case of White Opinion on Affirmative Action for Blacks. *Social Cognition, 8*, 73–103.

Kiousis, S., Mitrook, M., Wu, X., & Seltzer, T. (2006). First- and Second-Level Agenda-Building and Agenda-Setting Effects: Exploring the Linkages Among Candidate News Releases, Media Coverage, and Public Opinion During the 2002 Florida Gubernatorial Election. *Journal of Public Relations Research, 18*(3), 265–285.

Koopmans, R. (2004). Movements and Media: Selection Processes and Evolutionary Dynamics in the Public Sphere. *Theory and Society, 33*(3/4), 367–391.

Kriesi, H. (2010). The Role of Predispositions. In H. Kriesi (Ed.), *Enlightening or Manipulating?* (pp. 143–167). Hampshire: Palgrave Macmillan.

Kriesi, H., Bernhard, L., & Hänggli, R. (2009). The Politics of Campaiging—Dimensions of Strategic Action. In F. Marcinkowski & B. Pfetsch (Eds.), *Politik in der Mediendemokratie*. Wiesbaden: VS Verlag für Sozialwissenschaften.

Kriesi, H., Fossati, F., & Bernhard, L. (2019). The Political Contexts of the National Policy Debates. In L. Bernhard, F. Fossati, R. Hänggli, & Hp. Kriesi (Eds.), *Debating Unemployment Policy: Political Communication and the Labour Market in Western Europe* (pp. 43–70). Cambridge: Cambridge University Press.

Matthes, J. (2009). What's in a Frame? A Content Analysis of Media Framing Studies in the World's Leading Communication Journals 1990–2005. *Journalism & Mass Communication Quarterly, 86*(2), 349–367.

Mazzoleni, G. (1987). Media Logic and Party Logic in Campaign Coverage: The Italian General Election of 1983. *European Journal of Communication, 2*, 81–103.

McCombs, M. E., & Shaw, D. L. (1972). The Agenda-Setting Function of Mass Media. *Public Opinion Quarterly, 36*(2), 176–187.

Mermin, J. (1999). *Debating War and Peace: Media Coverage of U.S. Intervention in the Post-Vietnam Era*. Princeton, NJ: Princeton University Press.

Nelson, T. E. (2004). Policy Goals, Public Rhetoric, and Political Attitudes. *The Journal of Politics, 66*(2), 581–605.

Norris, P., Curtice, J., Sanders, D., Scammell, M., & Semetko, H. A. (1999). *On Message: Communicating the Campaign.* London: Sage.

O'Keefe, D. J. (2002). *Persuasion* (2nd ed.). Thousand Oaks, CA: Sage.

Pan, Z., & Kosicki, G. M. (1993). Framing Analysis: An Approach to News Discourse. *Political Communication, 10*(1), 55–75.

Pfetsch, B. (2003). Politische Kommunikationskultur; ein theoretisches Konzept zur vergleichenden Analyse politischer Kommunikationssysteme. In F. Esser & B. Pfetsch (Eds.), *Politische Kommunikation im internationalen Vergleich; Grundlagen, Anwendungen, Perspektiven* (pp. 393–418). Wiesbaden: Westdeutscher Verlag.

Price, V., & Tewksbury, D. (1997). News Values and Public Opinion: A Theoretical Account of Media Priming and Framing. In G. A. Barnett & F. J. Boster (Eds.), *Progress in Communication Sciences: Advances in Persuasion* (Vol. 13, pp. 173–212). Greenwich, CT: Ablex.

Scheufele, D. A. (1999). Framing as a Theory of Media Effects. *Journal of Communication, 49*(1), 103–122.

Scheufele, D. A. (2000). Agenda-Setting, Priming, and Framing Revisited: Another Look at Cognitive Effects of Political Communication. *Mass Communication and Society, 2&3*(3), 297–316.

Schulz, W. (1976). *Die Konstruktion von Realität in den Nachrichtenmedien.* Freiburg and München: Verlag Karl Alber.

Schumpeter, J. A. (1976 [1942]). *Capitalism, Socialism and Democracy.* London: Allen and Unwin.

Selb, P. (2003). *Agenda-Setting Prozesse im Wahlkampf.* Bern: Haupt.

Shoemaker, P. J., & Reese, S. D. (1996). *Mediating the Message: Theories of Influences on Mass Media Content* (2nd ed.). White Plains, NY: Longman.

Sides, J. (2006). The Origins of Campaign Agendas. *British Journal of Political Science, 36*(3), 407–436.

Sigal, L. (1973). *Reporters and Officials.* Lexington, MA: D.C. Heath.

Smith, G. (1976). The Functional Properties of the Referendum. *European Journal of Political Research, 4*(1), 1–23.

Smith, D. A., & Tolbert, C. (2001). The Initiative to Party: Partisanship and Ballot Initiatives in California. *Party Politics, 7,* 738–757.

Smith, D. A., & Tolbert, C. (2004). *Educated by Initiative: The Effects of Direct Democracy on Citizens and Political Organizations in the American States.* Ann Arbor: University of Michigan Press.

Sniderman, P. M., & Theriault, S. M. (2004). The Structure of Political Argument and the Logic of Issue Framing. In P. M. Sniderman & S. M. Theriault (Eds.), *Studies in Public Opinion: Attitudes, Nonattitudes, Measurement Error and Change* (pp. 133–165). Princeton, NJ: Princeton University Press.

Tilly, C. (1978). *From Mobilization to Revolution.* Boston, MA: Addison-Wesley.
Tilly, C. (1986). *The Contentious French.* Cambridge: *Cambridge* University Press.
Tilly, C. (1995). *Popular Contention in Great Britain, 1758–1834.* Cambridge: *Cambridge* University Press.
Tuchman, G. (1978). *Making News a Study in the Construction of Reality.* New York: The Free Press.
Wolfsfeld, G. (1997). *Media and Political Conflict: News from the Middle East* (Reprint ed.). Cambridge, MA: Cambridge University Press.
Zaller, J. R. (2003). A New Standard of News Quality: Burglar Alarms for the Monitorial Citizen. *Political Communication, 20,* 109–130.
Zaller, J. R. (2005 [1992]). *The Nature and Origin of Public Opinion.* Cambridge: Cambridge University Press.

CHAPTER 3

Research Design and Data

WHERE DIALOGUE IS MOST LIKELY

I address the leading questions of this book (*Under what conditions will we see dialogue in the media? What are the driving mechanisms? What is the role of dialogue in the Public Opinion formation process?*) by using a most-similar system design and analyzing three most likely cases. I opt for a most-similar system design because it allows many factors to be controlled for, and in such a way isolates the factors responsible for more or less dialogue. Furthermore, since dialogue is normatively desirable (see Chapter 1), I aim at finding as much dialogue in the news as possible. Thus, I analyze debates where dialogue is most likely. But where is dialogue most likely in the news media?

The most likely cases are *direct-democratic* campaigns. In these campaigns, the chance of finding dialogue in the news media is high for various reasons. First, in this context the *issue is given*. The involved actors are forced to talk about the topic at hand. They can hardly take up a separate topic from the news and in such a way detract from the discussion. This constraint pushes dialogue. Indeed, Simon (2002) showed for US senate elections that little dialogue occurs unless (among other factors) the campaign's arena is limited to one issue. Second, direct-democratic campaigns confront voters with a *binary choice*—either in favor of (pro) or against (con) the issue-specific proposition at stake. This binary situation implies the presence of a pro and a contra camp.

R. Hänggli, *The Origin of Dialogue in the News Media*,
Challenges to Democracy in the 21st Century,
https://doi.org/10.1007/978-3-030-26582-3_3

The presence of competing camps guarantees competing information flows because both camps would like to be present in the media with their viewpoints. Third, the issue is *salient* in direct-democratic campaigns. This factor has also been supported empirically: Critical or salient issues bring more dialogue into the media (Simon 2002; Kaplan et al. 2006). Fourth, direct-democratic campaigns are of *limited duration*, with a clear beginning and a clear end. This implies the intensification of flow in frame communication and increases the incentives to participate in the discussion.

Dialogue in the news media is most likely in *Swiss* direct-democratic campaigns. Thus, I investigate direct democracy in Switzerland. The Swiss context further promotes dialogue in the media because, firstly, direct-democratic instruments are led by the elite in this country. The elites are constitutionally bound to inform and communicate with the citizen public[1] and exercise their campaigning role with a certain restraint. They provide the voters with a balanced diet of information and are reluctant to dominate the opinion formation in the general public. Second, all organizations with an interest in the issue at stake can, and often do, participate in this context. Typically, several actor types are involved: large political parties ("large pol. parties"), small political parties ("small pol. parties"), economic interest groups and unions ("econ. interest groups"), citizens' interest groups, church organizations and SMOs ("citizens' int. group"), the minister in charge of the campaign issue and the public administration ("authorities"), and finally ad hoc campaign committees ("ad hoc"). Blumer (1948) noted that the formation of public opinion takes place *within and between the organizations* and not between individuals, and is the product of a discussion among societal actors. Thus, the involvement of a variety of actors increases the diversity of views and in so doing also the chances of dialogue. Third, these campaigns take place frequently in Switzerland. Nowhere else are direct-democratic instruments more developed than here (Kriesi and Trechsel 2008: 49). Between 1960 and 2015, a total of 401 referenda and initiatives were held at the national level in Switzerland. All actors involved know exactly how direct democracy works and the actors can apply their energy to the issue at stake. It is routine action and usually follows the same pattern. Aside from Switzerland, direct-democratic

---

[1] 05.054 Message on the citizens' initiative "Popular sovereignty instead of government propaganda" from June 29, 2005, BBl 2005 4384.

instruments are used frequently in California and a few other American states. In contrast to the USA, however, Swiss direct-democratic campaigns are organized by the elites. In the USA, the government has less control over the direct-democratic process (De Vreese and Semetko 2004; Bowler and Donovan 2006).

The logic of a most-similar system design is helpful in working out the relevant driving factors. The crucial role of limitation to one issue (Simon 2002), or the salience of the issue (Simon 2002; Kaplan et al. 2006) for dialogue in the news has been empirically shown. Thus, in order to provide more insights, we need to keep these factors constant. By keeping the direct-democratic setting constant (most-similar system design), I can elaborate on the influence of actors' choices, campaign, and channel characteristics. However, although I concentrate on the Swiss direct-democratic setting, the findings are not restricted to these direct-democratic debates (see implications in Chapter 1).

Swiss Direct-Democratic Institutions

Different types of direct-democratic instrument are created by the Swiss constitution, with my study consisting of two optional referendums and one initiative. These two types of instrument share in common the fact that they need to be called for by the citizens. In contrast, the source of proposition differs for each of the two instruments. Referendums concern propositions from government, while initiatives are usually put forward by the people. The optional referendum intervenes at the end of the decision-making process and allows citizens to demand a popular vote on laws passed by parliament. It requires 50,000 signatures to be gathered within 100 days of the adoption of an act by parliament. It can also be initiated at the request of eight cantons, but this has happened only once since 1874. If an optional referendum is demanded, the legislative act must be submitted to a popular vote, effectively giving the electorate a veto on government legislation. Initiatives, on the other hand, generally occur at the beginning of the decision-making process and have an agenda-setting function. To force an initiative, the signatures of 100,000 citizens must be gathered within 18 months. The proposed changes can relate to individual items in the constitution or even the constitution as a whole. Before a people's initiative is put to a popular vote in the country, parliament will issue a recommendation to accept or decline it. The Swiss government and parliament, in contrast to the practice in the USA, discuss the text of the initiative before it is submitted to the popular vote and provide it with a voting recommendation, almost always on the side of rejection.

Direct-democratic instruments are not only frequently used; they also exert a profound impact on the political system. The most important impact is derived from the optional referendum and is of an indirect nature. The optional referendum hangs like a sword of Damocles over the legislative process (Neidhart 1970) because the involved actors always have to fear that any political actor may submit the bill to the optional referendum, thus potentially ruining the entire bill. As a consequence, formal and informal institutional mechanisms have been developed in order to avoid this risk of veto. These mechanisms have transformed Swiss democracy into a negotiation democracy. In the pre-parliamentary and parliamentary phases, negotiations take place in which political actors try to find a compromise that is sufficiently strong to avoid a popular vote. Along with federalism, it leads to the establishment of "concordance" or "consensus democracy" (Linder 1999: 24).

RELEVANT POLICY DOMAINS—ACTORS, INTERESTS, AND COALITIONS

The three cases we analyze can be categorized under two of the policy domains highest among voters' priorities, namely immigration and the economy. This adds to their salience. The optional referendum, called by the left against the revised asylum law and put to the voters on September 24, 2006, and the initiative "for democratic naturalizations", organized by the populist right and put to a vote on June 1, 2008, both belong to the immigration policy domain. The optional referendum against the revision of corporation tax, initiated by the left and for which people went to the ballot box on February 24, 2008, comes under the policy domain of economy. Table 3.1 displays these three campaigns in terms of institutional instrument, policy domain, and configuration of the dominant coalition in this domain.

Immigration and the Populist Right

Immigration issues and policies have become increasingly salient and high profile in recent years in the politics of Western European nations.

Table 3.1 Classification of three campaigns in terms of institutions and policy domains

Instrument	Policy domain	
	Immigration policy	Economic policy
Optional referendum	Asylum law (centre-right coalition)	Corporation tax (centre-right coalition)
Initiative	Naturalization initiative (centre-left coalition)	–

This can be largely attributed to the processes of globalization and denationalization (Kriesi et al. 2006, 2008), which have created movements of people into Western Europe from other parts of the world. These immigrants often come from places previously seen as far away and culturally distinct, leading some people within indigenous populations to perceive them as a threat to established cultures, traditional ways of life and their own economic prospects. New populist, right-wing parties and movements have emerged in many European countries to mobilize and exploit these fears by demanding harsher and more restrictive immigration policies. On the other hand, those arguing for more liberal and relaxed immigration policies and defending migrants' rights tend to belong to parties on the left (Koopmans et al. 2005). They are joined on this side of the debate by NGOs, human rights groups, religious associations, and labor unions (other economic interest groups tend to stay out of this policy domain).

What sets the situation in Switzerland apart from other Western European countries is that these direct-democratic campaigns give the opposing sides an opportunity to mobilize their constituencies around institutionally binding proposals. The populist right use an initiative to promote more restrictive immigration policies, while a coalition on the left use an optional referendum to prevent punitive changes to existing law. Therefore, by selecting these two propositions our study looks at cases representing each side of the immigration policy debate.

With the two sides in this policy domain being diametrically opposed and entrenched in their views, the position of the *moderate right* becomes crucial. Attempting to achieve a balance between representing the generally conservative views of their supporters and a wariness of being too closely associated with the populist or far right, they form varying alliances, often in favor of the status quo. Therefore, they tend to align themselves with the left in opposing the populist right's initiatives, e.g., the naturalization initiative, but also support the right in their opposition to the left's referendums, for instance, against the revised asylum law.

Neo-Liberal Tax Reforms

In contrast to the cases in the immigration policy domain, where firm left/right positions and voting traditions do not always hold, the third case—the corporation tax referendum—presents a classic confrontation between the left and the united right on a class-based economic issue (although the rise of this issue on the Swiss policy agenda is also due to some of the same processes of global competition as those driving the immigration issue).

Traditionally, Switzerland has offered relatively low rates of business tax. However, from the 1990s onwards, as international competition for capital investment has intensified, the federal government has taken action to further reduce charges for particularly sensitive parts of the economy, such as mobile factors of production like capital and labor. As is the case in many Western countries, the issue of fiscal reform in Switzerland—on both the tax and expenditure side—has become a major ideological battleground for neoliberals and free marketeers. However, unlike elsewhere, in Switzerland those wanting to reform the tax code must take into account the system's direct-democratic nature. Indeed, the framework of Switzerland's highly complex, federal economic system—including the levying of specific taxes—is part of the constitution, so any modification of this framework implies a compulsory referendum. It is unsurprising, therefore, that at federal level there has been a succession of votes broadly related to fiscal reform (Kriesi and Bernhard 2012).

The Cases: Asylum Law, Naturalization, and Corporation Tax

In the following section, we will look at the specific cases in turn and how parliamentary debates and government decisions prefigured each issue and prestructured the choices around them.

The Asylum Law Referendum

Having introduced the asylum law above, some more context and background to the campaign is useful here. Accompanying the referendum on the asylum law was a vote on reform of immigration law, also accepted with a convincing majority. Government proposals on each reform had been toughened during parliamentary debate in Spring 2004 as a result of pressure from the populist right (SVP), with the support of the moderate right. The SVP had put forward a radical asylum initiative two years previously, which, although narrowly rejected, had been supported by 49.5% of the popular vote and more than half of all cantons. This led the moderate right to be more receptive to SVP demands for a hardening of the asylum and immigration reforms.

The Naturalization Initiative

The so-called naturalization initiative of the Swiss People's Party (SVP) was rejected by 63.6% of voters on June 1, 2008. A comprehension of the naturalization process in Switzerland is important for understanding the impetus behind the SVP's initiative. Local municipalities play a central role in the process, but there have always been political as well as administrative considerations and the naturalization procedure varies significantly from canton to canton, and within individual cantons, even from one local area to another (Helbling and Kriesi 2004; Helbling 2008). Rather than being decided centrally, individual naturalization decisions can be taken by general assemblies of local citizens, or by local parliaments, executives, or naturalization committees. Prior to a 2003, individual cases could even be decided by popular vote. In that year, federal judges outlawed such ballots in reaction to an infamous vote in the city of Emmen, where the populace rejected a series of applications for Swiss citizenship by people from the former Yugoslavia (while approving those by applicants from Italy). It was shown that, although these popular votes were limited in number, where they did take place the rejection rate for applicants was far higher than in the rest of Switzerland (Helbling and Kriesi 2004). The judges argued that justification was needed for rejecting naturalization requests, and that such justification was not possible in a direct-democratic vote.

In reaction to this Federal Court decision, in 2004 the SVP launched its popular initiative, which proposed that the procedures used for

Table 3.2 Main frames of each campaign

Asylum	Naturalization	Corporation tax
Human. trad. Rule-of-law Abuse Efficacy	Rule-of-law People final say Mass naturalization	Tax equity Tax loss SME (small and medium-sized enterprise) Competitiveness

naturalizations, and in particular whether individual applications were put to a popular ballot, should be the decision of voters in any given municipality. The initiative went even further than this in prohibiting any appeal against local rejections of naturalization applications and indeed demanding that the naturalization process become an entirely political one, rather than administrative, with decision-making power in the hands of the citizens only. Thus the initiative's pro camp advocated that people should have the final say (*people final say*), and also that "mass naturaliza- tions" should be stopped (*mass naturalization*), whereas the con camp called for fair procedures that complied with basic rights (*rule-of-law*). Table 3.2 presents an overview of the main frames in each campaign.

The Swiss government recommended that the initiative be rejected, arguing that it violated international law, in particular the European Convention on Human Rights, the UN's International Covenant on Civil and Political Rights, and the UN convention against racism. The debate in parliament was not without controversy, with some members of the moderate right expressing considerable sympathy for the proposal. In the end a clear majority recommended its rejection, but parliament did make a significant concession to the populist right in the form of a suggested modification to the law on civic rights. This counter-proposal, to come into force if the initiative were rejected, retained the possibility of local general assemblies deciding on naturalization applications, but on the proviso that explicit justifications should be provided for rejec- tions, with these justifications being cited during the assemblies and potentially forming the basis of later appeals. The parliamentary and direct-democratic debates varied slightly in this case, with parliament concerned predominantly with procedures for naturalization.

In light of early opinion polls, the clarity of the verdict in this case (63.6% against the proposal) came as a surprise, unlike the outcome of the asylum law vote (67.7% in favor of the new law). Such a movement from pro to con position cannot be explained through campaign activities alone, but seems also to be connected to SVP internal conflicts, which reduced both the mobilization of their members and the persuasion effect on non-party members (Longchamp et al. 2008: 10). As leaders of the pro campaign, this vote was the first important test of the SVP's new opposition politics and overall strategy. Having won the federal elections in Autumn 2007, by the end of that year the party had been outmaneuvered in the composition of the coalition government. In fact, their coalition partners, the Social Democrats (main left-wing party of Switzerland) and Christian Democrats (CVP: center to center-right party, originally the Catholic-Conservative Party [KKP]) had essentially brought down the SVP leader. While respecting the party's claim to two out of the total of seven government seats, they refused to reelect both of its incumbent ministers, and instead of the SVP's charismatic leader Christoph Blocher (the incumbent Minister of Justice), parliament chose another member of the party—Evelyne Widmer-Schlumpf—to replace him. In reaction to this, the SVP proceeded to exclude its two newly elected ministers from the party and chose to adopt a systematically oppositional stance within parliament. This whole process and exclusion procedure preoccupied both the SVP and the Swiss public in the lead up to the vote on the naturalization initiative, causing the campaign for the initiative to begin just five weeks before the vote.

The Corporation Tax Referendum

The outcome of this vote was also unexpected, this time in its closeness. Opinion polls before the vote had suggested a clear lead for the pro camp and given Swiss voters' generally favorable attitude toward neoliberal tax reforms it came as a surprise that, on February 24, 2008, the revised corporation tax was accepted in a referendum with the slimmest possible majority of 50.5%. The post-vote survey helped to explain this movement toward the con position by revealing that the public had perceived the proposal to be complex and had experienced difficulties deciding which way to vote. For this reason, many settled on their choice only in the latter stages of the campaign, and of those who were undecided until two weeks before the vote, the majority opted against the proposal (56%) (Hirter and Linder 2008). Not only were the pro camp overly optimistic based on the early opinion polls and reduced their campaigning activity in the run-up to the vote, the messages and arguments of the contra camp also resonated well with an external event happening at the time (the UBS subprime crises, see Chapters 6 and 7).

The corporate tax reform consisted of three elements, the core one being a reduction of the tax levied on large shareholder dividends. This measure was designed to alleviate the double imposition of dividend tax, which Switzerland is one of the last OECD member states to practice. The second component involved the possible mitigation of cantonal tax on capital, and the third provided special measures for ownership inheritance in private, non-incorporated companies.

The main frames of this campaign are shown in Table 3.2. Opponents of the reform focused on matters of fairness or "tax equity" and warned that the reduction in tax take, in terms of both direct and indirect taxes, would create a shortfall of several hundred million Swiss francs (tax loss). The supporters of the new law used the frame of a necessary nurturing of small- and medium-sized enterprises (SME) and argued that the reform would boost the economy by encouraging investments (competitiveness).

In order to boost its chances of success, the reform represented a political compromise between the business community, the cantons and parties of the right. The business community restrained their desire to banish the double imposition of dividend taxes altogether in order to keep onside the cantons, who had proven to be a formidable adversary in a previous 2004 vote on the tax package. Thus, a compromise was reached whereby the reform, rather than removing the tax entirely, instead proposed reducing it to 50 or 60% for investors holding at least 10% of the shares in company property or private property, respectively. The 10% qualification, already in force in several cantons, was another compromise introduced by parliament in order to limit cantonal loss of tax revenue, whereas the government had proposed to reduce the tax for all shareholders, regardless of size of shareholding. In this way, the new law could carry the support of the cantons, with seventeen (out of the 26) cantons having already introduced such a tax reduction for large shareholders. It also ensured that the benefits of the reduction were felt mainly by the owners and investors of myriad small- and medium-sized companies, often considered to be the engine and backbone of the Swiss economy and whom the whole package was designed to strengthen in the first place.

The autonomy of the cantons in matters of tax was also carefully considered in the second element of the reform, which introduced the potential for cantons that levy a tax on profits to also suppress their tax on capital, but did not oblige them to do so and gave them control over details of the process. Finally, the law involved an element of mitigation for companies undergoing a period of transition, with measures designed to facilitate the transfer or inheritance of a company from one generation of owners to the next, or to alleviate the financial burden on self-employed people looking to close down their business (Kriesi and Bernhard 2012).

CAMPAIGN SELECTION

The case selection is based on a "focused comparison" (King et al. 1994: 43ff) and is helpful for working out the mechanism of the origin of competing messages and of dialogue. I am able to compare the campaigns with regard to four criteria—their complexity, familiarity, imbalance in terms of financial resources, and expected closeness of the vote (see Appendix for more information on these indicators). Simplifying a little, I can classify the campaigns in the following way: As we can see in Table 3.3, the corporation tax case constitutes a complex object. In addition, the corporation tax case and the naturalization initiative were unfamiliar issues. The lack of familiarity suggests that, in these two cases, the campaigners enjoyed a greater degree of latitude than for the asylum issue.

Furthermore, the budgets of the three investigated direct-democratic campaigns can be roughly estimated based on the interviews with the campaigners. We asked them about the budget of their campaign as well as the estimated budget of their opponents' campaign. In addition, we double-checked the information with our own estimation of budgets based on the number and size of advertisements placed. In the naturalization initiative, around 0.8 million Swiss francs were spent.

Table 3.3 Complexity and familiarity, imbalance in financial resources, and expected closeness of the three proposals

	Complexity	Familiarity	Imbalance in financial resources	Expected closeness of the outcome
Asylum	Low	Familiar	Balanced	Close
Naturalization	Low	Unfamiliar	Imbalanced	Close
Corporation Tax	High	Unfamiliar	Very imbalanced	Not close

The asylum law involved expenditure of 2.8 million Swiss francs, whereas the budget for the corporate tax reform rose to around 7.0 million Swiss francs. The pro camp was far ahead of the contra camp in terms of financial resources in the corporate tax reform. Advantages such as this have been extremely rare in Swiss direct-democratic campaigns (Kriesi and Bernhard 2012). The resources for the pro camp came mainly from the business interest associations, and the amount invested by them signals the singular importance that the business community attributed to this particular reform. By contrast, in the asylum law campaign, the two camps were able to draw upon almost the same budget. The naturalization initiative and the asylum law campaigns were evaluated as close races whereas the corporate tax reform was not perceived as close. I will go on to suggest that dialogue is more likely if the issue is simple and familiar, if the financial resources are balanced, and if the race is expected to be close.

DATA COLLECTION

Content Analysis of Campaign Material and Media Content

The content analysis is most important for my study. In all three campaigns, we conducted a content analysis of the media input (=press releases and documents written for media conferences), political advertisements, letters to the editor, and of the media's news reporting. Additionally, direct mails and information for members were coded in the asylum law campaign. All material was coded in the same manner,[2] with three levels of analysis—the level of the article, the political actor, and the argument (details, see Appendix).

Eighteen newspapers and two TV news programs were included in the study of the news media. We selected the most important elite newspapers (which we call "elite"), free newspapers ("free"), regional newspapers ("regional"), tabloid newspapers ("tabloid"), and public service TV news ("TV") both in the German-speaking and in the French-speaking part of the country[3] (see Table 3.4 for the list). We made sure that the

[2]The codebook is available upon request.
[3]The daily newspapers selected were those with the highest total audience for German-speaking as well as French-speaking Switzerland. Concerning TV, we concentrated on

Table 3.4 Media analyzed in content analysis

Type	Media	Language
Elite	Le Temps	French
	Neue Zürcher Zeitung	German
	NZZ am Sonntag	
	Sonntagszeitung	
Free	20 Minutes	French
	20 Minuten	German
Regional	24 heures	French
	Tribune de Genève	
	Aargauer Zeitung	German
	Basler Zeitung	
	Berner Zeitung	
	Die Südostschweiz	
	Neue Luzerner Zeitung	
	St. Galler Tagblatt	
	Tagesanzeiger	
Tabloid	Le Matin	French
	Blick	German
	Sonntagsblick	
TV news	le journal	French
	Tagesschau	German

selected media covered all relevant media types. For the asylum law, the media coverage was analyzed over a period of 16 calendar weeks. This campaign started earlier than the other two campaigns because the issue was important to many organizations on the contra-side and they tried to frame the issue before the summer holiday had started. The other two campaigns were shorter; the coverage over thirteen calendar weeks before the vote was analyzed in both. In the case of the naturalization initiative, the attention paid to the first 100 days of a newly elected member of the Federal Council delayed the beginning of the campaign. Only when the event marking the end of these first 100 days had passed did the campaign and the media coverage begin in earnest. The vote about the tax reform took place in February. Such votes usually imply shorter campaigns because they do not start until after the Christmas break. In all three cases, we covered the direct-democratic campaign from the start to the end.

public service TV, as commercial and privately owned TV plays only a marginal role in Switzerland. We did not analyze media from the small Italian-speaking part of the country.

Table 3.5 Total number of articles and arguments coded by campaign and channel

	Asylum	Naturalization	Corporation tax
Number of articles			
News media	559	380	327
Media input	92	69	88
Political ads	371	327	434
Letters to the editor	223	257	272
Direct mail	19	–	–
Info for members	106	–	–
Number of arguments			
News media	2455	1909	2066
Media input	1061	782	1056
Political ads	1818	1467	1286
Letters to the editor	597	989	1057
Direct mail	324	–	–
Info for members	2099	–	–

Table 3.5 shows the total number of articles and arguments which were coded. The highest number of newspaper articles and documents directed toward the media (media input) were found in the asylum law campaign. The average media article contains about five arguments whereas around twelve arguments are found in a piece of media input. In the corporate tax reform, we find the highest number of political ads and letters to the editor.

Expert Interviews with Political Actors

To a minor extent, I relied also on data collected in interviews. The conversations considering the strategies of the political actors were conducted with the campaign managers of *all* political organizations who took part in the campaign under scrutiny. In other words, we interviewed one person per organization. The campaign manager is the person responsible for the campaign, i.e., for the strategy, message, communications, campaign actions, cooperation, timing, budget, etc. Table 3.6 gives an overview of the number and type of organizations interviewed. We distinguish between five types of organization, called actor types: the department of the minister (=Swiss Federal Councilor) responsible for the issue and other governmental actors, the political parties, the economic interest groups including unions, the ad hoc campaign

Table 3.6 Number and type of political organization interviewed, by campaign

	Asylum		Naturalization		Corporation tax	
	Contra	Pro	Contra	Pro	Contra	Pro
Parties (large parties)	10 (2)	6 (3)	10 (4)	3 (1)	7 (2)	5 (3)
Citizens' interest groups	15	2	7	3	3	0
Economic interest groups	4	3	4	1	3	10
Ad hoc committees	4	0	1	1	0	0
Department of minister	0	2	3	0	0	2
n per camp	33	13	25	8	13	17
n total		46		33		30

Note The numbers of large parties are indicated in brackets

committees, and citizens' interest groups including church organizations. In the case of the asylum law, we had 46 different interlocutors. Thirty-three organizations belonged to the challengers' camp, which illustrates that the campaign against the asylum law mobilized a large number of collective actors, especially parties and citizens' interest groups. In the naturalization case, we interviewed 33 organizations, again with a much larger number from the contra camp (25) than the pro camp (8). Half of the conversations were held with parties and citizens' interest groups from the contra camp. In the tax reform campaign, the economic interest groups were particularly active. Overall, we interviewed 30 organizations in this case, 17 on the pro side, of which 10 were economic interest groups. The number of actors varies in each campaign since the organizations do not have sufficient resources to campaign every time. The involvement of an organization depends not only on the importance of the issue for that organization, but also on the number of important issues on the agenda in a given year.

We conducted two face-to-face interviews with each campaign manager—one at the outset of the campaign, and one after the citizens' vote. This design is motivated by the fact that questions relating to expectations are preferably asked prior to the vote, whereas evaluation questions only make sense after the end of the campaign.

Panel Study (Chapter 8)

Public opinion was captured by means of two (three in the asylum law) panel surveys in the French- and German-speaking parts of Switzerland. In all surveys, the first panel wave was fielded before the campaign

Table 3.7 Details of three panel studies

Study details (panel waves, date of interviews)	N	% female	Mean age (SD)
Panel study I: Asylum			
Wave I (7/4–7/20/2006)	1725	52.2	48.5 (17.1)
Wave II (8/28–9/2/2006)	1415	53.7	49.3 (17.0)
Wave III (9/25–9/30/2006)	1094	54.6	50.4 (17.1)
Panel study III: Naturalization			
Wave I (4/7–4/25/2008)	1251	51.3	48.5 (16.8)
Wave II (6/2–6/20/2008)	999	50.2	49.6 (16.7)
Panel study II: Corporation tax			
Wave I (1/9–1/23/2008)	1251	50.3	50.2 (16.3)
Wave II (2/25–3/7/2008)	1001	50.4	50.2 (16.4)

started and the final survey took place after the date of vote. The computer-assisted telephone interviews (CATI interviews) were conducted by a single company.

For each campaign, we conducted a panel study. The structure of the questionnaire remained comparable across the three campaigns and differed only in terms of their thematic focus. Table 3.7 lists the relevant information pertaining to the panel studies. As can be seen in this table, in the study about the asylum law campaign, participants were interviewed three times, while there were only two waves of interviews in the other two studies. The first interviews always took place before the campaign started. The final wave was started after the vote.

ARGUMENTS AS LINKS BETWEEN THE DATA COLLECTION INSTRUMENTS

The questions concerning the arguments were linked between all relevant actors in the political campaigns. In content analysis and interviews, we included questions about the very same arguments (Table A.4). First, we asked the politicians about the importance of each argument in their campaign and their position on these arguments. For instance, they were asked about the importance of the argument "the abuse of asylum policy must be stopped" and how much they agreed with it. In the content analysis, we coded how often the argument "the abuse of asylum policy must be stopped" was mentioned in the campaign material and in the news media and whether or not it was used offensively or defensively. Such an integrated approach in data collection enables us to trace the flow of arguments from political actors to mass media reporting. Finally, in the panel survey, we asked the survey respondents whether they were aware of the most important arguments (Table A.5) and whether they agreed with them. For instance, our interviewees were asked whether they had heard the argument "the abuse of asylum policy must be stopped" and how much they agreed with it. Such an integrated approach in data collection enables us to trace the flow of arguments from political actors via mass media reporting to the public (see Hänggli et al. 2012, for a more detailed description).

REFERENCES

Blumer, H. (1948). Public Opinion and Public Opinion Polling. *American Sociological Review, 13*(5), 542–549.

Bowler, S., & Donovan, T. (2006). Direct Democracy and Political Parties in America. *Party Politics, 12*(5), 649–669.

De Vreese, C. H., & Semetko, H. A. (2004). News Matters: Influences on the Vote in a Referendum Campaign. *European Journal of Political Research, 43*(5), 701–724.

Hänggli, R., Schemer, C., & Rademacher, P. (2012). Toward a Methodological Integration in the Study of Political Campaign Communication. In H. Kriesi (Ed.), *Political Communication in Direct Democratic Campaigns: Enlightening or Manipulating?* (pp. 39–53). Hampshire: Palgrave Macmillan.

Helbling, M. (2008). *Practicing Citizenship and Heterogeneous Nationhood: Naturalizations in Swiss Municipalities.* Amsterdam: Amsterdam University Press.

Helbling, M., & Kriesi, H. (2004). Staatsbürgerverständnis und politische Mobilisierung: Einbürgerungen in Schweizer Gemeinden, Schweiz. *Zeitschrift für Politikwissenschaft, 10*(4), 33–58.

Hirter, H., & Linder, W. (2008). Analysis of the Federal Votes of February 24, 2008 (Analyse der eidgenössischen Abstimmungen vom 24. Februar 2008). *Vox Analysis.* Berne: University of Berne.

Kaplan, N., Park, D. K., & Ridout, T. N. (2006). Dialogue in American Campaigns? An Examination of Issue Convergence in Candidate Television Advertising. *American Journal of Political Science, 50*(3), 724–736.

King, G., Keohane, R. O., & Verba, S. (1994). *Designing Social Inquiry: Scientific Infer-Ence in Qualitative Research.* Princeton, NJ: Princeton University Press.

Koopmans, R., Statham, P., Giugni, M., & Passy, F. (2005). *Contested Citizenship. Immigration and Cultural Diversity in Europe.* Minneapolis: University of Minnesota Press.

Kriesi, H., Adam, S., & Jochum, M. (2006). Comparative Analysis of Policy Networks in Western Europe. *Journal of European Public Policy, 13*(3), 341–361.

Kriesi, H., Grande, E., Lachat, R., Dolezal, M., Bornschier, S., & Frey, T. (2008). *West European Politics in the Age of Globalization.* Cambridge University Press.

Kriesi, H., & Bernhard, L. (2012). The Context of the Campaigns. In H. Kriesi (Ed.), *Political Communication in Direct-Democratic Campaigns: Enlightening or Manipulating?* (pp. 17–38). Hampshire: Palgrave Macmillan.

Kriesi, H., & Trechsel, A. H. (2008). *The Politics of Switzerland.* Cambridge: Cambridge University Press.

Linder, W. (1999). *Schweizerische Demokratie - Institutionen, Prozesse, Perspektiven.* Bern.

Longchamp, C., Bucher, M., Ratelband-Pally, S., & Imfeld, M. (2008). Meinungsumschwung bei Gesundheitsartikel und Einbürgerungsinitiative. Stabile Mehrheit gegen die Initiative „Volkssouveränität statt Behördenpropaganda". *Medienbericht* zur 2. Welle der Trendstudie „Abstimmungen vom 1. Juni 2008" im Auftrag der SRG SSR idée suisse. Gfs.bern.

Neidhart, L. (1970). *Plebiszit und pluralitäre Demokratie: eine Analyse der Funktion des schweizerischen Gesetzesreferendum.* Bern: Francke.

Simon, A. (2002). *The Winning Message: Candidate Behavior, Campaign Discourse, and Democracy.* New York: Cambridge University Press.

PART II

Empirical Outcomes

CHAPTER 4

Frame Construction for Media Input (Strategic Framing Choices)

INTRODUCTION[1]

In order to win a political campaign, political actors try to achieve an *emphasis* effect (Druckman 2001, 2004), i.e., to lead the media or individuals to focus on certain aspects of an issue rather than others when constructing their opinions (Druckman 2001: 230). They frame the issue at stake strategically and "campaign on behalf of competing ways of understanding what is at issue" (Sniderman and Theriault 2004: 158). I argue that political actors face at least three strategic framing choices. I investigate these three strategic choices exclusively in the press releases and documents written for press conferences (=media input) in this chapter because this is the crucial channel in the frame-building process. The first aim of the campaigners is to bring their frames into the earned media coverage, because the news media transport their message the furthest and for free.

We collected and coded all the press releases published at the national level in these three campaigns. Thus, I can confidently state that the press releases and documents analyzed are more or less a full reflection of what the media or the citizens directly received from the campaigners.

---

[1] Part of this chapter or an earlier version has been published previously (Hänggli and Kriesi 2010: Asylum Law; Hänggli and Kriesi 2012: Naturalization Initiative; Hänggli et al. 2012).

© The Author(s) 2020
R. Hänggli, *The Origin of Dialogue in the News Media,*
Challenges to Democracy in the 21st Century,
https://doi.org/10.1007/978-3-030-26582-3_4

We did not code documents published at the subnational level, discussions in informal meetings or personal exchanges or explanations by individual actors. Information that is not public or is irrelevant at the national level does not influence the general populace. Furthermore, informal conversations between journalists and political actors are irrelevant for the content of the stories as we found journalists to be independent of lobbying activities. As one journalist of a quality paper mentioned, "we are too strong for political actors to exert pressure on us." The influence of political actors on journalists is reduced to invitations to public talks or political discussions, or attempts to place their own articles in a newspaper or letters to the editor.

THE THREE STRATEGIC CHOICES

In order to win a campaign, the political actors face three strategic choices (Hänggli and Kriesi 2010). First, they are expected to search for a frame which they believe has the capacity to become a *strong substantive frame*. This is a frame that finds attention and is convincing. I call this choice the "Substantive Emphasis Choice." Indeed, to find information that matters to citizens—in Lupia's term (2016: 15), to find "the sweet spot"—is a key task. Lupia (2016) takes note of how educators can communicate effectively with an audience. Framing is a crucial element of this process and concerns "choices about which attributes [of complex issues] to emphasize" (Lupia 2016: 133). To do so, educators can connect an issue to values that a citizen already holds. Non-academic advisors also point to this aspect. To arouse an eager want in others, we need to see things from their point of view and to combine our desires with their wants (Carnegie 2010[1936]). To find strong arguments, Lupia (2016: 75, 134) recommends speaking to the fears and aspirations of prospective learners. In order to do so, educators need to learn about the values that are important to the audience and choose the argument that is in line with these values. However, on its own "understanding values will not be sufficient to choose an effective frame" (Lupia 2016: 134). The argument also needs to be convincing—informative in Lupia's term (2016: 15)—while Achen and Bartels (2016: 309) argue that addressing ongoing concerns in a language spoken by a target group is crucial to court the support of that group. Second, the political actors have to decide how much importance they will attach to the frames of the opponents compared to their own frames. This choice is labeled the

"Oppositional Emphasis Choice." According to conventional wisdom, political actors should focus on the issue or issue attributes for which they enjoy an advantage. Riker's (1996) "dominance principle" formulates this type of strategy: "when one side has an advantage on an issue, the other side ignores it." Issue ownership theory (Petrocik 1996) suggests that political parties tend to follow this recipe, which means that they essentially talk past each other in political campaigns.

As a consequence, yes and no campaigners fighting against each other would be expected to rely essentially on different frames. However, under some conditions there are reasons to expect the political actors to counter-argue the strong frames of their opponents. In other words, there are reasons to expect dialogue. Firstly, if the campaign is restricted to one issue, political actors tend to talk to each other (Simon 2002). They cannot switch to another topic. Secondly, there are strategic reasons to enter into dialogue. Jerit shows that dialogue (in her words engagement) is "more effective at increasing support for reform" (Jerit 2008: 1) than avoiding an argument, while Jacobs and Shapiro (2000: 150) argue that dialogue is the strategic choice if neither side has complete control in a debate. Political actors know that the media offer dialogue in direct-democratic campaigns. Indeed, they do not have control of the debate in the media. Thus, they counter-attack their opponent's line of argument. In this way, they anticipate the media logic and adapt their communication strategy accordingly (Cook 1989; Entman 1989; Jacobs and Shapiro 2000; Jerit 2008). To expect political actors to counter-argue is also in line with research on framing effects and on persuasion, which teach us that political actors can reduce their opponents' influence if they counter-frame (for an overview, see, for instance, Chong and Druckman 2007: 109f., or de Vreese and Lecheler 2012: 296ff.). In an experimental setting, Druckman and Nelson (2003) found that counter-framing and heterogeneous discussions do indeed limit framing effects by prompting deliberative processing and offering reformulations of the problems. From the literature on persuasion, we know that "[t]wo-sided messages influence attitudes more than one-sided messages" provided that the "message refutes opposition arguments" (Perloff 2010: 186). Thus, we can expect political actors to engage in and promote dialogue because they are likely to be more influential if they do so. Thirdly, the pro camp of a referendum has a special incentive to engage in dialogue as they seek policy change and have to explain why they want it (Riker 1996: 69). Fourthly, political actors want to be credible. If the public is likely to be preoccupied with the issue of the campaign (as is the case in our settings), it is considered important for candidates to establish their credentials on this issue. By releasing press documents on the major pro and contra arguments, political actors are more likely to be seen as concerned and responsive and in such a way increase their credibility (Ansolabehere and Iyengar 1994). Thus, we expect political actors to react to the frames of their opponents.

Issue complexity is expected to handicap dialogue because the topic is more difficult. Political actors might first have to explain what the issue at stake is about and to build frame ownership before they can discuss among each other. In addition, an *imbalance in financial resources* between the two camps is also expected to decrease dialogue. Kaplan et al. (2006: 730) argue that the camps are unable to talk about everything they might wish to talk about. Money helps them to address more aspects. In our cases, money is often an indicator for campaign importance. If more money is involved, it means that political actors are more active and produce more input material. If the difference in financial terms increases, the activities of the camps become more unequal, and as a consequence, the possibilities to engage in dialogue become more unequal.

In contrast, *issue familiarity* is expected to facilitate dialogue because the political actors have to explain less what the proposal is about and can concentrate on the discussion with the other camp. Furthermore, according to Kaplan et al. (2006) and Kahn and Kenney (1999: 81–86), the *expected closeness* of a vote or an election (as measured before the campaign) increases dialogue. Kahn and Kenney find that candidates involved in close races tackle their opponent's policy agenda and issue position more often than is the case for less competitive races because it is particularly worthwhile to refute the opponent's line of argument in this situation. Thus, the political actors will counter-argue as much as possible for strategic reasons. Basinger and Lavine (2005) confirm this pattern and explain the mechanism behind this finding as follows: In more competitive campaigns, voters are more motivated to form an opinion as this opinion matters and can make a difference. As a consequence, they rely more on issue or ideological voting rather than on partisan cues. This tendency for a greater reliance on issue voting also increases the motivation of the political actors to discuss the topic and not allow their opponents to dominate the information flow or to persuade voters.

In this chapter, we also investigate dialogue at the frame level, i.e., frame dialogue. *Frame dialogue* (=frame convergence) is the extent to which two camps converge with regard to *one* particular frame of an issue (see Appendix for details). Thus, instead of looking at all the main frames of a campaign, it concentrates on *one* frame, e.g., the "humanitarian tradition" frame, and explores the extent to which opposing viewpoints of this aspect are present. Frame dialogue is highest if both the pro and contra position on this frame are equally present, and lowest if only one perspective is present.[2] In order to distinguish between the two measures of dialogue, I speak of dialogue (=campaign dialogue) and frame dialogue. At the frame level, I hypothesize that *salience* (Damore 2005) of the frame in the media increases frame dialogue in media input. When a frame receives attention in the media, it might become important to the voters too, and the political actors might be forced to take a position on it. Thus, the political actors are expected to use a salient frame more often.

If political actors refer to the frames of their opponents, they can do so either *offensively* or *defensively*. As introduced in Chapter 2, the offensive use of opponents' frames corresponds to what Sides (2006) has called "*trespassing*": Political actors may use strong images, issues or issue attributes of their opponents in order to appear responsive to the general public. Sides also refers to this strategy as "*riding the wave*" and shows in his analysis of the 1998 American presidential campaign that it is widely used. Even more widespread, however, may be the defensive use of opponents' frames: Political actors may feel forced to react to the successful frames of their opponents and to adopt *counter-frames* to offer rebuttals and to counter-attack their adversaries. A fully fledged framing strategy of a political actor should not only mobilize his or her own constituency and the neutrals, but should also try to "neutralize and discredit the framing efforts of adversaries and rivals, keeping their potential supporters passive" (Gamson 2004: 250). I expect political actors to prefer their own substantive frames and to rely on defensive strategies only

---

[2]We use frame dialogue only in this chapter for three reasons. First, frame dialogue is less important because we are more interested in the overall dialogue than in the dialogue about a certain frame. Second, the average frame dialogue in a campaign is similar to the ordinary measure of dialogue. It is not necessary to show the same results twice. Third, I wish to illustrate that there is a certain degree of dialogue on all frames, and for this reason, it is interesting to present these results here.

insofar as their opponents' framing is successful, or they anticipate their opponents' framing to be successful. In most cases, political actors are expected to use their opponents' frame defensively (i.e., counter-frame). They use the opponent's frame offensively (i.e., trespass) only if such a frame is credible, people have firm beliefs about it (for instance that a particular outcome or consequence of a law will occur), and a strong value is involved.

Concerning the third choice, the political actors have to decide how much importance they will attach to the campaign *contest* compared to the *substantive* content of the campaign. This is the "Contest Emphasis Choice." In general, I expect that the political actors would like to get their substantive message across and place a high priority on their chosen substantive frame(s). This choice deals with style, i.e., how things are said. Historical figures such as Aristotle and Machiavelli realized that this is an important rhetorical element. In fact, the three choices characterize public debates—the first two (Substantive Emphasis and Oppositional Emphasis Choices) define the range of views and the last one (Contest Emphasis Choice) defines the style of a public debate (Hänggli and van der Wurff 2019). To summarize the hypotheses: First, the strategic actors are expected to search for a frame which they believe has the capacity to become a *strong substantive frame* ("Substantive Emphasis Choice"). Second, yes and no campaigners fighting against each other are not expected only to rely on different frames, but rather to engage in dialogue. If the political actors refer to the frames of their opponents, they are expected to do so predominantly *defensively*, where their opponents' framing is successful or they anticipate their opponents' framing to be successful ("Oppositional Emphasis Choice"). Dialogue is probably handicapped by *issue complexity* (high in the corporate tax reform) and *an imbalance in financial resources*. In contrast, *issue familiarity* (high in the asylum law) and *expected closeness* (high in the naturalization initiative and the asylum law) are expected to increase dialogue. At the frame level, I hypothesize that the *salience* of a frame in the media increases dialogue. Third, I expect that the political actors would like to get their substantive message across and place a high priority on their chosen substantive frame(s) ("Contest Emphasis Choice").

RESULTS

Substantive Emphasis Choice: Reasons for Frame Choice

Based on hypothesis 1, the strategic actors are expected to search for a strong substantive frame ("Substantive Emphasis Choice"). But how do political actors find their strong arguments?

The reasons for their choice of argument (Table 4.1) mainly concern two aspects. On the one hand, campaigners look for arguments which find attention, and on the other hand, they want to convince them. To find attention, campaigners want to connect with their target group, and so they prefer emotional arguments. But campaigners are also particularly looking for convincing arguments. They justify their argument choice by saying that the argument is convincing, comprehensive, factual, or represents values well embedded in the country (valence arguments) or the value(s) of their own organization. If they choose an argument that represents a value of an organization, the value must be of key importance to that organization, which is then motivated to talk about the concerned aspect. Some also have credibility in mind. They pick arguments on which their organization is particularly credible. Some think a good argument needs to show the way in which the law can(not) solve problems: For instance, an actor of the contra camp argued that the new asylum law was a bluff package that would not reduce abuse. By using the abuse perspective, he wanted to show that the expected consequence was unrealistic and that the law would not solve problems.

Finally, individual campaigners mentioned other reasons for picking an argument, such as the additional perspective it brings into the discussion, its potential to find attention, or the internal agreement within a committee. This internal agreement was particularly difficult to achieve in one case because many different organizations were brought together in one committee. They had different understandings of the topic and what a campaign should look like and so had to choose the argument everybody agreed with. Often, a good argument unifies many of these different reasons.

Substantive Emphasis Choice: How to Find Strong Arguments?

Politicians and campaigners have a pretty good understanding of the persuasive power of an argument from the signature collection phase and

Table 4.1   Reasons for argument choice

Reasons	Examples of statements in interviews	Overall aim
Emotional argument	It is emotional It touches people It makes people feel involved It elicits sympathy It makes people angry	To find attention
Receives attention	Argument attracts attention but is not too extreme	
Convincing argument	It is convincing (mentioned several times) It convinces conservatives It is most convincing as opinion poll shows	To be convincing
Comprehensible argument	It is comprehensible It is easy to understand/people understood it It is not too abstract We reach people with it It reduces complexity to a core message Even the most ignorant person can understand it It can be demonstrated in an appealing manner It connects with the everyday experiences of people	
Factual statement	It is based on facts It has an empirical basis It can be supported by facts It is verifiable It is a factual statement It argues that anger/emotion is not a good guide for action	
Culturally embedded argument (valence argument)	It is true The opponent/the other camp agrees upon this aspect too It is well received It cannot be rejected It is capable of winning a majority	
Speaker is credible with it/argument represents speakers' value(s)	We are credible with this message Each organization picks the argument they are most credible with We reach our target group with this argument	
Argument represents organizations' value(s)	The organization advocates the value behind the argument It is a fundamental aspect of the law and it is a fundamental value for us	
Demand for problem solving	It shows that new proposal does (not) solve a problem It shows that proposal is (un-)necessary The argument shows that the implementation is (not) workable	
Other reasons	Argument brought in another perspective It was the one we internally agreed upon	Others

Note The exact wording of the question was: Which was your best argument? Why?

from everyday life experience. By interacting with many different people, they talk about the topic in the street, at work, in their leisure time, and at home. In this way, they can test different arguments and develop a good feeling for strong arguments. Additionally, many of them have had wide experience with campaigns. In the aftermath of the votes, a publicly financed survey (VOX analysis) is available. Among other information, it provides details about individually relevant reasons for the vote. This gives campaigners the possibility of learning which arguments have been convincing. Some themes are recurring, and it can happen that frames are already established and ready to be re-used. This was the case with the humanitarian tradition frame that was used in the asylum law (see below). This frame was an invention of the postwar period. After the Second World War, Switzerland was criticized by the international community for its attitude to Nazi Germany. Many accused Switzerland of having achieved neutrality by cooperating economically, while remaining politically uninvolved. The aim was to improve the country's reputation, so after 1945 the idea of a humanitarian Switzerland was invoked.[3]

My work shows that campaigners find strong arguments through a process of trial and error. This gives them experience, and over time, they develop an intuition for which arguments work and which do not. Before or during a campaign, some (mainly individual) campaigners rely on self-financed and not necessarily representative opinion polls in order to decide about the convincingness of arguments. One campaigner also admitted the limits of his evaluation capacity: "You never know how convincing an argument is because votes are anonymous."

However, Kriesi and Hänggli (2019) show that the policy-specific messages are based on deep core beliefs in general. Strategic action or reactive behavior can reduce this link. In other words, campaigners use messages linked to core values but keep some room to maneuver when it comes to their communication strategy (Bernhard 2012).

---

[3] https://www.republik.ch/2018/08/01/die-humanitaere-schweiz-ist-eine-erfindung-der-nachkriegszeit?utm_source=newsletter&utm_medium=email&utm_campaign=republik%2Fnewsletter-editorial-eine-rede-zum-1-august-und-ein-besuch-am-gericht, October 2018.

Main Frames

Table 4.2 provides an overview of the main frames produced and expressed by political actors in the three campaigns under scrutiny. The corresponding relative frequencies are written in bold and show that we arrive at one or two main frames for each camp in each campaign. As becomes clear from Table 4.2, the campaigners predominantly address their own frame(s). On average, 45%[4] of the arguments of the contra camp fall into their most important frame, whereas the pro camp focused on arguments that fall into its most important frame in one-third of cases. With the asylum law, each side used two main substantive frames. On the contra side, the "*humanitarian tradition*" frame (=human. trad.) was used most often (=core frame). This frame maintained that the new asylum law violated human dignity and human rights, endangered religious norms, and that it was contrary to the Swiss humanitarian tradition. The second important frame of the no camp can be labeled the "*rule-of-law*" frame. This frame maintained that the provisions of the new law undermined the rule-of-law, that they violated international law (e.g., the Geneva Convention), that certain provisions of the new law violated the principle of proportionality, and that the risk of judicial errors would increase. On the pro side, the "*abuse*" frame constituted the core substantive frame. This argued that there were too many so-called bogus asylum seekers in the country, and that Switzerland needed instruments to fight the abuse of its asylum system. The second most important substantive frame of the pro side is a positive frame, which promises a more efficient implementation of the asylum legislation. It does so in general terms, but also by pointing to specific improvements such as greater flexibility for the Swiss member states (the "cantons"), especially with respect to returning failed asylum seekers (the pro side calls them "illegal") to their home countries. I call this the "*efficacy*" frame. Both sides used additional frames, which are summarized under "others" in Table 4.2.

The analysis identifies only one main frame for the opponents of the naturalization initiative. In order to avoid arbitrary decisions, the "*rule-of-law*" frame asks for fair procedures that comply with basic rights. By contrast, the pro side conceived naturalizations as political acts and not as administrative ones. Therefore, it is not surprising that its key frame

---

[4] $(38.8 + 49 + 48.5)/3$.

Table 4.2 Substantive and contest frames (percentage shares), and dialogue levels of substantive frames in media input: by campaign and camp

Campaign	Asylum			Naturalization			Corporation tax		
	Contra	*Pro*	*Frame dialogue*		*Contra*	*Pro*	*Frame dialogue*		*Contra*	*Pro*	*Frame dialogue*
Substantive frames											
Human. trad.	**38.8**	24.8	80.1	Rule-of-law	**49.0**	19.6	61.7	Tax equity	**48.5**	7.7	30.0
Rule-of-law	**21.5**	9.3	62.2	People final say	21.9	**39.3**	66.8	Tax loss	**22.3**	8.4	58.9
Abuse	17.6	**26.9**	77.0					SME	5.6	**38.4**	23.4
Efficacy	4.0	**17.3**	36.1	Mass naturalization	17.5	**20.6**	86.6	Competitiveness	14.1	**27.3**	63.6
Others	13.9	16.1		Others	5.0	7.5		Others	4.3	11.3	
All substantive	95.9	94.3		All substantive	93.2	87.9		All substantive	94.8	93.1	
Dialogue			69.9				69.3				41.5
Contest frames	4.1	5.7			6.5	13.1			5.2	6.9	
Total (%)	100	100			100	100			100	100	
n	726	335			675	107			462	594	

is concerned with the claim that people should have the final say (*people final say*). Aside from procedural aspects, the proponents of a yes vote adopted a rather xenophobic discourse. They stated that "*mass naturalizations*" had to be stopped. This frame included the idea that there are too many foreigners in Switzerland and also alluded to crimes that occurred during the campaign, in particular those committed by recently naturalized persons.

Regarding the corporate tax reform, each side again used two main substantive frames. The opponents of the corporate tax reform mainly focused on matters of "*tax equity.*" They argued that the tax cuts introduced an unfair privilege for the well-off and went against the principle of fair taxation. They even claimed that the reform was unconstitutional. This line of reasoning applied mainly to a controversial provision that included a reduction in tax rates on dividends for shareholders disposing of at least a ten percent stake in a corporation. To a lesser extent, the opponents warned that the reform would lead to a shortfall of several hundreds of millions of Swiss francs with respect to both direct and indirect taxes. More specifically, a powerful argument stated that the old-age pension scheme would suffer if people accepted the proposal. I decided to label this kind of argument as the "*tax loss*" frame.

The proponents of the new law framed the reform in terms of a necessary fostering of small and medium-sized enterprises (SMEs), which form the backbone of the Swiss economy. The "*SME*" frame dominated the yes campaign. It stated that these companies needed to benefit from a set of planned measures aimed at reducing financial and administrative burdens. The second most important frame of the pro side turned the public's attention to the overriding importance of the reform for the Swiss economy. The "*competitiveness*" frame maintained that the new law would boost the economy by encouraging investments and the creation of jobs.

Oppositional Emphasis Choice: Campaign Dialogue

The second hypothesis predicts that yes and no camps not only rely on different frames, but also engage in dialogue ("Oppositional Emphasis Choice"). Dialogue is expected to be lower in complex issues (corporation tax) and when there is an imbalance in financial resources (high in the corporation tax), whereas it should be higher in familiar issues (asylum law), or if the result is expected to be close (the naturalization initiative and to a lesser extent the asylum law reform). Thus, we expect the lowest level of dialogue in the corporate tax reform and the highest level in the asylum law. The results in Table 4.2 show, first of all, that political actors address their opponents' frames. There is dialogue. As introduced in Chapter 1, the dialogue measure works with the absolute differences between the two camps in the share of attention each camp devoted to a certain frame, divides the sum by 2 in order to calibrate the measure to the range between 0 and 100, and subtracts that sum from 100 in order to convert the measure to one of similarity rather than dissimilarity (see *Appendix* for formula). Dialogue of 100 would mean that each camp talks equally about the different perspectives, whereas 0 would mean that no exchange on perspectives takes place. On average, dialogue in the three direct-democratic campaigns is 60.2. This equates to both camps talking about their two most important frames in seven of ten cases (distributed equally on both frames) and in three of ten cases about their opponents' most important frames (again distributed equally). A figure of 60.2 is much higher than the average (44.1) found in the study by Kaplan et al. (2006) regarding American candidate television advertising aired in the US Senate campaigns from 1998 to 2002. By contrast, it is lower than the mean (75.3) of dialogue in US presidential campaigns from 1960 to 2000 (Sigelman and Buell 2004). However, the two immigration campaigns reach a level which is as high as that observed in US presidential campaigns. In addition, these previous measurements are less demanding because they only look at issue convergence and do not test whether the same frames are discussed. The *frame dialogue* also seems to be quite high (58.8 compared to a mean of 24.9 in the study by Kaplan et al. [2006]). It again equates to each camp discussing its own arguments seven times and the argument of the opponent three times. Thus, I conclude that both campaign and frame dialogue are present in the press releases in Swiss direct-democratic campaigns.

Second, the results in Table 4.2 show that the degree of dialogue varies between campaigns. The *dialogue* levels are much higher for the immigration ballots (69.9 for the asylum law and 69.3 for the naturalization initiative) than for the campaign on corporation tax (41.5). The first two results are comparable to a situation where both camps emphasize their two most important frames 6.5 times out of ten and the frames of their opponent in 3.5 out of ten times (again, distributed equally on the two frames). The corporation tax result is comparable to a situation in which both camps talk about their two most important frames eight out of ten times and about their opponent's most important frames two out of ten times. The results provide support for my hypothesis, with the exception that familiarity seems to be less important for dialogue. The tax reform was the most complex issue and the campaign most dominated by one side in terms of financial resources of all the campaigns since the beginning of the 1980s. In addition, the tax reform was evaluated as the most predictable race. Accordingly, the level of dialogue should indeed be lowest in the tax reform campaign. Based on the high level of dialogue in the other two campaigns, we can consider closeness of the race to be important. The naturalization campaign was expected to be the closest run, while the asylum law was perceived as moderately close. Since campaign dialogue level in the most familiar issue (asylum law) is not higher than in the least familiar issue (naturalization initiative), familiarity seems to be less important. Complexity could be the crucial variable: If the issue is easy to understand, people can catch up easily and become familiar with the issue in a short space of time.

Oppositional Emphasis Choice: Frame Dialogue

We will now turn to frame dialogue and look at whether media frame salience increases dialogue. The *salience* of the frame in the media (measured as the relative frequency in news media) was hypothesized to increase dialogue. In the case of the asylum law, the "humanitarian tradition" and the "abuse" frames were the most salient media frames (Chapter 6). Both are characterized here by a high level of frame-specific convergence. In the interviews, the campaigners from the contra camp reported that they felt obliged to counter the abuse frame because it was so prevalent in the public discussion. This provides support for our hypothesis. However, salience does not always increase frame dialogue. In the naturalization and tax reform campaigns, the political actors did not converge on the most salient media frames. As we will see below (Table 4.3 ignorance of opponents' arguments, Table 4.4 strategic avoidance) this has to do with the strategic thinking of political actors. They try to ignore and avoid arguments which they cannot convincingly counter-argue.

Table 4.3 looks at how the political actors dealt with the strongest argument of their opponent (we included this question in the

Table 4.3 How did you treat your opponents' strongest argument?

	Asylum		Naturalization		Corporation tax	
	Contra	Pro	Contra	Pro	Contra	Pro
Counter-argued	–	–	79.2	62.5	61.5	35.2
Ignored	–	–	20.8	37.5	15.4	52.9
Included (absorbed)	–	–	0.0	0.0	23.1	11.8
n per camp			24	8	13	17
n total				32		30

Note Answers in percentage (except the *n* values). Since we did not ask this question for the asylum law, the first two columns are empty

Table 4.4 Did you try to avoid certain arguments?, by camp and campaign

	Asylum		Naturalization		Corporation tax	
	Contra	Pro	Contra	Pro	Contra	Pro
Avoided argument(s)	24.2	53.9	52.0	62.5	38.5	52.9
Avoided argument(s) on principle	18.2	23.1	24.0	50.0	15.4	0.0
Strategic avoidance: Avoided argument(s) because opponent could profit	21.2	61.5	40.0	25.0	23.1	47.1
n per camp	33	13	25	8	13	17
n total		46		33		30

questionnaire only after the first campaign). It shows that in three of four cases, the camps primarily counter-argued. This is the primary strategy and the basis of dialogue! Ignorance was the dominant strategy for the pro camp in the tax reform, with inclusion (absorbance) generally less important. In the naturalization initiative, the proposal was short and gave less leeway to ignore or include arguments than the more complex and long proposal of the corporate tax reform.

Let us explore the ignorance strategy in more depth. In the second face-to-face interviews, we asked campaigners whether they avoided certain arguments in general, on principle or because an opponent could profit. If they did so, we asked them which arguments they avoided. Table 4.4 shows the percentage of campaigners doing so. The categories are not mutually exclusive. In five of six cases, the most frequent answer is to avoid arguments in general. This overall answer includes different reasons, but mainly that the argument does not belong to the issue, or is not convincing. How do campaigners decide whether an argument fits into the core of an issue? The law is the basis for doing so. Campaigners discuss different aspects and decide which aspect(s) of the law is most important. For instance in the asylum law, campaigners from both the pro and contra camp did not want to argue that the law creates different classes of foreign people. For moderate pro forces, this argumentation was too extreme, too likely to wake resentments. For the contra camp, this argumentation belongs more to the debate about free movements of persons and goes too much into the detail of the campaign. An organization from the contra camp avoided referring to black market work. For this campaigner, black market work should primarily be linked to social standards, social benefits, labor laws, and the abuse of people. In their view, black market work should not primarily be linked to asylum and migration. For precisely this reason, they did not want to push this argument and thereby strengthen the link between black market work and migration. In Table 4.4, we see that campaigners exclude some arguments on principle ("Avoided argument(s) on principle"). For instance, in the asylum law campaigners of the contra camp refused to engage with an argument based on the Holocaust. Similarly, in the naturalization initiative, organizations of the pro camp avoided the argument "the boat is full" or "we have too many foreigners" (mass naturalization frame). Indeed, these argumentation lines would be provocative, with campaigners wary of referring to the Holocaust. In the naturalization initiative, the contra camp avoided mentioning that "this poll damages the image of Switzerland" (others frame). Here, they wanted to avoid image damage by not promoting this perspective.

Argument avoidance based on strategic reasons was present too. Here, two different categories of ignored arguments need to be distinguished: on the one hand, ignorance of an argument which is present in the debate (emphasized by the other camp) and on the other hand, ignorance of arguments mainly absent in the debate (not or only weakly promoted by the other camp). Let us first discuss the former. In the corporation tax case, the pro camp applied this strategy most. They believed that the contra arguments "this tax reform harms the old age and survivors insurance (AHV)" (tax loss frame) and "a tax relief for major shareholders is unfair" (tax equity frame) would help the contra camp. They were based on calculations of how much money would be lost tax-wise. In the view of the pro camp, these factual arguments could not be successfully counter-argued. Furthermore, an organization of the contra camp avoided "This tax reform advances SMEs" (SME frame), while another organization ignored "This tax reform advances investments and creates new jobs" (competitiveness frame). Both of these are *valence* arguments, because as with valence issues (Schneider 1972), voters take one side on them. Almost everybody is in favor of SMEs and likes creating new jobs. Similarly to factual arguments, valence arguments are more difficult to rebut. In the naturalization initiative, the pro camp avoided "this initiative brings discriminatory and arbitrary naturalization decisions" and "naturalizations have to be in accordance with the rule of law" (both belong to the rule-of-law frame). The first argument is also rather factual. Most interviewees agreed that the procedure proposed by the initiative would be arbitrary. The second argument is a valence argument. Rule-of-law is a well-accepted and positively loaded principle in Switzerland, which is hard to rebut. In the asylum law, this strategy was not mentioned at all.

Let us now look at the second category of ignored arguments, those *not* promoted by the opposite camp but thought to be convincing for their position. In the asylum law, the pro camp deselected the argument "the new law is the most restrictive one in the whole of Europe" (others frame) because they thought it would help the contra camp. Meanwhile, the contra camp avoided "the new law makes integration easier" (others frame—integration) for the same strategic reason. In the naturalization campaign, the argument "we need to make a gesture against the criminality of foreigners" was avoided by the contra camp. In the corporate tax reform, the pro camp avoided "this tax reform makes the tax system even more complicated." These examples were mentioned in the interviews after the vote. They show that some perspectives with the potential to be convincing for the opposite position are kept secret if the side that stood to benefit from these arguments did not think about or choose them, and the media did not elaborate on them. Since no actor promoted these arguments, they remain unimportant in the public debate. They belong to the category of "other" frames.

Oppositional Emphasis Choice: Frame Dialogue—Offensive or Defensive Use?

Let us go back to content analysis data and to the question of counter-arguing. Is the widespread use of the opponents' arguments a sign of (offensive) trespassing or of (defensive) counter-framing? Hypothesis 2 expected a defensive use of counter-framing. There is a rather unequivocal answer to this question. The two camps use their opponents' frames defensively in almost all cases. In other words, we find little trespassing (=offensive use of the opponents' frames), but mainly counter-framing (=defensive use) in all of the communication channels. The one exception to this general finding is the pro camp in the asylum campaign, which does some trespassing (18.1%)[5] with respect to the contra camp's "humanitarian tradition" frame. In this particular case, the pro camp made use of a double-edged argument by endorsing the concern advanced by their adversaries. In the first step, its actors pointed out that they were strongly in favor of the humanitarian tradition of Switzerland. In a second step, they maintained that the revised law would strengthen this claim because it would help to fight against abuse, thereby helping those asylum seekers who really deserved protection. This clever counter-framing strategy found its expression in slogans that combined both aspects: fighting against abuse and maintaining the humanitarian tradition. For instance, the pro camp endorsed the "humanitarian tradition" argument, but accused the contra camp of falsely claiming that the new law constituted a threat to this tradition. Or, the pro camp used the "humanitarian tradition" frame offensively by accusing the contra camp of tolerating or even stimulating asylum abuse (which, it claimed, had endangered this very tradition). In another example, the pro camp dismissed the contra camp's complaint that the new law violates the UN Charter of Children's Rights and claimed that the law is compatible with this charter. These types of message were intended to appeal to moderate and cross-pressured voters in order to assure victory. Arguments discussing the humanitarian tradition are also valence arguments. Based on the insights above, we can assume that valence arguments that connect to a negative emotion (e.g., fear) might become controversial and

---

[5] Numbers not presented here, see Table 6.1. Calculation: share of offensive use of "humanitarian tradition" counter-frame from total use of "humanitarian tradition" counter-frame: 4.5/(4.5 + 20.3).

Table 4.5 Contest frames in the naturalization initiative: Percentage shares by camp and actor type

Camp	Contra					Pro	
Actor type	Authorities	Ad hoc committees	Parties	Economic interest groups	Citizens' interest groups	Parties	Ad hoc committees
Personal attacks	1.7	4.0	2.0	9.2	6.6	8.1	0.0
Conflicts	**5.6**	0.0	2.0	4.1	0.5	**8.1**	0.0
All contest frames	**7.2**	4.0	4.1	13.3	7.1	**16.2**	0.0
Power by actor type (mean)	41.1	18.0	8.9	8.3	5.0	80.0	18.0
n	108	25	246	98	198	86	21

are counter-argued, whereas valence arguments that connect to a positive emotion (e.g., feeling proud) might be less counter-argued (they were avoided), except where they can be countered offensively as was the case in the "humanitarian tradition" frame.

Contest Emphasis Choice

Next, we will look at whether political actors primarily used substantive or contest frames. As expected, contest frames such as personal attacks and conflicts are only rarely used by political actors in Swiss direct-democratic campaigns. As depicted in Table 4.2, the proportion of contest frames is somewhat higher in the naturalization and tax reform campaigns, especially in the case of the pro camp in the naturalization initiative. This might be due to the fact that a former member of the Federal Council from the populist right-wing party (SVP), Christoph Blocher, was not re-elected and was instead replaced by another person from the same party, Eveline Widmer-Schlumpf, on December 12, 2007. As she accepted the elected position, she was thrown out of the SVP, and a small minority of her supporters split off from the party. The issue was contentious and emotional, and the naturalization initiative was the first vote for which Widmer-Schlumpf was the Federal Councilor responsible.

Table 4.5 provides a more detailed overview of the comparatively high share of contest frames in the naturalization initiative. It shows the use of the contest frames by different actor types. It can be seen that it was the most powerful actor types, i.e., the authorities and the political parties of the pro camp, who campaigned with significantly more conflict frames. In fact, it appears that the dispute between Christoph Blocher, the SVP, and Eveline Widmer-Schlumpf caused the *quarreling* actors to rely more on these frames. Blocher and the SVP belonged to the political parties of the pro camp, and Widmer-Schlumpf to the authorities. Whereas the parties of the pro camp used both personal attacks and conflicts, the authorities on the contra side mainly emphasized the conflict and refrained from making personal attacks.

In the tax reform campaign, the political parties of the pro camp also used more contest frames than the other actor types. Since both campaigns took place soon after the non-re-election of Blocher, I assume that the actors involved used more contest frames than would otherwise have been the case. However, in general, we can conclude that in Swiss direct-democratic campaigns, framing is primarily accomplished in substantive terms.

Conclusion

We can summarize the results according to the three strategic choices of framing which we have outlined in this chapter. With regard to the "Substantive Emphasis Choice" and the "Oppositional Emphasis Choice," we find that political actors tend to emphasize their own frames, but they do not exclusively revert to this behavior and do engage in dialogue. We have established that dialogue at the issue level varies according to the complexity of the issue (less dialogue in complex issues), to the imbalance in financial resources (less dialogue in the presence of imbalance) and to the expected closeness of the race (more dialogue in close campaigns) at the campaign level. Surprisingly, issue familiarity is not important for dialogue. At the frame level, we note that frames present in the debate generally are highly discussed and counter-framed. In general, it has been shown that addressing the frames owned by opponents is largely achieved defensively rather than offensively, that is, by means of counter-framing rather than trespassing. We have briefly explored the exception of offensive counter-framing, and found it was a successful way of using the argument of the opposing side: A promising counter-framing strategy consists of endorsing the argument held by the adversary and simultaneously framing it in a manner disadvantageous to them. We also find that factual or valence arguments referring to positive emotions cannot be easily rebutted. For these frames, we find lower degrees of frame dialogue except if they can be countered offensively (humanitarian tradition frame). With regard to the conceptualization of strong frames in communication, we see that political actors deal with their opponents' strong frames primarily by counter-framing. This is in line with my measure of a strong frame, which is defined as a frame that provokes a defensive reaction by opponents and/or that resonates in the media. With regard to the third choice, the "Contest Emphasis Choice," we have shown that the political actors mainly focus on substance in direct-democratic campaigns, i.e., they mainly rely on substantive framing. We found that the dispute between Christoph Blocher, the SVP, and Eveline Widmer-Schlumpf caused the quarreling political actors to rely significantly more on conflict frames in the naturalization campaign.

Interaction Between Context (Campaign Type, Country) and Frame Construction

The "Substantive Emphasis Choice"—the choice of a strong substantive frame—is the most important choice and is quite independent of the campaign type. To win political power, the political actors "must compete, and a central aspect of this competition is their effort to define the terms of political choice" (Sniderman 2000: 75). However, the campaign type does matter with regard to the second and third choices. The "Oppositional Emphasis Choice" (how much priority the political actors give to the opponents' substantive frame(s) compared to their own frames) might become more complicated in proportional election campaigns because more sides are involved and an actor has to attend to more than one opponent. Since the issue is not given in election campaigns, dialogue might take place at the issue level (not at the frame level). However, it still seems likely that dialogue will occur, with journalists perhaps more important for scrutinizing information. Indeed, Banda (2015) shows for U.S. Senate elections that candidates respond to their opponents for strategic reasons, particularly in competitive elections which garner more media attention. In public debates, it is possible for only one camp to be involved and thus for there to be no competition regarding alternatives. If only one side is campaigning, its interpretation could become highly influential. This is a very different situation than we have in direct-democratic campaigns, and such a situation would be characterized by less dialogue. It will render the second choice more relevant in public debates in general. Hence, it is not surprising that Entman's (2003) cascading model addresses the very question of whether frame contestation arises in public debates. From my point of view, it appears that public debates on *foreign policy* issues bear the highest risk of a dominant frame situation because government monopolizes information, which impedes opposition. Such one-sided situations seem to be rare in terms of everyday politics. This is why I consider the typical research objects of the indexing approach (Bennett 1990; Bennett et al. 2007; Mermin 1999) as rather atypical cases. More frequently, debates on *technical issues* also risk becoming a one-sided situation. Here, I am referring to issues that become relevant as a result of digitalization, such as discussions on privacy or security issues in social networks or on transparency of advertising in web search results (the list could easily go on longer). These topics require technical knowledge and powerful actors pursuing their business interests can monopolize information. The "Contest Emphasis Choice" (the priority of the substantive frames compared to the campaign contest) might be more important in electoral campaigns, in which candidates might analyze the rationale and strategy underlying the rhetoric and positions of their opponents or emphasize and attack some of their personal characteristics. Indeed, contest frames are dominant in media election coverage in many countries (Kaid and Strömbäck 2008: 424). An increase in contest frames reduces the room for substantive dialogue. In public debates, the behavior of political actors is also decisive for the extent of the substance (e.g., Jackson 2011). Furthermore, I do not expect more contest frames generally as long as the public debate is two-sided. However, when something goes wrong and scandalous information is released or leaked, the situation can become one-sided and more contest-oriented (see Hänggli and van der Wurff 2019).

I expect the "Substantive Emphasis Choice" and the "Oppositional Emphasis Choice" to also be quite independent of the differences between countries. For instance, in Denmark, the yes camp also campaigned with one main message (de Vreese and Semetko 2004: 172). By contrast, we might find more contest frames ("Contest Emphasis Choice") and thus less room for substantive dialogue in countries with less control by elites, because extreme and non-government actors rely more on contest frames. The same expectation holds for countries with a media-oriented political communication culture.[6] Media orientation increases the use of news values and in such a way the use of contest frames. For instance, in U.S. presidential election campaigns, contest frames are more important due to commercialization of the media, the important role of TV in general and the involvement of political advertisements on TV in particular, and because of the majoritarian democratic system (Kaid and Strömbäck 2008; Strömbäck and Kaid 2008). By contrast, Hardmeier (2003: 251) reached the conclusion that only seven percent of articles used an emotional or personalized style of coverage in Swiss parliamentary election campaigns.

References

Achen, C. H., & Bartels, L. M. (2016). *Democracy for Realists. Why Elections do not Produce Responsive Government.* Oxford: Oxford University Press.

Ansolabehere, S., & Iyengar, S. (1994). Riding the Wave and Claiming Ownership over Issues: The Joint Effects of Advertising and News Coverage in Campaigns. *Public Opinion Quarterly, 58*(3), 335–357.

Banda, K. K. (2015). Competition and the Dynamics of Issue Convergence. *American Politics Research, 43*(5), 821–845.

Basinger, S., & Lavine, H. (2005). Ambivalence, Information, and Electoral Choice. *American Political Science Review, 99*(1), 169–184.

Bennett, W. L. (1990). Toward a Theory of Press-State Relations. *Journal of Communication, 40*(2), 103–125.

Bennett, W. L., Lawrence, R., & Livingston, S. (2007). *When the Press Fails: Political Power and the News Media from Iraq to Katrina.* Chicago: University of Chicago Press.

Bernhard, L. (2012). *Campaign Strategy in Direct Democracy.* Hampshire: Palgrave Macmillan.

Carnegie, D. (2010) [1936]. *How to Win Friends and Influence People.* UK: Simon & Schuster.

[6]When comparing the results with those of de Vreese and Semetko (2004: 101, 174), we find less substance (measured as issue frames) in the Danish referendum campaigns. Since Denmark is classified as a similar country to Switzerland, we would not expect large differences, and those we found are probably caused by different coding procedures. In my analysis, the argument was the unit of analysis, whereas de Vreese and Semetko's study is based on the topic of the story. In order to attract the attention of the reader, the media might use strategic frames in their headlines or leads, but still use substance in the article.

Chong, D., & Druckman, J. N. (2007). A Theory of Framing and Opinion Formation in Competitive Elite Environments. *Journal of Communication, 57*(1), 99–118.

Cook, T. (1989). *Making Laws and Making News. Media Strategies in the U.S. House of Representatives.* Washington, DC: Brookings Institution.

Damore, D. F. (2005). Issue Convergence in Presidential Campaigns. *Political Behavior, 27*(1), 71–97.

de Vreese, C. H., & Semetko, H. A. (2004). News Matters: Influences on the Vote in a Referendum Campaign. *European Journal of Political Research, 43*(5), 701–724.

Druckman, J. N. (2001). The Implications of Framing Effects for Citizen Competence. *Political Behavior, 23,* 225–256.

Druckman, J. N. (2004). Political Preference Formation: Competition, Deliberation, and the (Ir)relevance of Framing Effects. *American Political Science Review, 98*(4), 671–686.

Druckman, J. N., & Nelson, K. R. (2003). Framing and Deliberation: How Citizens' Conversations Limit Elite Influence. *American Journal of Political Science, 47*(4), 729–745.

Entman, R. M. (1989). *Democracy Without Citizens: Media and the Decay of American Politics.* New York: Oxford University Press.

Entman, R. M. (2003). Cascading Activation: Contesting the White House's Frame After 9/11. *Political Communication, 20,* 415–432.

Gamson, W. A. (2004). Bystanders, Public Opinion, and the Media. In D. A. Snow, S. A. Soule, & H. Kriesi (Eds.), *The Blackwell Companion to Social Movements* (pp. 242–261). Oxford: Blackwell.

Hänggli, R., & Kriesi, H. (2010). Political Framing Strategies and Their Impact on Media Framing in a Swiss Direct-Democratic Campaign. *Political Communication, 27*(2), 141–157.

Hänggli, R., & Kriesi, H. (2012). Frame Construction and Frame Promotion (Strategic Framing Choices). *American Behavioral Scientist, 56*(3), 260–278.

Hänggli, R., & van der Wurff, R. (2019). Quality of Public Debates. In L. Bernhard, F. Fossati, R. Hänggli, & H. Kriesi (Eds.), *Debating Unemployment Policy: Political Communication and the Labour Market in Western Europe.* Cambridge: Cambridge University Press.

Hänggli, R., Bernhard, L., & Kriesi, H. (2012). Construction of the Frames. In H. Kriesi (Ed.), *Political Communication in Direct Democratic Campaigns: Enlightening or Manipulating?* (pp. 69–81). Hampshire: Palgrave Macmillan.

Hardmeier, S. (2003). Amerikanisierung der Wahlkampfkommunikation: Einem Schlagwort auf der Spur. In P. Sciarini, S. Hardmeier, & A. Vatter (Eds.), *Schweizer Wahlen 1999* (pp. 219–255). Bern: Haupt.

Jackson, D. (2011). Strategic News Frames and Public Policy Debates: Press and Television News Coverage of the Euro in the UK. *Communications, 36*(2), 169–193.

Jacobs, L. R., & Shapiro, R. Y. (2000). *Politicians Don't Pander.* Chicago: University of Chicago Press.

Jerit, J. (2008). Issue Framing and Engagement: Rhetorical Strategy in Public Policy Debates. *Political Behaviour, 30*, 1–24.

Kahn, K. F., & Kenney, P. (1999). *The Spectacle of U.S. Senate Campaigns.* Princeton: Princeton University Press.

Kaid, L. L., & Strömbäck, J. (2008). Election News Coverage Around the World: A Comparative Perspective. In J. Strömbäck & L. L. Kaid (Eds.), *The Handbook of Election News Coverage Around the World.* New York: Routledge.

Kaplan, N., Park, D. K., & Ridout, T. N. (2006). Dialogue in American Campaigns? An Examination of Issue Convergence in Candidate Television Advertising. *American Journal of Political Science, 50*(3), 724–736.

Kriesi, H., & Hänggli, R. (2019). The Positioning of the Actors in the Public Debates. In L. Bernhard, F. Fossati, R. Hänggli, & H. Kriesi (Eds.), *Debating Unemployment Policy: Political Communication and the Labour Market in Western Europe.* Cambridge: Cambridge University Press.

Lupia, A. (2016). *Uninformed.* Cambridge: Cambridge University Press.

Mermin, J. (1999). *Debating War and Peace: Media Coverage of U.S. Intervention in the Post-Vietnam Era.* Princeton: Princeton University Press.

Perloff, R. M. (2010). *The Dynamics of Persuasion. Communication and Attitudes in the 21st Century.* Routledge.

Petrocik, J. R. (1996). Issue Ownership in Presidential Elections, with a 1980 Case Study. *American Journal of Political Science, 40*(3), 825–850.

Riker, W. H. (1996). *The Strategy of Rhetoric: Campaigning for the American Constitution.* New Haven: Yale University Press.

Schneider, W. (1972). *Electoral Behavior and Political Development.* Harvard: Harvard University, Center for International Affairs.

Sides, J. (2006). The Origins of Campaign Agendas. *British Journal of Political Science, 36*(3), 407–436.

Sigelman, L., & Buell, E. H. (2004). Avoidance or Engagement? Issue Convergence in U.S. Presidential Campaigns, 1960–2000. *American Journal of Political Science, 48*(4), 650–661.

Simon, A. (2002). *The Winning Message: Candidate Behavior, Campaign Discourse, and Democracy.* New York: Cambridge University Press.

Sniderman, P. A. (2000). Taking Sides: A Fixed Choice Theory of Political Reasoning. In A. Lupia, M. D. McCubbins, & S. P. Popkin (Eds.), *Elements of Reason: Cognition, Choice, and the Bounds of Rationality* (pp. 67–84). Cambridge, UK: Cambridge University Press.

Sniderman, P. M., & Theriault, S. M. (2004). The Structure of Political Argument and the Logic of Issue Framing. In P. M. Sniderman & S. M. Theriault (Eds.), *Studies in Public Opinion: Attitudes, Nonattitudes, Measurement Error and Change* (pp. 133–165). Princeton: Princeton University Press.

Strömbäck, J., & Kaid, L. L. (2008). *The Handbook of Election News Coverage Around the World*. New York: Routledge.

CHAPTER 5

Frame Promotion: The Variation of Strategic Framing Choices in Different Communication Channels and Over Time

There is dialogue in the media input, this much is clear. Yet we know little about how dialogue varies in different communication channels and over time. I will explore these two aspects in this chapter. For this purpose, I investigate how the political actors vary their framing choices in the different communication channels and over time. This is called the promotion process of frame building. To examine the variation in the communication channels, I compare the results with the findings regarding the media input channel from Chapter 4. The media input channel is the baseline or reference category. As introduced in previous chapters, I distinguish between mediated (media input and letters to the editor), unmediated (political advertisements and direct mail), and internal (info for members) channels. In the mediated channels, campaigners must cater to the needs and values of journalists, while the unmediated channels offer campaigners control over the content and form of the message. Both mediated and unmediated channels target the general public, while the internal channel is aimed at members.

The comparison between the channels is worth studying for three reasons. First, in the media input, campaigners must satisfy journalists. Thus, news values may determine their framing strategies. By comparing

---

A paper summarizing the most important aspects of frame promotion in the naturalization initiative (one, not all three campaigns) was published in Hänggli and Kriesi (2012).

© The Author(s) 2020
R. Hänggli, *The Origin of Dialogue in the News Media*,
Challenges to Democracy in the 21st Century,
https://doi.org/10.1007/978-3-030-26582-3_5

the media input (press releases and documents written for media confer-ences) with the unmediated channels, we can evaluate the ways in which anticipation of the media role influences the framing of the media input. In the media input, the political actors anticipate the expectations and working routines of the journalists and try to frame the issue in their favor under these circumstances. In the unmediated channels, we can observe how political actors frame an issue if they address their audience directly. Second, successful strategic communication depends on coordi-nating messages across all publications (Norris et al. 1999: 67). As such, despite some variation across channels, there should also be some simi-larity between them. To my knowledge, the way in which political actors rely on the same message across different channels in direct-democratic campaigns has never been investigated. Third, the differences between the channels should draw the reader's attention to the fact that the results can vary depending on the type of communication channel. For instance, Iyengar (1991) explores the mechanisms by which television has impoverished political discourse. It is possible the results might have looked different if he had relied on another channel. It is worthwhile to study the variation in the three strategic framing choices over time for the simple reason that we know little about it.

Direct mail and information for members were coded only in the asy-lum campaign, as limited resources in terms of time and money restricted analysis in the two other campaigns. Nevertheless, I consider it impor-tant to include them in my investigation. First of all, it is imperative to theoretically distinguish between these channels. Second, the results of one campaign can still provide insight into the potential empirical results of another campaign. More problematic is the fact that I use only those letters that were published and appeared in the newspapers, rather than all of the letters sent to the editors (roughly one-third of letters sent were published). It is standard practice that critical letters to the editor are also published, or that the balance between pro and con is maintained. In addition, the content of the letters should relate as far as possible to texts published in the newspaper and should be of a certain quality, i.e., not offensive or untrue. However, the published letters are not necessarily a representative sample of all letters sent to the editors. In other words, we do not know to what extent our results reflect the input letters. It is also possible that journalists edited the letters published in the newspapers. In addition, not all of the published letters come from the political actors or are the result of their strategic framing.

Nevertheless, there are reasons to look at published letters to the editor. The letters section can be seen as an open forum for public debate, which "thrives on minimal editorial intervention" (Wahl-Jorgensen 2007: 154). Editors and journalists see their profession as "a calling in the service of democracy, free speech, and the public" (Wahl-Jorgensen 2007: 154). Or, as Gans (2003: 21) pointed out, "journalism views itself as supporting and strengthening the roles of citizens in democracy". In addition to these democratic ideals, editors also offer an economic justification for minimal editorial intervention in the letters section (Wahl-Jorgensen 2007: 154). They explain that allowing all citizens to submit letters will boost the newspaper's popularity and its success in the market. Thus, it is because of democratic ideals and market success that editors are reluctant to edit. There are also practical constraints that prevent editors from radically altering the letters: Editors work under a constant deadline, with the knowledge that the paper has only limited space for letters. The selection criteria are similar across different types of newspapers (Wahl-Jorgensen 2007: 68): Editors prefer short, coherent letters, which are submitted exclusively to the respective newspaper, and by different locally tied writers. In particular, editors avoid letters which appear to be part of an orchestrated letter-writing campaign. Campaigners have thus adapted their strategies accordingly. In direct-democratic campaigns, political actors draft a short letter containing their main frames and request that their members and volunteers personalize and submit it as a letter to the editor. Alternatively, they teach their supporters how to write quality letters to the editor.

Before we start with the investigation of the framing choices, let me illustrate the use of the different channels. First, a look at the total number of articles in the different channels (Table 5.1) provides us with a general idea of the importance of these channels. In the asylum law campaign, the figures indicate that the contra camp was much more active than the pro camp in producing arguments for media input, direct mails and information for members. It produced more than twice as many articles for the news media and many more direct mails and information for members. By contrast, the pro camp produced more than twice as many political ads. This suggests that the two camps followed different strategies: While the contra camp relied much more on its internal channel and on media news reporting, the pro camp relied heavily on paid advertisements. This is a result of the organizational structure of the two camps—heterogeneous and decentralized (contra) versus predominance

Table 5.1 Total number of articles coded of the two camps, by campaign and communication channel

	Contra					Pro				
	Media input	Letters to editor	Ads	Direct mail	Info for members	Media input	Letters to editor	Ads	Direct mail	Info for members
Asylum	63	148	116	18	96	29	75	255	1	10
Naturalization	60	163	24			9	94	303		
Corporation Tax	39	116	15			50	156	419		

of the major parties, especially of the new populist right (pro)—and of the access to resources. The contra camp has access to more personnel, the pro camp to more money (Bernhard 2012). A very similar pattern can be observed in the naturalization initiative. In both cases, the populist right-wing party (SVP) had the lead in the pro camp campaign and used the political advertisements channel more often. In the corporate tax reform campaign, the pro camp was also highly involved with political advertisements. This time, the most powerful Swiss economic interest group (economiesuisse) was the leading actor in the pro camp. Finally, the numbers of media input are related to the number of participating actors. The more actors, the more media input was produced.

Second, Fig. 5.1 presents the weekly development of the frames in the media input, the letters to the editor, and the political advertisements of the two camps in the three campaigns. In the asylum law campaign, the panels show that the contra camp launched its media input at well-chosen moments (two peaks), while the pro camp's media input was not time-related. Instead, the pro camp ran a low but steady stream of ads that contained its key frame, which it increased heavily toward the end of the campaign. The same can be found in the naturalization initiative.

In the corporate tax reform campaign, we find two peaks in both camps, indicating that both camps carefully chose moments to submit input to the media. The peaks are characteristic of the media input, and their high amplitude indicates media conferences. The fact that political actors pause between media conferences explains the steepness. It also represents an anticipation effect of the media logic. In the interviews, political actors made clear that they were careful not to organize too many media conferences. Otherwise, they feared that journalists would no longer come. In the asylum law campaign and the corporate tax reform, we find media input more than ten weeks before voting. In the asylum law, this finding goes back to the institutional routine of the contra camp: Bernhard (2012) finds that opponents launch their campaigns much earlier with respect to the referenda than supporters. However, in the case of the corporate tax reform, the *pro* camp was also active early in the campaign. In this case, it employed a "planting the seed" strategy (Iyengar and McGrady 2007: 140) with an early media input. From the beginning, the pro camp wanted to present its core frame in order to influence opinion leaders and the media. In the naturalization initiative, the campaign started later (Chapter 3) because the minister was new in office. In addition, the highest peak in the media input occurs six

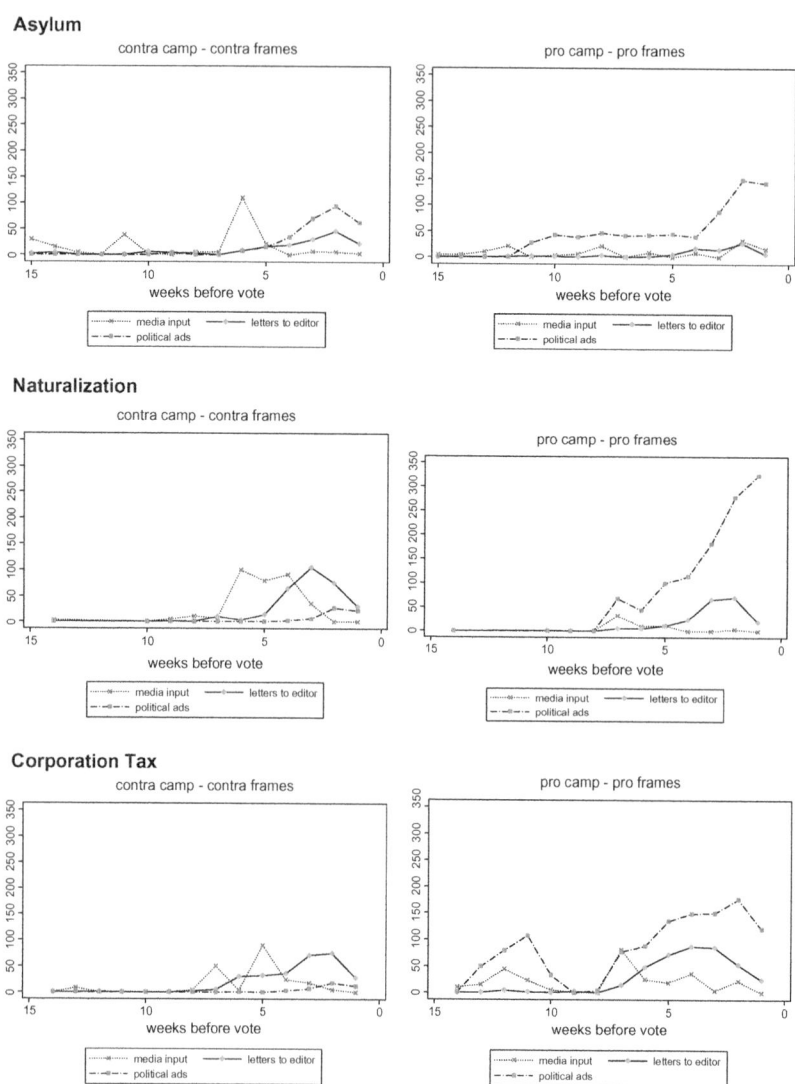

Fig. 5.1 Weekly development of the frames in the media input, the letters to the editor and the political advertisements of the two camps in the three campaigns

or seven weeks before the vote takes place. This is the beginning of the "critical period" of media coverage (Chapter 6).

Letters to the editor increase five to seven weeks before the vote occurs, and peak two or three weeks before the vote, when the public has received voting material and has begun voting (primarily by mail). In the graphs of the pro camps in the asylum law campaign and the naturalization initiative, we see an increase in the use of political advertisements in the final stages of the campaign. With this additional effort, the campaigners tried to get out the vote. I call this the "mobilizing strategy". The contra camps lacked advertising money, but also slightly increased their paid media efforts in the final stages of the campaign due to this "mobilizing strategy". In the corporate tax reform campaign, we see many pro camp ad arguments early in the campaign. The pro camp also followed a "planting the seed" strategy in the advertisements. The direct mail and information for members channel are not presented because the delivery date, i.e., timing, is less important and less well known.

Let us now turn to the three framing choices. For each choice, I will discuss the variation in the communication channels first, followed by the variation over time. Afterward, we will look at the results. For the same reason as mentioned above (delivery date is less important and less well known), the direct mail and the information for members channels are omitted when looking at the variation over time.

Variation by Communication Channel: Substantive Emphasis Choice

As introduced in Chapter 2, strategic actors first have to search for one or two frames which they believe have the capacity to become a strong substantive frame ("Substantive Emphasis Choice"). Because the letters to the editor are mediated and scrutinized by journalists, I expect them to have a set of frames similar to that found in the media input. In the political advertisements—in contrast to the media input—I expect political actors to focus more on their core frame for three reasons: First, advertising provides candidates with much greater control over their message than does news coverage. However, advertisements are less credible messengers than news media coverage (Iyengar and McGrady 2007: 164). Thus, political actors have an incentive to use the message that makes them appear most credible, i.e., their core message.

Second, advertising allows campaigners to shape their message to spe-cifically target those voters who are most pivotal to the outcome of a vote. Campaigners use the frame they believe will most effectively mobi-lize swing voters. Third, an advertisement focusing on one message can be used to grab the attention of the news media (Iyengar and McGrady 2007: 191). This may be especially relevant with regard to posters, but it can also be seen in advertisements.

For direct mail, I expect the political actors to choose the "Substantive Emphasis Strategy" similarly to advertisements, because both channels can reach citizens directly. Thus, I expect them to focus more on the core frame here as well. In the information for members, political actors communicate with motivated or better-informed read-ers. Members may be able to handle more frames, and they might also want to become more informed and more aware of different arguments. As a result, campaigners may promote their message using more than one frame. Thus, with regard to variation of the "Substantive Emphasis Choice" in the different communication channels, I expect results in let-ters to the editor to be similar to those in media input. I suspect that political actors focus more on their core frame in political advertisements and in direct mail, whereas they may have a wider focus in terms of infor-mation for members than they have in media input. I do not expect any variation between campaigns.

Variation by Communication Channel: Oppositional Emphasis Choice

The extent to which the two camps converge on the same frames is defined as dialogue (Chapter 1). From the letters section, we are already aware that editors strive for an open forum and "aim to create dialogue" (Wahl-Jorgensen 2007: 66). I expect the level of dialogue in the letters to be similar to that found in the media input. In the mediated chan-nels, political actors anticipate the media logic and adapt their commu-nication strategy accordingly (Cook 1989; Entman 1989; Jacobs and Shapiro 2000; Jerit 2008). They assume that the media offer dialogue and they want to ensure that they are in the media with the best possible counter-frames. For this reason, they provide the counter-frames them-selves. In their political advertisements and direct mail, campaigners fol-low issue ownership theory and emphasize issues on which they enjoy an advantage over their opponent (Iyengar and McGrady 2007: 142). This also appears to be plausible for frames. In addition, there are no political advertisements on television in Switzerland. Normally, ads in newspapers or flyers are small (half a newspaper page), decreasing the chance of dialogue. They often include no more than a short, catchy message, and thus do not lend themselves to extensive debate. As a consequence, it is expected that campaigners will engage in less dialogue with regard to ads and direct mail than they will with regard to the media input. When speaking to their own constituency in their information for members, political actors focus primarily on their own arguments. For this reason, I expect fewer opponents' frames in the information for members than in the media input.

Hence, with regard to the variation of the "Oppositional Emphasis Choice" in the different communication channels, I expect a similar amount of dialogue in letters sections to that in media input. By contrast, campaigners are expected to use fewer opponents' frames in their political advertisements, direct mail and information for members than they use in media input. In accordance with the results found in Chapter 4, I hypothesize that issue complexity and inequality of financial resources will reduce dialogue in all channels, whereas expected race closeness will increase convergence.

OPPOSITIONAL EMPHASIS CHOICE: OFFENSIVE OR DEFENSIVE USE?

With regard to the "Oppositional Emphasis Choice", campaigners must also decide whether to use their opponents' frames offensively (=trespassing) or defensively (=counter-framing). To my knowledge, it has never been investigated how this choice varies by communication channel. It has been argued that campaigners "have enough rhetorical freedom when designing campaign messages that an amenable frame can likely be found for nearly any issue" (Sides 2007: 467). In a similar way, the campaigners have enough rhetorical freedom to talk effectively about their rival's frame. Typically, political actors rely on goal ranking, issue categorization, institutional role assignment (Nelson 2004), or direct rebuttal (Jerit 2009) when debating the framing of an issue. In all of these prominent framing tactics, the rival frames are downplayed in a *defensive* way. Thus, I expect the offensive use of opponents' frames to be used rarely in all channels. In the media input channel, a message will have to be selected by journalists. Acting as gatekeepers (White 1950; Breeds 1955), journalists determine what message is put forth. Trespassing by the political actors may make messages less credible, potentially reducing the offensive use of frames in this channel. On the other hand, journalists may prefer to take an offensive stance, thereby motivating the political actors to increase the offensive use of frames. There might be more trespassing in the letters to the editor than in the media input for several reasons. First, the letters to the editor serve as an open forum for public debate. Often, an argument as presented by the opponent, i.e., in the offensive way, is included in order to react to it. Often, an opponent's argument is presented, i.e., in the offensive way, in order to react to it. It is also possible that a writer discusses different positions of the same argument, thus including the offensive and the defensive usage of it. Furthermore, there might be less strategic or camp-bound behavior in this channel than in media input. A letter writer might use an argument in his or her own way, which differs from the way in which the camps use it. Political ads and direct mail focus on a camp's core frame, which is indicative of campaigners who are interested neither in their opponents' frames nor in trespassing. For the same reason, I do not expect much trespassing in the information for members channel.

VARIATION BY COMMUNICATION CHANNEL: CONTEST EMPHASIS CHOICE

In general, I expect political actors to rely primarily on substantive frames in all their communication channels. Letters to the editor are rejected if they put a paper at risk of a libel suit, alienate advertisers, threaten readers or journalists with violence, or are racist. In all other cases, editors accept letters even if they are "uncomfortable with the tenor of the debate" (Wahl-Jorgensen 2007: 155) because they believe that letters which highlight conflict or attack other persons will encourage dialogue (Wahl-Jorgensen 2007: 67f., 154f.). In addition, a letters section can also perform a "safety valve" function (Wahl-Jorgensen 2007: 80) by allowing readers to vent their anger. In this way, a letters section serves a therapeutic function and helps readers to cope with their emotions. Consequently, I expect more contest frames in letters sections than in other channels. Although primarily the result of angry readers, the greater share of contest frames may also be a result of strategy on the part of volunteers, who want letters to appear authentic.

With regard to political ads, I expect that newspaper editors, who depend on advertising revenue, will refuse to print advertisements that are too aggressive in order to avoid alienating other potential advertisers. Nevertheless, contest frames, i.e., personal attacks and criticism, are still possible. It is well known that in the USA, campaigners rely heavily on negative or attack advertisements (Iyengar and McGrady 2007: 147ff.). Typically, consultants differentiate between critiques of performance, which focus on opponents' records, and character assassinations, in which opponents are portrayed as immoral people. As a result of several factors, however, both tactics appear to be insignificant in Swiss direct-democratic campaigns. First, the opponent's character is not at stake. Second, the Swiss consensus democracy is based on power sharing, which handicaps clear responsibilities and performance critiques. Third, the Swiss culture is less confrontational than in the USA. As a result, I expect political actors to use arguments in their advertisements instead of contest frames, such as attacks.

For similar reasons, I expect the same for direct mail, whereas I anticipate more contest frames in the information for members. In this channel, campaigners may resort to using misleading, unsubstantiated, and even outright false allegations against opponents. Such attacks can reinforce the division between in- and out-groups in such a way as to strengthen the ties of organization members. In line with the results of Chapter 4, I expect more contest frames in the naturalization initiative campaign because of the dispute between Christoph Blocher and Eveline Widmer-Schlumpf. Thus, with regard to the variation in the "Contest Emphasis Choice" in the different communication channels, I hypothesize that I will find more contest frames in letters to the editor than in media input. Political actors, however, will rely primarily on substantive frames in political advertisements and in direct mail. In information for members, they may also use more contest frames. I also expect to find more contest frames in the naturalization initiative.

VARIATION OVER TIME: MANAGEMENT OF EVENTS

In order to understand changes over time, we discuss both the management of events and the variation in framing choices over time. We start with the management of events. In an ideal campaign, each political actor hopes to enjoy a regular stream of favorable news coverage, while his opponent suffers from a lack of attention or poor coverage. In the real world, the campaigners have to compete for media attention. The "nuts and bolts" of press management are the strategic scheduling of events, i.e., the scheduling of opportunities to promote the message. Put simply, events must be designed and scheduled to attract maximal news coverage. There are three types of event: *genuine*, *mediated*, and *staged* events (Kepplinger and Habermeier 1995; Kepplinger 1998: 662). Genuine events are provided by the daily routine of the policymaking process (e.g., parliamentary votes), mediated events are triggered by key events and influenced by the media (e.g., the World Economic Forum, elections), and staged events, or so-called pseudo (Boorstin 1992) events (e.g., press conferences or demonstrations), are produced only in order to obtain media attention. Staged events would not occur without the mass media since their inherent goal is to transport the message to the media and ultimately to the audience (Schmitt-Beck and Pfetsch 1994: 114). Staged events have to pass the selection logic of the media. News value research has found that events pass the media logic more easily if they carry news factors such as unexpectedness, damage, controversy, relevance, or reach (Schulz 1997; Eilders 1997: 67, 259). Direct-democratic campaign events are neither genuine nor mediated events. Most events happening during direct-democratic campaigns are staged events.

Besides the strategic management of events, a second practice to promote one's own frame could be to play one media outlet against another (Iyengar and McGrady 2007: 134). The abundance of journalists covering a campaign provides the campaigners with the option of awarding access to sources on the basis of the anticipated quality of their coverage. Theoretically, this is above all an option for the minister. His campaigner reported that the minister basically has unlimited media attention. However, according to an informal, traditional conception, the minister is expected to exercise his or her campaigning role with a certain restraint (Kriesi 2009). Based on this norm, the minister is not expected to play the media against each other. The other campaigners do not have recourse to this opportunity, because they are less prominent. Playing one source against another seems to be better suited for exclusive stories or unforeseen events such as the announcement of a new party strategy or a resignation of a party's president, which include a high inherent news value. Thus, we cannot expect to find this practice in direct-democratic campaigns. Let us discuss the variation in framing choices next.

Variation Over Time: Substantive Emphasis Choice

Do the political actors vary their "Substantive Emphasis Choice" over time? Campaigners should not waffle or flip-flop between the frames (Iyengar and McGrady 2007: 129). Rather, they should stay on message (Norris et al. 1999; Perron 2007) or on their core frame, which they chose according to the "Substantive Emphasis Choice". Staying on message means the capacity to repeat the central campaign message, even when challenged by journalists, opponents, or simply by the campaign environment. This promotion practice goes hand in hand with the well-known advice put forward by the issue ownership theory (Petrocik 1996), which states that political actors should focus on the issue or issue attribute for which they enjoy an advantage. Of course, if a message is failing, it might be better to jettison plans and adapt to the circumstances. Nevertheless, strategic communication is based on the principle of planning for all eventualities and developing a popular message well in advance of the crucial phase of the campaign. Thus, I expect the campaigners to stay on their core frames in all channels in all campaigns.

Variation Over Time: Oppositional Emphasis Choice

How do the campaigners vary the level of dialogue ("Oppositional Emphasis Choice") over time? In real-world debates, framing strategies such as alternate frames (=promotion of one's own frames) and direct rebuttals (=counter-frames) (Jerit 2009) are common. Gilland and Marquis (2006) document that, in contrast to Riker's so-called dominance principle, there is no concentration on a smaller number of frames over the course of a direct-democratic campaign. Koopmans supports this notion, stating that he does not expect a "long-term tendency towards an increasingly uniform public discourse [...] [P]ublic discourse is kept alive by the small minority of 'distortions' or 'mutations'" (Koopmans 2004: 389). Based on this reasoning, I also expect there to be no concentration on a smaller number of frames toward the end of the campaign in the media input or in the letters to the editor. In other words, I expect a constant behavior of political actors over time. In the political advertisements, I expect to find less dialogue, but I do not have a specific hypothesis about variation over time here. In addition, I expect no variation between the campaigns.

Variation Over Time: Contest Emphasis Choice

How do the campaigners vary the "Contest Emphasis Choice" over time? Campaigners of ad hoc committees in the asylum law campaign and of economic interest groups in the corporate tax reform campaign believed themselves to have more influence on the frame-building process before the "crucial phase" started. Based on their experience with the media, these campaigners presumed that scarcity in terms of media attention increases during the "crucial phase" when more actors are involved. To compensate for this increasingly scarce media attention, the political actors might increase the news value of their events (Schulz 1997) by becoming more aggressive or increasing the conflict toward the end of a campaign. This means that they might increase their contest frames in the media input toward the end. For the other channels or between campaigns, I do not expect any variation.

Results

Variation by Communication Channel: Substantive Emphasis Choice

Table 5.2 gives an overview of the substantive and contest frames in the media input, letters to the editor, and political advertisements in all three campaigns, i.e., the asylum, naturalization, and corporation tax campaigns. For the asylum law, Table 5.2 also shows the frames for direct mail and the information for members. The main frames of each camp (Chapter 4) are in bold. Let us look first at the substantive frames in the different communication channels. Overall, it is clear that the shares of substantive frames in the media input are highly correlated with the shares of the substantive frames in the other channels ($r = 0.87$). We already know that in the media input, the most important frame of the contra camp makes up 45% of the arguments, whereas the pro camp focused on its most important frame in one-third of its arguments (Chapter 4).

The findings in the letters sections are similar to those in the media input of all three campaigns, and they are in line with my hypothesis that we find a similar set of frames in both mediated channels. In the political advertisements, the political actors increase the frequency of their main frame. With one exception, this rises to about 50%. This result

Table 5.2 The main substantive frames of the two camps, by communication channel: percentages

Asylum

	Contra					Pro				
	Media input	*Letters to editor*	*Political ads*	*Direct mail*	*Info for members*	*Media input*	*Letters to editor*	*Political ads*	*Direct mail*	*Info for members*
Substantive										
Human. trad.	38.9	36.1	35.7	47.0	33.3	24.8	15.5	13.3	11.1	12.5
Rule-of-law	21.9	4.9	14.8	9.2	18.8	9.3	5.3	3.8	0.0	5.7
Abuse	17.6	19.4	16.9	14.0	11.7	26.9	30.1	53.1	55.6	21.9
Efficacy	4.0	6.4	3.5	4.1	3.0	17.3	7.3	2.8	11.1	24.0
Others	13.9	23.5	28.5	21.0	25.2	16.1	26.7	26.0	22.2	32.3
All	96.3	90.3	99.3	95.2	92.0	94.3	85.0	99.0	100.0	96.4
substantive										
Contest	4.1	9.7	0.7	4.8	8.0	5.7	15.1	1.0	0.0	3.7
Total (%)	100	100	100	100	100	100	100	100	100	100
n	726	395	569	315	1907	335	202	1249	9	192

(continued)

Table 5.2 (continued)

Naturalization

	Contra			Pro		
	Media input	*Letters to editor*	*Political ads*	*Media input*	*Letters to editor*	*Political ads*
Substantive						
Rule-of-law	**49.0**	**48.1**	**52.3**	19.6	26.3	14.4
People final say	21.9	21.7	28.4	39.3	36.3	23.6
Mass naturalization	17.5	10.8	0.0	20.6	19.1	58.1
Others	5.0	5.6	14.7	7.5	9.7	3.9
All substantive	93.4	86.2	95.4	86.9	91.4	100.0
Contest	6.5	13.9	4.6	13.1	8.6	0.0
Total (%)	100	100	100	100	100	100
n	675	628	109	107	361	1358

Corporation tax

	Contra			Pro		
	Media input	*Letters to editor*	*Political ads*	*Media input*	*Letters to editor*	*Political ads*
Substantive						
Tax equity	**48.5**	**49.2**	**60.0**	7.7	17.9	3.1
Tax loss	**22.3**	13.1	**31.1**	8.4	4.1	2.1
SME	5.6	12.9	0.0	**38.4**	**31.6**	**49.0**
Competitiveness	14.1	14.5	6.7	27.3	**32.4**	**45.1**
Others	4.3	2.5	0.0	11.3	6.6	0.2
All substantive	94.8	92.2	97.8	93.1	92.6	99.6
Contest	5.2	7.8	2.2	6.9	7.4	0.4
Total (%)	100	100	100	100	100	100
n	462	449	45	594	608	1241

shows that the camps generally focus on one message and indeed focus most on their main frame in their advertisements (see Figs. 5.2): In every second argument, they use their core frame. Nevertheless, in the other half, they speak about something else—using their own second frame or their rival's frame. There is one exception, the asylum law campaign, in which the contra camp focused less on one frame (not shown). This can be explained in two ways: First, as the interviews revealed, the contra camp perceived the abuse frame to be so strong that they felt the need to counter-frame it, even in their own advertisements. Second, the contra camp also used a higher proportion of "other" frames because many organizations with different foci and different frames were involved in one committee.

The campaigners in the asylum law case use a similar strategy in their direct mail to that in the advertisements. The communication documents of both channels are directed in an unmediated way toward the public. In the communication with the members, the political actors have a wider focus. They use their main frame on average only 27% $(=(33+21)/2)$ of the time. The pro camp even promoted the "efficacy" frame more than the "abuse" frame.

In general, the core frame of the media input also remains the core frame of the other channels. However, there are three exceptions. The first is found in the naturalization initiative. The core frame of the pro camp in the media input is the "people final say" frame, whereas in the political advertisements, this is used in only 23.6% of all frames. Instead, the "mass naturalization" frame is used 58% of the time. This result reflects a change in the strategy of the pro camp. The campaigner responsible for this strategic change explained in an interview that toward the end of the campaign, the pro camp changed its strategy because the campaigners received feedback from their activists indicating that the "people final say" frame was not convincing. In addition, the pro camp had more funds available than they had originally planned. This allowed them to publish a significant number of political advertisements in the last three weeks of the campaign. They tested different arguments and decided to promote primarily the "mass naturalization" frame. As a result, we see the "mass naturalization" frame emphasized in their advertisements (Fig. 5.2a). The pro camp reused its well-known advertisement from the 2004 naturalization of second- and third-generation immigrants campaign. Because the end of the campaign was nearing, the pro camp was unable to change its core frame in the other channels too.

(a)

(b)

Fig. 5.2 Political advertisements of the two camps in the naturalization initiative. **a** Advertisement of the populist right in support of its initiative. **b** Advertisement of the moderate right's contra campaign

The second exception is found in the corporate tax reform. The core frame of the pro camp is the "SME" frame. Nevertheless, in the letters to the editor, the "competitiveness" frame is emphasized and the "tax equity" frame was discussed more frequently than in the other channels. This indicates that the "SME" aspect was not particularly controversial. The third case is found in the asylum law campaign, in which the pro camp promoted the "abuse" frame the most in the media input. This is not the case in the information for members, in which they relied more on the "efficacy" frame, most frequently used by the moderates of the pro camp. Thus, in this communication channel, it is the frame of the moderate part of the pro camp that is more visible, while the extreme part of the pro camp dominated the other channels.

Dialogue by Communication Channel: Oppositional Emphasis Choice

Looking at the non-bold numbers in the first three rows of Table 5.3, we see that in the media input, both sides address the main frames of the opposing camp on average once in every four arguments. They address primarily the most important frame of the opposing camp and, secondarily, the other camp's next most important frame. The pattern in the letters to the editor is similar to that found in the media input. On average, the opponents' frames are again used in 25% of the promoted frames. This suggests that the two main frames on both sides were strong, such that neither side could ignore the frames of their opponents. Instead,

Table 5.3 Use of opponents' main frames in the different communication channels

		Contra	Pro	Average
Media input	Asylum law	21.6	34.1	**25.1**
	Naturalization	39.4	19.6	
	Corporation tax	19.7	16.1	
Letters to the Editor	Asylum law	25.8	20.8	**25.8**
	Naturalization	32.5	26.3	
	Corporation tax	27.4	22.0	
Political ads	Asylum law	23.4	17.1	**18.7**
	Naturalization	28.4	14.4	
	Corporation tax	6.7	5.2	
Info for members	Asylum law	14.7	18.2	**16.5**
Direct mail	Asylum law	18.1	11.1	**14.6**

Note Example for the calculation: 19.4 + 6.4 = 25.8 (contra frames in letters to the editor in the asylum law)

both frames elicited strong defensive reactions from opponents in both channels. In all *other* channels, the political actors address their opponents' frames only around 15% of the time.

Let me illustrate here with a few examples what dialogue means. Opponents of the asylum law discussed the "wrong information of the pro camp". Discussing the abuse frame, the contra camp argued that contrary to what the responsible department claimed (pro camp), there has been more than one wrong decision out of 530,000 since 1964 and that the Federal Council also knows this. Thus, because the proposed law prohibited assistance for asylum seekers whose claims have been refused, tightening the law might hit those who have been truly persecuted. In the corporate tax reform, the contra camp contended that the argument regarding tax equity is wrong. In summary, they argued that contrary to what the pro camp says, double taxation is not a problem because the revenue raised is reinvested and not lost to the economy. Furthermore, they claimed that the national expert group "rechtsform-neutrale Unternehmensbesteuerung" and the Federal Council (pro camp) also argued this way in the letter accompanying the proposal. In the naturalization initiative, a representative of the liberal party (an actor on the contra side) discussed the arguments of the pro camp; thus: "We reject the quantitative element of the contra camp campaign (too many naturalizations, mass naturalization frame). We should not decide about naturalizations based on an upper limit but based on the integration to Swiss circumstances. Those who are sufficiently integrated and willing to participate in our political life, should be allowed to do so". On rare occasions, we also find dialogue of lower quality. For example, the contra camp was repeating an argument of the pro camp (that the courts allegedly want a further facilitation of naturalizations that will lead to more naturalizations of criminals or welfare state abusers—a frame not important for the debate) but merely by saying that it is populistic, purely demagogic, or just stupid, rather than discussing it. In this case, we would also see contest frames. However, this low-quality dialogue occurs only rarely and predominantly on less important, other, frames.

Table 5.4 shows the level of dialogue (convergence) in the different communication channels of the three campaigns. A figure of 100 would mean that they speak about the same frames to the same extent, while 0 would indicate that they used completely different frames. The highest level of dialogue is found in the letters to the editor in all three campaigns.

Table 5.4 Dialogue in the different communication channels

	Channel	Asylum	Naturalization	Corporation tax	Mean (over all three campaigns)
Letters to editor	Mediated	72.6	72.5	56.1	67.1
Media input		69.9	69.3	41.5	60.2
Political ads	Unmediated	51.1	39.5	13.1	34.6
Info for members	or internal	50.5			(50.5)
Direct mail		38.6			(38.6)

In all three campaigns, the dialogue level of the ads is lower than in the mediated channels. In the asylum law, the level of dialogue in the ads is higher than in the other two campaigns because in this case many actors of the contra side came together in one key coalition, which then struggled with its different heterogeneous interests. They were not able to compromise on one single message but needed to include different messages in their ads representing different perspectives, thus increasing the level of dialogue. Regarding the remaining channels, we find the lowest level of dialogue in the direct mail, while in the communication to members we observe a level of convergence similar to that found in the political advertisements. Even though there is variation in the level of dialogue in the ads, the results support my expectation that the levels of dialogue in the mediated channels should be higher than in the unmediated and internal channels. With regard to the differences between the campaigns, we find further support for the idea that complexity and inequality of financial resources reduce dialogue (Chapter 4). The tax reform was the most complex issue and the one that has been most financially dominated by a single camp since the early 1980s. Across all communication channels, we find the lowest levels of dialogue in the corporate tax reform campaign. In contrast to the media input results (Chapter 4), we do not find more dialogue in the closer race (naturalization initiative). Thus, I conclude that the expected closeness of outcome may be of minor importance for dialogue.

Table 5.5 The offensive use of opponents' frames in the communication channels: percentage of adversaries' frames which were used offensively

Channel	Contra	Pro
Letters to editor	6.9	8.9
Info for members	0.6	6.2
Political ads	0.0	4.5
Media input	0.0	3.6

Note The percentage shares are averaged over opponents' core and second frame and over campaigns. The direct mail channel is not presented because of the small number of cases

Oppositional Emphasis Choice: Offensive or Defensive Use?

Table 5.5 shows the percentage of offensive use (=trespassing) of opponents' frames in each channel. The defensive use of opponents' frames (=counter-framing) is not shown but can be easily calculated (100% − offensive use = defensive use). Overall, the two camps use their opponents' frames defensively in the overwhelming majority of cases in every channel. In other words, we find few instances of trespassing and an emphasis on counter-framing in all communication channels. Most examples of offensive use of the opponents' frames are found in the letters section. Across all channels, we see no systematic variation over time. Campaigners nearly always counter-frame their opponents' frames if they use them at all, i.e., use them in a defensive way (not shown).

Variation by Communication Channel: Contest Emphasis Choice

Let us look again at Table 5.2. As expected, contest frames, such as personal attacks and conflicts, are rarely used by political actors in Swiss direct-democratic campaigns, regardless of the communication channel. In the letters to the editor, the proportion of contest frames is, with one exception, higher than that of media input. Even though I rely on the published letters to the editor, I can assume that the share of contest frames in the letters submitted is not significantly different: First, letters contain the writer's name and are submitted by locals. This allows for personal attacks. Second, as argued in the theoretical section, the editors strive for minimal intervention and allow attacks because they believe dialogue will emerge from controversial letters. On average, 10% of all statements in the letters section are contest frames. The pro camp in the naturalization initiative campaign is an exception in using so many contest frames in the media input that the share of contest frames is higher in media input than in letters to the editor. In the political ads, the political actors generally refrain from using contest frames. As a result, contest frames are used, on average, in only 1.5% of the statements in the ads. Similarly, in the direct mail, the political actors use contest frames on average only 2.4% of the time; in communications with their members, contest frames appear in only 5.8% of cases.

However, as we see in Table 5.2, substantive frames predominate in all channels. Thus, we can state that in Swiss direct-democratic campaigns, framing is done primarily in substantive terms across all channels. With the exception of the pro camp in the asylum law campaign, there are more contest frames in the naturalization initiative because of the dispute between Christoph Blocher, the populist right-wing party (SVP), and Eveline Widmer-Schlumpf. In the asylum law campaign, AUNS, a citizens' interest group from the conservative right who campaigned on the pro side, prepared several aggressive draft versions of letters.

Variation Over Time: Management of Events

Let us look at the patterns over time. Generally, we can state that direct-democratic campaigns are characterized by similar information over time. This is confirmed by one journalist of a regional newspaper: "Often, there is no change over time in a campaign. I notice an organization the first time but tend to ignore it if it promotes its frame(s) a second or third time". Thus, one can say that political actors can promote their frames at least once. In fact, political actors in direct-democratic campaigns rely on *staged* events such as media conferences and media releases. Across the three campaigns, every ad hoc committee and all large political parties[1] involved hold at least one media conference. In the tax reform campaign, the economic interest groups were also active with a media conference. In the three cases, six to nine media

---

[1] By "large political parties", I refer to the five strongest parties in the Swiss multi-party system: the Swiss People's Party (SVP), the Social Democrats (SP), followed by the Liberal Party (FDP) and the Christian Democratic Party (CVP), each with a vote share of between 7 and 29%. These four parties form the coalition government. The fifth, the Green Party (GPS), has not been part of the government coalition so far.

conferences took place during a campaign (i.e., in the three months before the vote). The small parties, or the citizens' interest groups, did not organize a media conference on their own due to a lack of resources or know-how, as they reported in the interviews. However, in coalition with larger parties, they were also present in conferences. If coalitions held a media conference, different organizations spoke in order to increase the credibility of the message. In addition, the most prominent or powerful speaker of each organization promoted the message in order to increase the chance of media attention. Almost all media conferences were held in the Swiss capital Bern, as this is where political events take place: The parliament is located in Bern, the important media outlets have journalists on the ground and most parties and citizens' interest groups are also resident here.

The most common form of staged event is the press release. More than thirty press releases were found in every campaign. In the asylum law, the contra camp also relied on a concert, one demonstration, and street theater. In the tax reform campaign, a citizens' interest group of the contra camp produced an informative videotape that elaborated the tax issue. In the interviews, this citizens' interest group remarked that they did not fit well into the direct-democratic discourse for two reasons: Firstly, they believe that they have a broader perspective because they consider the global situation and international law to a greater extent. Secondly, they point to their longer time horizon. They are not tied to the electoral cycle as political parties are. They can deal with topics such as the reform of the financial system, which usually last for several years.

In order to attract maximal news coverage, the campaigners produce staged events actively but also *reactively*. They can actively attract media attention by informing about their position and the issue at stake only once. This kind of information subsequently loses its news value. The campaigners have to compensate for this loss by finding new opportunities to promote their frames, and thus they become *reactive*. Four different ways can be found to achieve this: reaction to events in one's own camp, to the opponent, to the media, and to facts. Let us illustrate these four types of reaction with examples from the three campaigns. First, the campaigners react to events occurring in their *own camp*. This is particularly suited to large political parties, who often organize a convention to adopt a position or recommendation for the vote and take it as an opportunity to promote their message concerning the next direct-democratic vote: In the asylum law campaign, the right-wing party (SVP) reported on their convention and announced that the senior party members were also in favor of the new law. In the tax reform campaign, the Christian Democrats (CVP) stated that the women of their party also supported the reform. This promotion practice seems to be especially relevant for the large parties because they often announce their position early in the campaign.

Second, the campaigners react to their *opponent's camp*. For instance, in the asylum law campaign, the pro camp promoted the abuse frame, claiming that the new law was needed in order to prevent abuse. The contra camp felt compelled to react and organized a media conference called "the untruths of the pro camp" and counter-framed the abuse argument. In addition, it invited three asylum seekers to speak about their experiences. These asylum seekers had been sent back to their native countries, in which they had been imprisoned. The contra camp alleged that these cases were judicial errors. Most importantly, they argued that the number of judicial errors was much higher than the pro camp claimed and that the new law would increase this number even more. On the very same day, the pro camp, in turn, reacted to the conference of the contra camp. This time, the responsible department of the state administration (SEM) responded with a press release in which it refuted the accusation of the contra camp. It argued that while asylum seekers were, indeed, occasionally imprisoned for short periods, the arrests were often aimed at clarifying the asylum seekers' identification or were made for reasons not relevant to the asylum process, such as due to non-political criminal acts. On another occasion in the asylum law campaign, the contra camp claimed that the information bulletin produced by the government and sent to each citizen did not contain accurate information.

Third, the campaigners also react to the *media*. For example, in the naturalization initiative campaign, the pro camp reacted to a TV program (Rundschau), claiming that the program's descriptions of the circumstances were misleading. Also in the naturalization initiative campaign, the right-wing party (SVP) announced that the former minister and head of the party (Blocher) and the responsible minister and excluded party member (Widmer-Schlumpf) would participate in the Swiss TV debate show (Arena) and added their message to this announcement. It appears that the right-wing party tends to be more reactive to the media than the other political actors.

Fourth, the campaigners react to *facts* appearing in the course of the campaign. During the asylum law campaign, it emerged that an asylum seeker (Solongo Chinbat) had abused the system. The pro camp reacted

Fig. 5.3 Ad of social democrats (*Note* Marcel Ospel is presented as primary beneficiary of the tax reform)

to this fact with a press release in which it used the case to further promote their message: it claimed that a new law was needed in order to prevent such abuse. In the tax reform campaign, the argumentation of the Social Democrats—who were in charge of the contra-committee during the campaign—resonated well with external events happening at the same time. The Social Democrats mainly argued that the tax cuts were an unfair privilege for the well-off and went against the principle of fair taxation (tax equity). They even claimed that the reform was unconstitutional. This line of reasoning mainly applied to a controversial provision that included a reduction in tax rates on dividends for shareholders who held at least a ten percent stake in a corporation. In the final phase of the campaign, the Social Democrats reacted to the UBS subprime crisis and presented individuals who would profit from the reform (Fig. 5.3). By that time, the subprime crisis of UBS had become a political issue: On December 10, 2007, UBS had unveiled 11 billion Swiss francs (10 billion US dollars) of subprime write-downs and announced that it had obtained an emergency capital injection from the Singapore sovereign fund and an unnamed Middle East investor. On January 30, 2008, UBS announced that it would write down 4.4 billion Swiss francs (4 billion US dollars) in bad investments for the year 2007 and would report a net loss of 12.5 billion Swiss francs (11.4 billion US dollars) in the fourth quarter of 2007. On February 14, 2008, UBS confirmed a net loss of 4.4 billion Swiss francs (4.0 billion US dollars) in 2007. For many people, these losses of a major Swiss bank went strongly against the very high bonuses some managers were being awarded. Toward the end of the campaign, on February 14, the Social Democrats made an explicit link to UBS and to the President of the Board of Directors of UBS AG, Marcel Ospel (Fig. 5.3). They claimed that controlling and major stockholders such as Ospel would be the primary beneficiaries of the tax reform. In the naturalization initiative campaign, the pro camp reacted to a murder carried out by a recently naturalized person and emphasized the importance of saying yes to the vote. Overall, the campaigners tend to use media conferences actively, whereas in the press releases they tend to act more reactively. Anything that might give the political actors an additional opportunity to further promote their message or increase its credibility is used as a reason for a media release.

Next, we look at the usage of the practice of playing one media outlet against another (Iyengar and McGrady 2007: 134). As expected, the interviews with the campaigners reveal that playing one source against another is not used in direct-democratic campaigns. Normally, the campaigners send their media releases to all media outlets and invite all of them to their media conferences. Sometimes, they might have mailing lists which do not include all of the media outlets. However, they do not intend to play the newspapers against each other or deliver their message exclusively: The missing newspapers are not interested or did not subscribe to the mailing list, and it would be a fruitless endeavor to send the message to all of them. Nevertheless, playing one source against another did occur on one occasion. In the tax reform campaign, a tabloid newspaper (Blick) refused to accept an advertisement from the major Swiss union (SGB). The union used the slogan "I am not stupid", copying Europe's largest retailer for consumer electronics (Media Markt). For the SGB, the slogan and its link to Media Markt fit very well with the issue at stake, because major shareholders of Media Markt are people who would typically benefit from the tax reform. The advertisement showed a photograph of a major Media Markt shareholder and stated that he would benefit from the tax reform. Blick refused to show the advertisement, ostensibly because it could harm the personal rights of this major shareholder. For the campaigner, another reason seemed to be more plausible: Blick did not want to upset Media Markt because it was one of its important advertisers. The campaigner then tried to exploit the story and informed other media outlets. The popular TV news program "10vor10" was not interested. Finally, it was covered by a regional newspaper, which produced an article called "Blick refuses an advertisement of the SGB". This is a case in which a campaigner played one source against another. However, this is the only occurrence in the three campaigns investigated. It can thus be seen as the exception that proves the rule.

Variation Over Time: Substantive Emphasis Choice

At the frame level, the empirical results from the three campaigns also show that the campaigners generally stay on frame. The main frames are promoted from the very beginning and no new frame appears in the course of the campaign. In addition, the most important frame of a camp remains the most important over time across all channels. Thus, it can be stated that campaigners do not normally change their "Substantive Emphasis Choice" during a direct-democratic campaign. As already mentioned, there is one exception to this general behavior: The main frame of the pro camp at the beginning of the naturalization campaign was the "people final say" frame. Toward the end of the campaign, however, the pro camp emphasized the "mass naturalization" frame the most in their advertisements.

Dialogue Over Time: Oppositional Emphasis Choice

Figure 5.4 shows the level of dialogue (convergence) in media input, letters to the editor, and political ads on all three cases taken together over time. For media input, we see that the political actors converge on the most important frames in around 60% of the cases when they are active with media input (from eight to three weeks before the vote takes place). They continue to use their opponents' frames during the whole campaign. In the letters to the editor, the level of dialogue decreases slightly in the fourth week before the vote but subsequently increases again. Further research will have to elaborate on this finding, but it might be possible that dialogue in the letters is most alive toward the end. In the political advertisements, the dialogue level varies more than in the other

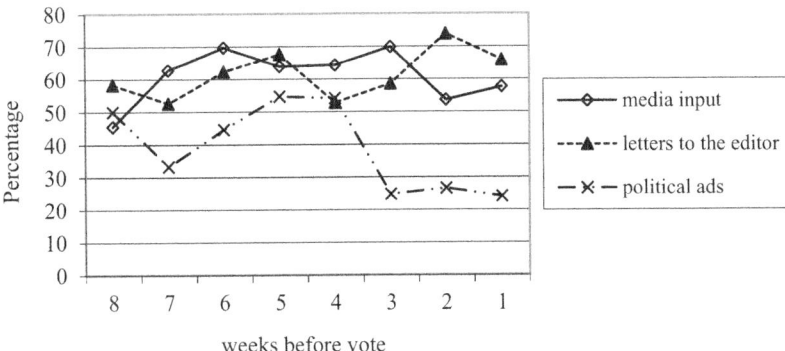

Fig. 5.4 Dialogue over time and in the different communication channels (*Note* In weeks 15–9, there were too few observations)

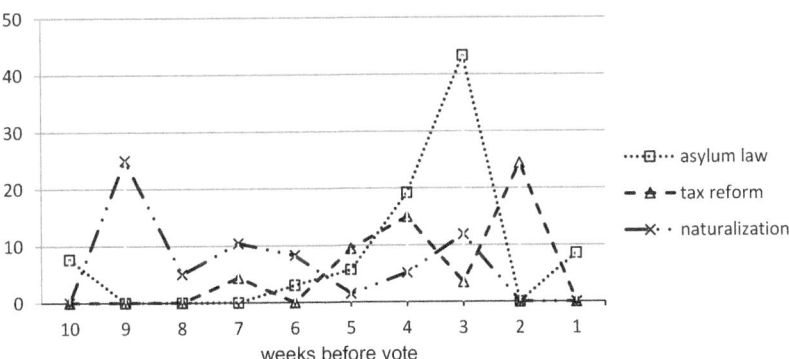

Fig. 5.5 Share of contest frames in media input over time

channels. It drops to very low levels in the last three weeks, when political actors are most active.

Variation Over Time: Contest Emphasis Choice

Figure 5.5 shows the share of contest frames over time in the media input. In the asylum law and corporate tax reform, the campaigners increased the usage of contest frames in media input before the end of the campaign. There were more contest frames at the beginning in the naturalization initiative.

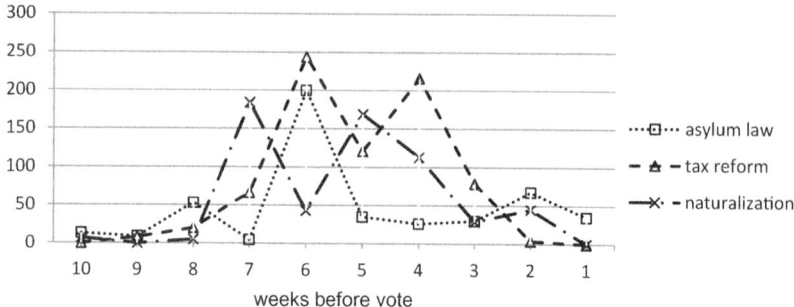

Fig. 5.6 Number of frames in media input over time

However, Fig. 5.6 (when seen alongside Fig. 5.5) shows that the higher shares of contest frames occur when there is little activity with media input. In general, there are few contest frames at all and there is not a great deal to explain. With regard to the use of contest frames over time in the other channels, there is no variation (not shown).

CONCLUSION

The key finding of this chapter is that there is more dialogue in the mediated channels. From a normative perspective, this is an important finding because dialogue is important to the democratic process. Citizens are able to make more informed decisions when they are exposed to different frames, and the likelihood of vote manipulation is reduced when citizens are exposed to counter-frames (Druckman 2004; Chong and Druckman 2007). The finding that political actors provide more dialogue in mediated channels also demonstrates that the political actors anticipate the role of the media. They offer more dialogue in the media input. Finally, this result is also relevant to research regarding media-based politics because we show that there are differences between the channels. The degree of dialogue in the advertisements and direct mails is lower than in the other communication channels. Thus, media input (and—as will be reported in Chapter 6—news media coverage) is capable of providing dialogue. Political advertisements and direct mails have functions other than that of providing dialogue. They should mobilize citizens to vote or should provoke an intensive public debate.

In greater detail, with respect to the "Substantive Emphasis Choice" and the "Oppositional Emphasis Choice", we find that political actors generally also use their main frames in channels other than the media input. We saw that the political actors stay on their frame with one exception: In the naturalization initiative, the pro camp switched from the "people final say" frame to the "mass naturalization" frame in its ads toward the end of the campaign. The "people final say" frame was not proving to be convincing. The fact that political actors stay on message across channels validates the findings of the media input. The core frames in the media input remain the core frames in the advertisements, which shows that the frames used in the media input are not used simply to placate journalists, but also shows the preference of the campaigners if they are in sole control of their message. We saw that the frame emphases in the letters section are similar to those found in the media input. In the political advertisements, with two exceptions, the core frame of the media input appears more frequently. Similar results have been found for direct mails. Accordingly, the political actors pay more attention to their opponents' frames in the media input and in the letters to the editor than in the advertisements and direct mails because the *mediation* motivates them to enter into dialogue with each other. Furthermore, we find instances of counter-framing rather than trespassing, which was virtually absent. It has to be kept in mind that the results of the letters to the editor channel cannot be claimed to be generally valid. Looking at the *published* letters instead of the *submitted* letters might have introduced a selection bias. We have no idea how the distribution of frames represented in this channel was altered because of journalists' selection.

We can also note that issue complexity and inequality of financial resources reduce dialogue (Chapter 4). However, expected closeness of the race does not seem to influence dialogue. We do not find more convergence in the closer race (naturalization initiative). With regard to variation over time, it can be concluded that dialogue does not disappear over the course of the campaign. In the media input, dialogue remains high until campaigners stop promoting their message. In the letters to the editor, the level of dialogue is also high and even increases moderately toward the end. In the political advertisements, the dialogue level varies most, but remains rather low during the last three weeks of the campaign when the campaigners rely most on this channel.

Concerning the "Contest Emphasis Choice" in the different communication channels, we show that in direct-democratic campaigns the political actors often refrain from using contest frames in their ads and in direct mail, whereas we find more contest frames in the letters to the editor and in the communication with members than in the media input. In the communication with members, attacks are used to strengthen the division between members and non-members, whereas the letters section might also help readers to vent anger. In line with the findings of Chapter 4, we notice more contest frames in the naturalization initiative. There is not much variation over time. However, toward the end of the campaign, we identify more contest frames in the media input.

Interaction Between Context (Campaign Type, Country) and Frame Promotion

In election campaigns, the frame promotion process is probably more important than in direct-democratic campaigns. This is related to the fact that election campaigns are not restricted to one issue and have more the character of a race. In addition, election campaigns generally involve more resources than direct-democratic campaigns. In our cases, the budget was between 0.8 and 7.0 million Swiss francs (see Chapter 3), whereas in the 1995 elections for the Swiss Parliament, the parties in the three largest Swiss cantons (=subnational level units similar to states in the US context) alone spent around 7.8 million (Kriesi 1998: 3). We also know that at the cantonal level, parties use 12% of their budget for direct-democratic campaigns, whereas they spend 30% for elections (Brändle 2001: 163). Thus, I can conclude that in election campaigns parties spend more money, which will increase the importance of the frame promotion process. This does not necessarily influence the level of dialogue. In public debates, different channels are probably less important. However, if scandalous information is released, social media channels might be important and there may be a lot of change over time, as the situation becomes less predictable.

Regarding variations between countries, I expect the frame promotion process to be more important in countries with a media-oriented political communication culture because the media logic increases the willingness to spend money. This expectation is supported by the fact that more resources are involved in US campaigns. For the general election, Obama's campaign committee raised more than $650 million in 2008 and more than $400 million in 2012.[2] However, these election

[2]http://en.wikipedia.org/wiki/Barack_Obama_presidential_campaign,_2012, May 2019.

campaigns are considered to be outliers, as nowhere else is such a high amount of the budget used for election campaigns (Nassmacher 2002: 9). As a consequence, I expect the promotion process to be more important in US presidential election campaigns than anywhere else. Despite this difference, I expect *similar patterns* in the frame promotion process of different countries, as found in this study. In particular, I expect also that elsewhere the actors will try to stay on message, will use more dialogue in mediated channels, and will increase the use of the contest frames toward the end of a campaign. In Denmark, for instance, De Vreese and Semetko (2004: 172) report that the political actors did, in fact, stay on message (although they ultimately failed with this strategy because the message was discredited). In addition, the Danish campaigners also increased the use of contest frames toward the end of the campaign (2004: 99). In a similar way to Switzerland, they also rely on a traditional or routinized mode of campaigning (De Vreese and Semetko 2004: 172), which means that their campaign communication was not particularly sophisticated or targeted.

References

Bernhard, L. (2012). *Campaign Strategy in Direct Democracy.* Hampshire: Palgrave Macmillan.

Boorstin, D. J. (1992 [1961]). *The Image: A Guide to Pseudo-Events in America* (25th Anniversary Edition). New York: First Vintage Book Edition.

Brändle, M. (2001). Die finanziellen Mittel der Parteien. In A. Ladner & M. Brändle (Eds.), *Die Schweizer Parteien im Wandel.* Zürich: Seismo.

Breed, W. (1955). Social Control in the Newsroom: A Functional Analysis. *Social Forces, 33*(4), 326–335.

Chong, D., & Druckman, J. N. (2007). Framing Public Opinion in Competitive Democracies. *American Political Science Review, 101*(4), 637–656.

Cook, T. (1989). *Making Laws and Making News. Media Strategies in the U.S. House of Representatives.* Washington, DC: Brookings Institution.

De Vreese, C. H., & Semetko, H. A. (2004). News Matters: Influences on the Vote in a Referendum Campaign. *European Journal of Political Research, 43*(5), 701–724.

Druckman, J. N. (2004). Political Preference Formation: Competition, Deliberation, and the (Ir)relevance of Framing Effects. *American Political Science Review, 98*(4), 671–686.

Eilders, C. (1997). *Nachrichtenfaktoren und Rezeption: Eine empirische Analyse zur Auswahl und Verarbeitung politischer Information* [News Factors and

Reception: An Empirical Analysis of the Audience's Selection and Retention Processes in Political Communication]. Opladen: Westdeutscher Verlag.

Entman, R. M. (1989). *Democracy Without Citizens: Media and the Decay of American Politics*. New York: Oxford University Press.

Gans, H. J. (2003). *Democracy and the News*. New York: Oxford University Press.

Gilland, K., & Marquis, L. (2006). Campaigning in a Direct Democracy: Three Case Studies. *Swiss Political Science Review, 12*(3), 63–81.

Hänggli, R., & Kriesi, H. (2012). Frame Construction and Frame Promotion (Strategic Framing Choices). *American Behavioral Scientist* (Special Issue), 260–278.

Iyengar, S. (1991). *Is Anyone Responsible? How Television Frames Political Issues*. Chicago: The University of Chicago Press.

Iyengar, S., & McGrady, J. A. (2007). *Media Politics: A Citizen's Guide*. New York: W. W. Norton.

Jacobs, L. R., & Shapiro, R. Y. (2000). *Politicians Don't Pander*. Chicago: University of Chicago Press.

Jerit, J. (2008). Issue Framing and Engagement: Rhetorical Strategy in Public Policy Debates. *Political Behaviour, 30,* 1–24.

Jerit, J. (2009). How Predictive Appeals Shape Policy Opinions. *American Journal of Political Science, 53*(2), 411–426.

Kepplinger, H. M. (1998). Inszenierung. In O. Jarren, U. Sarcinelli, & U. Saxer (Eds.), *Politische Kommunikation in der demokratischen Gesellschaft. Ein Handbuch mit Lexikonteil* (pp. 662–663). Wiesbaden: Opladen.

Kepplinger, H. M., & Habermeier, J. (1995). The Impact of Key Events on the Presentation of Reality. *European Journal of Communication, 10*(3), 371–390.

Koopmans, R. (2004). Movements and Media: Selection Processes and Evolutionary Dynamics in the Public Sphere. *Theory and Society, 33*(3/4), 367–391.

Kriesi, H. (1998). Einleitung. In H. Kriesi, W. Linder, & U. Klöti (Eds.), *Schweizer Wahlen 1995* (pp. 1–16). Bern: Haupt.

Kriesi, H. (2009). The Role of the Federal Government in Direct-Democratic Campaigns. In N. Stéphane & V. Frédéric (Eds.), *Rediscovering Public Law and Public Administration in Comparative Policy Analysis: A Tribute to Peter Knoepfel* (pp. 79–96). Bern: Verlag Haupt.

Nassmacher, K.-H. (2002). Die Kosten der Parteitätigkeit in westlichen Demokratien. *Österreichische Zeitschrift Für Politikwissenschaft, 31,* 7–20.

Nelson, T. E. (2004). Policy Goals, Public Rhetoric, and Political Attitudes. *The Journal of Politics, 66*(2), 581–605.

Norris, P., Curtice, J., Sanders, D., Scammell, M., & Semetko, H. A. (1999). *On Message: Communicating the Campaign*. London: Sage.

Perron, L. (2007). *How to Overcome the Power of Incumbency in Election Campaigns?*. Zürich: Institute of Political Science.

Petrocik, J. R. (1996). Issue Ownership in Presidential Elections, with a 1980 Case Study. *American Journal of Political Science, 40*(3), 825–850.

Schmitt-Beck, R., & Pfetsch, B. (1994). Politische Akteure und die Medien der Massenkommunikation. Zur Generierung von Öffentlichkeit in Wahlkämpfen. In F. Neidhardt (Ed.), *Öffentlichkeit, öffentliche Meinung, soziale Bewegungen. Kölner Zeitschrift für Soziologie und Sozialpsychologie, Sonderheft 34* (pp. 106–138). Opladen and Wiesbaden: Westdeutscher Verlag.

Schulz, W. (1997). *Politische Kommunikation theoretische Ansätze und Ergebnisse empirischer Forschung zur Rolle der Massenmedien in der Politik.* Opladen: Westdeutscher Verlag.

Sides, J. (2007). The Consequences of Campaign Agendas. *American Politics Research, 35*(4), 465–488.

Wahl-Jorgensen, K. (2007). *Journalists and the Public: Newsroom Culture, Letters to the Editor and Democracy.* Cresskill: Hampton Press.

White, D. M. (1950). The "Gate Keeper": A Case Study in the Selection of News. *Journalism Quarterly, 27,* 383–390.

CHAPTER 6

Frame Edition: Choices of Journalists

Introduction

In this chapter, we shall explore the contribution of journalists. Following Strömbäck and Nord (2006), one can distinguish between a process level and a content level of news making. At the process level, the journalists and political actors negotiate and battle over when and where the news is reported. At the content level, the journalists and political actors negotiate and battle over how the news is framed. The process level is of minor importance here. Since direct-democratic campaigns are well institutionalized, the news media report on the issue when political actors become active and the issue is salient in the news. Thus, it is more relevant to look at the content level (which I call frame edition). As was shown in Chapters 4 and 5, the political actors construct and promote the main frames in the public discourse in direct-democratic campaigns. But do journalists also contribute to the framing of news? I argue that when reporting on direct-democratic campaigns, journalists face at least four choices which are relevant for frame building. First, journalists decide on how to balance the messages of both camps ("Balancing Choice"). Second, they decide whose messages they want to cover ("Range of Views Choice"). The power of the frame promoter will be important for this choice. Once certain messages are available, journalists decide on the weight they will give to available messages ("Story Choice"). In this regard, the salience of frames in the media input and

© The Author(s) 2020
R. Hänggli, *The Origin of Dialogue in the News Media*,
Challenges to Democracy in the 21st Century,
https://doi.org/10.1007/978-3-030-26582-3_6

the role of the government minister responsible become important. Finally, journalists decide whether to investigate official claims or provide interpretations ("Interpretation Choice"). Through their decisions, journalists contribute to the dialogue in the news.

Journalists' Choices

Balancing Choice

First, the journalists decide on the degree to which they want to balance out the messages of the two camps ("Balancing Choice"). Journalism has always had many functions: Among others, it provides information, interprets news, entertains people, and sometimes also advocates politically. The advocacy function was central when newspapers began to emerge, in many cases (including Switzerland) based on the initiative of political parties in the late eighteenth to early nineteenth centuries (Hallin and Mancini 2004; Blumler and Kavanagh 1999). At this time, the newspaper served a political party and was financed by subsidies from political actors. In this model, the journalist is a political advocate or "political journalist", i.e., a publicist who wants to influence public opinion in the name of a political faction. By the late nineteenth century, another model of journalist was beginning to emerge—the "professional journalist". The "professional journalist" is a neutral provider of information, independent of partisanship, or particular interests. This second model of journalism is often connected to a commercial media. Commercial media are financed by advertisements, and their purpose is to make money. In reality, "political journalists" also adopt norms of political balance, and no "professional journalist" is fully neutral or free of any political ties. Nevertheless, these two models of journalism differ in the strength of connections between journalists and political actors. The difference between the two models is expressed in more general terms by the concept of political parallelism (Hallin and Mancini 2004; Blumler and Gurevitch 1995 [1975]; Seymour-Ure 1974). Political parallelism means the degree to which the "structure of the media system paralleled that of the political system" (Hallin and Mancini 2004: 27). It exists when a media outlet can be aligned with a general political tendency and has a number of different components.

Political parallelism can, as already mentioned, be manifested in journalistic norms and practices. "Perhaps most basically, it refers to *media content* – the extent to which the different media reflect distinct political orientations in their news and current affairs reporting" (Hallin and Mancini 2004: 28). If the media reflect both pro and contra viewpoints, they provide a rather balanced view, which is associated with a low level of political parallelism. Conversely, a one-sided or imbalanced proliferation of information is associated with a high level of parallelism. In the media systems of North and Central Europe, political parallelism is rather low and the neutral-informational professional journalism is dominant (Hallin and Mancini 2004). Accordingly, journalists in Switzerland are expected to give a more or less balanced account of messages from both camps. This expectation is in line with the ethical code for newspapers. Swiss newspapers are subject to the guidance of the Swiss Press Council, the self-regulatory authority for questions of media ethics. A core remit of this Council is to guarantee socially necessary discourse.[1] For referendums and initiatives, this means the provision of more or less equal coverage of pro and contra positions. This guidance is valid also in more challenging cases such as legally controversial initiatives like the minaret initiative (to prevent the construction of Mosque minarets) or the enforcement initiative (an initiative to automatically deport foreigners who commit certain crimes). Thus, I do not expect to find any differences between the campaigns as I anticipate the same professional ethos to be valid for all of the issues and for the country as a whole.

Range of Views Choice (Relevant for Frame Presence)

Second, journalists have to decide which messages they want to cover. I call this the "Range of Views Choice". This choice is relevant for the presence or absence of a frame in the news. In this regard, power plays an important role. Numerous studies have shown that media attention is biased toward the more powerful actors (e.g., Gans 1979; Wolfsfeld 1997; Entman 2007). The so-called indexing hypothesis predicts that "[m]ass media news professionals (…) tend to 'index' the range of voices and viewpoints (…) according to the range of views expressed in mainstream government debate about a given topic" (Bennett 1990: 106). Conflict within the political elite is newsworthy and—based on the news values theory—expected to be reported. In other words, the actors

[1] http://presserat.ch/21690.htm, March 2019.

that dominate the decision-making process seem to get preferential access to the media (Danielian and Page 1994). Based on the findings of Höglinger (2008) and Tresch (2009), the same seems to be true for Switzerland. As stated by Tresch (2009: 85), "Swiss media mostly [...] largely reproduce existing hierarchies and structures of influence". The reporters rely on powerful actors because they provide a convenient and regular flow of information. It makes their job efficient because it eliminates the need to double-check facts (Hackett 1985). Thus, I expect the journalists primarily to cover the messages of powerful actors. The importance of power is expected to vary depending on the issue characteristics. In complex issues, journalists might rely most on powerful actors, because fewer political actors are capable of making their claims.

Story Choice (Relevant for Frame Frequency)

Third, journalists decide on the story of their article and with it the importance they wish to give to available frames ("Story Choice"). The interest of the journalists in selling their newspaper plays a role here. This choice is relevant for how often a frame is found in the news. Here, two different aspects are relevant. Firstly, studies of agenda building have shown that the salience of issues in the media input is positively related to the salience of issues in news media (Kiousis et al. 2006). The same process is expected to be at work at the frame level. The theoretical idea behind this is that journalists follow the political actors based on the professional norms in journalism. In Western democracies, the neutral-informational professional journalism is dominant (Hallin and Mancini 2004). Based on this neutral-informational norm, journalists should give an accurate account of important events, actors, and messages within the institutionalized arenas of the political system and make the political process transparent for the citizen public. The journalists are expected to disseminate information as neutral chroniclers and impartial observers. This norm is in line with the dissemination function of journalists (Shoemaker and Reese 1996) or the mirror approach, which conceives of the media as a mirror of political reality (e.g., Schulz 1976; McQuail 1992). Thus, the journalists are expected to report the frames *proportionately* to the degree to which they are promoted. The salience of a frame in the media input is the frequency with which it is mentioned in the media input of the political actor. I expect no variation depending on issue characteristic.

Secondly, journalists decide whether they want to meet the messages of the *minister responsible,* or in general, of very prominent institutional speakers in the debate, with a higher response than the messages of other actors. By minister, I am referring to a Federal Councilor. The Federal Council has seven members and constitutes the Swiss federal government. Federal Councilors are faced with a dual task: They are a member of the governing college, and they direct one of the seven federal ministries (Kriesi and Trechsel 2008). Based on the news values theory, the minister responsible for the proposition submitted to the vote is expected to garner disproportionately more media attention. Both the prominence and prestige of a given actor are expected to increase the news value of a frame promoted by this actor (Galtung and Ruge 1965; Schulz 1976; Price and Tewksbury 1997). Thus, the messages of the minister are expected to be represented in the news with disproportionate frequency.

As introduced in Chapter 3, there are two different direct-democratic instruments: initiatives and referenda. Both present the voters with a binary choice—either in favor of (pro) or against (con) the issue-specific proposition at stake. However, we can distinguish between the two according to the *source* of the proposition: Initiatives are propositions "from below", formulated by organizations representing groups of citizens, while referenda concern propositions "from above", i.e., legislative acts proposed by the government and adopted by parliament. Since, in the case of a referendum, the legislative act is worked out (sometimes over several years) and proposed by the government and its administration, I expect journalists to rely more on the minister in referendum campaigns than in initiative campaigns. In a referendum, the minister and his team have worked for several years on a topic. They are able to explain the proposal in detail. In addition, journalists are expected to cover the minister's messages more often in complex issues about which he and his administration are most knowledgeable. In complex issues, access to information is also more important and/or scarcer, which gives the minister an advantage. For low complexity cases, familiarity does not appear to be critical: Even when they are faced with unfamiliar issues, political actors and journalists should be able to compensate for their lack of knowledge.

Interpretation Choice

Since we are dealing with institutionally driven public debates (Livingston and Bennett 2003; Lawrence 2000), we expect journalists *not* to introduce new frames. These public debates are institutionally staged, e.g., in the direct-democratic arena, and are initiated and prepared by political actors. Journalists can therefore plan to rely on the input of political actors. This expectation is well in line with Wolfsfeld's key hypothesis (1997: 3): The political process is likely to be the driving force in the interplay between political actors and journalists. However, journalists might control or interpret the message offered by political actors. They might investigate official claims by asking experts about their opinion, help the reader to understand the topic by breaking it down to basics, or state the issue in narrative terms. This idea goes back to the interpretative function, which states that journalists help the reader to understand an issue by investigating official claims, providing interpretation, and analyzing complex problems (e.g., Weaver and Wilhoit 1991; Shoemaker and Reese 1996). I expect this choice to be more important in complex issues, for which the reader needs more help to understand the topic. We call it the "Interpretation Choice". Both the information function (also called the dissemination function), already discussed in terms of the "Balancing Choice", and the interpretation function are important in today's Western European journalism. Free newspapers are not expected to interpret. As we know from interviews with journalists, free daily newspapers have fewer resources available than other newspapers. At most, two journalists work on a topic and there is no time to provide other interpretations.

In summary, the hypotheses are as follows: First, journalists balance out the messages of both camps ("Balancing Choice"). Second, access to news coverage is restricted to powerful actors, particularly in complex issues ("Range of Views Choice"). Third, the salience of a frame in the media input is crucial for its frequency in the media, and the minister's frames are multiplied disproportionately, particularly in referendum campaigns and in complex issues ("Story Choice"). Fourth, journalists investigate official claims by asking experts and help the reader to understand the topic, particularly in complex issues ("Interpretation Choice").

OUTCOME: DIALOGUE

As a result of these choices (and those of political actors), we will find a certain degree of dialogue in the news. As introduced in Chapter 1, there is little consensus regarding what constitutes dialogue. Bennett et al. (2004) use the concept of "responsiveness", i.e., mutual reactions from the opposing political actors. Their concept entails political actors not only using their opponents' frame but also identifying the source of the opponents' frame. My approach is less demanding. Dialogue does not require that the actors refer to each other. For me, it is crucial that the audience learns about the position of a political actor on each frame. This requires both camps to be present in the media along with the frames of both camps (convergence). It seems less important that they refer to each other, because it is the *issue* at the fore and not the actors.

From a normative perspective, it is good when dialogue is high. Principally, dialogue corresponds to the news media's mediating function. The news media have to mediate the message of the political actors. This refers to "any acts of intervening, conveying, or reconciling between different actors, collectives, or institutions" (Mazzoleni and Schulz 1999: 249). In this way, the news media are an intermediary agent which transports meaning from the political actors to the audience and sometimes replaces interpersonal exchanges. The media fulfill this mediating function by setting limits on the range of the debated frames and by presenting a debate about these main frames. In Chapter 4, it was found that the political actors converge to some extent on the frames. The media are expected to converge even more on the same frames than the political actors, because of their mediating function. As mentioned in Chapter 1, there are more reasons why dialogue is normatively desirable: Majorities formed on the basis of public dialogue tend to be more legitimate than simple majorities. In addition, for democracy to function well, citizens must be able to become informed (e.g., Schudson 1998, 2000).

METHOD

In order to test the expectations formulated for journalists' choices, we apply an indirect procedure. Instead of asking journalists about their decisions, we compare media input and media coverage and are able to rely on hard data on media content. To test the "Range of Views Choice" and the "Story Choice", we use a zero-inflated negative binomial regression model. In this analysis (Table 6.2), we will investigate the lagged effect of power, of the counts in the media input, and of the minister variable.[2] Power is operationalized by a reputational indicator and

---

[2] I will use the following abbreviations for the variables: Media $(t-1)$ is the daily number of arguments reported in the media. Contra input $(t-1)$ and pro input $(t-1)$ are the daily number of arguments presented as input material by the contra and the pro camps, respectively. Minister $(t-1)$ is the minister dummy indicator. Power contra $(t-1)$ and power pro

is based on a set of questions asked in the second interviews referring to the list of all organizations involved (Kriesi et al. 2006; Bernhard 2012): The campaigners were first asked to name the organizations on the list which, from their point of view, had been particularly influential during the campaign. Next, they were asked to name the three most influential organizations and, finally, the most influential one. For each organization, a summary indicator reflects the number of times it was mentioned by the other respondents in answer to these questions: Mentions as "most influential" are coded as "3", mentions among the "three most influential" as "2", and mentions as "influential" as "1". The values of the indicator range from 0, for an organization that was never mentioned as influential, to 3 times the number of respondents, for an organization that would have been considered to be the most influential actor by all of them. Power (power) is the sum of *daily* power of each side, which corresponds to the total amount of power of the actors who promote frames for a given camp on a certain day. For example, two actors of the pro camp hold a media conference together, while no other actor of their camp is active on this day. Actor A is a powerful actor who scores 86 on the power measure, whereas actor B only reaches a score of 18. Together, they arrive at 104 points, the sum of daily power of the pro camp. Alternatively, one could use the mean or median of the power of the actors involved. The results show little change if we operationalize power differently. The salience of a frame in the media input (contra and pro) is the frequency with which a frame is mentioned in the media input of a camp. In addition, we use a dummy indicator for the frame-sponsoring of the minister responsible for the campaign (minister). We use the lagged effects of these variables because the political actors and the journalists do not communicate simultaneously, but in a sequence in which events produced by the political actors during the day are followed by the press of the next day.

We use a zero-inflated negative binomial regression model because we are dealing with count data, which are characterized by an excess

---

$(t-1)$ are the sums of daily power of the respective camps. Human. trad. and the remaining variables in the count model are dummy indicators for the four (three in the naturalization campaign) main framing categories, with the residual category ("others") forming the reference category. All independent variables are counts on the day before t $(t-1)$. The dependent variables are arguments on day t in the news media.

of zeros and overdispersion.[3] When interpreting zero-inflated models, it is easy to be confused by the meaning of the effect parameters (the incidence-rate ratios). Such models have two parts—an inflation model and a count model. The inflation model estimates the effects (incidence-rate ratios) of the factors under investigation on the possibility that an argument will not make it into the media, i.e., on the possibility of its absence from the media. The count model estimates the effects (incidence-rate ratios) of the factors under investigation on the frequency of an argument's presence in the media. These two models allow a distinction to be drawn between frame presence/absence in the media on the one hand and frame frequency in the media on the other hand. Accordingly, frame building can be conceived as being composed of two processes—the daily frame *absence/presence* and the daily frame *frequency*. In a similar way, Tresch (2009) defines two dimensions of standing (="having a voice in the media", see Ferree et al. 2002: 86): presence (=non-absence) and prominence. Since both absence and frequency are measured on a daily basis, I refer in this context to the daily frame absence/presence and daily frame frequency.

For the estimation of the models, we use a stacked file, with five (four in the naturalization campaign) cases for each day, one for each of the main frame categories, plus one for the residual category. We introduce a dummy variable for each of the main frames in order to control for their variable salience. In order to control for contemporaneous correlation,

---

[3]Overdispersion implies the presence of greater variability (statistical dispersion) in the predicted counts for a given value of x than would be expected based on the Poisson regression model. Stata provides a likelihood-ratio test for overdispersion. In addition, due to the excess zeros in the data, also called zero inflation, a zero-inflated count model is necessary. Greene (2000) has proposed the Vuong (1989) test for non-nested models in order to establish whether a zero-inflated model is necessary. Zero-inflated count models assume that there are two latent (i.e., unobserved) groups: an "Always Zero" and a "Not Always Zero" and that zero counts are generated by two independently operating processes. In the first process (Inflation Model), the zeros belonging to the "Always Zero" group are generated. An argument in this group has an outcome of zero with a probability of one. This process is binary; it generates zeros or ones. If this first process results in one, the second process is assumed to come into play: a negative binomial regression process (count model) which generates zeros of the "Not Always" group. An argument in this group might have a zero count, but there is a non-zero probability that it has a positive count.

we cluster the standard errors over time (=robust s.e.).[4] We also lag the dependent variable by one day so as to control for the autoregressive effect. Zero-inflated models may be very sensitive to the specification of the inflation model. It is therefore important to perform a sensitivity analysis (Steenbergen 2008; Long and Freese 2006) (available upon request).

Model Specification

Power is expected to be relevant for frame absence/presence (i.e., "Range of Views Choice") because powerful actors have preferential access to the media (Danielian and Page 1994), and a frame needs powerful actors in order not to be ignored. Weak political actors can make a great effort and provide many arguments, but they are weak and their frames will remain absent in the debate. Thus, the power of the actor promoting a frame, and not the salience of the frame in the media input, is crucial for frame absence/presence. Regarding minister status, it should be noted that this is not responsible for frame absence/presence either, because many powerful actors other than ministers promote their frames and find media coverage. We expect that access to the media in direct-democratic campaigns is not restricted to ministers but to powerful actors in general.

The salience of the promoted frame and the involvement of the minister are expected to become relevant for the frequency with which a frame appears in the media (i.e., for the "Story Choice"). First, in line with the mirror approach, the media are assumed to report the frames proportionately to the degree to which they are promoted. The more a frame is promoted, i.e., the more salient it is in the media input, the more the media will report it—under the condition that a powerful actor is promoting it. Second, the salience of a frame in the media input also indicates whether a frame is presented in a media conference or in a press release. High absolute numbers are found in media conferences. These normally find more media coverage and political actors have developed a sense of how many media conferences they can organize to find media attention and

---

[4]This correction was designed for linear models, and it is not completely clear whether it works as well for this kind of model. However, the results are also robust without the clustering (sensitivity analyses model s2).

do not make excessive use of them. Power is not included for the "Story Choice". First, it seems implausible that a frame presented in a media conference will find media attention proportionately to the power of the political actors participating in the conference. Power is crucial to get access to the debate, but it is prominence and prestige that are decisive for how much media coverage is gained. The presidents of parties or commissions, ministers, spokesmen, or spokeswomen are prominent or prestigious figures in general. In direct-democratic campaigns, such prominent actors can generally be expected to get disproportionately high media attention. Ministers or prominent figures have an advantage that does not hold for powerful actors in general, such as ordinary political parties or other powerful organizations without a prominent speaker. Second, power is defined as having an influence in the background and/or in the foreground. The organizations that are influential behind the scenes are not necessarily known in public. Sometimes they are even more influential because they stay incognito to the public. Thus, their frames cannot be expected to be covered more or proportionately to their power.

RESULTS

Balancing Choice

First, we will look at the ratio between pro and contra arguments in the media input and in the news media coverage ("Balancing Choice"). Table 6.1 reveals that in both immigration issue campaigns, the political actors of the contra camp promoted more frames than the political actors of the pro camp (media input). On the other hand, the pro camp was more active in the tax campaign. The ratio between pro and contra arguments

Table 6.1 Balancing: Number of arguments on each side by campaign and ratio of contra/pro arguments

	Media input			News media		
	Contra	*Pro*	*Contra/pro*	*Contra*	*Pro*	*Contra/pro*
Asylum	726	335	**2.2**	1528	927	**1.6**
Naturalization	675	107	**6.3**	1176	733	**1.6**
Corporation tax	462	594	**0.8**	943	1123	**0.8**

Note There is no difference between media types

is lower in the news media than in the media input for both immigration issues. This means that the media tend to balance out the difference between the contra and pro camp on these issues. In the tax campaign, the same ratio between contra and pro camp arguments is found in the media input and in the news media. In this campaign, the input was already quite balanced and the news media did not need to balance out further the news. Indeed, the ratio is most balanced in this case. From these findings, I conclude that, even though the news media do not report exactly the same amount of arguments on each side, they tend to balance the news.

In the second interview on the asylum law, the campaigners were asked in an open-ended question how the media should deal with their media input from a normative point of view. Several actors mentioned that the media should balance the news and that both camps should have a voice. In this regard, the media fulfill their expectation. In another open question, we asked them how the media dealt with their input. Many political actors from both camps answered that the media reported both perspectives. By contrast, Amnesty International and the right-wing party (SVP) were unhappy with the coverage. Amnesty International claimed that the newspapers from the German-speaking part of Switzerland were one-sided, whereas the SVP complained that they were often ignored, except when they were provocative. Based on the content analysis, there is no suggestion that the SVP was ignored. In both the asylum law and the naturalization initiative, it was the party that received the most attention in the news media. In the corporate tax reform, the SVP was less active. Interestingly, some political actors reported that the leader of the SVP (Blocher), who was also the responsible minister in the asylum law campaign, had received substantial media attention. This statement can be confirmed based on the content analysis. He was, in fact, the most important individual actor in the news media coverage of the asylum law. In this regard, the statement by Amnesty International finds more empirical support than the critique by the SVP. For both the naturalization initiative and the corporate tax reform, we posed questions in a closed manner. Almost no campaigner (between 0 and 3% of all political actors) reported that the media always ignored their media input or did not report their slogan. Thus, the interviews show that most of the political actors (except very few, including the SVP) perceived that they were treated well. This result is good from a normative perspective. The SVP might complain for strategic reasons, as they wish to nourish their closeness-to-the-people/anti-establishment image.

Range of Views Choice: Power

For the "Range of Views Choice", let us look at the lower part of Table 6.2 (Inflation Model). The lagged dependent variable (media [t−1]) controls for serial correlation and for continuing frame attention in the dependent variable. All power ratios are smaller than one. This means that power reduces the probability that a frame will be absent in the news media. In other words, the greater the power of the actors presenting the arguments of a given camp on a given day, the higher the chance that their argument will be covered in the media the following day. However, the corresponding ratios are not always significant. Thus, in the asylum law campaign, power has no significant impact on frame presence or absence in the media. This result meets my expectation that with familiar issues, access to the public debate is less restricted to powerful actors than it is in less familiar cases. The political actors anticipate this media routine in their coalition behavior (anticipatory effect of media). It is common for one political actor (often a large political party) to take the lead in a campaign and for weak actors to go along with it in order to find media attention. They *collectively* present their frames in order for the message of the weak actor to also be covered in the news on the next day.

In the naturalization initiative, the power of the contra camp is highly significant, while the power of the pro camp is not. There are two reasons for this lack of significance: First of all, only two actors were involved in the pro side, and one of them produced 75% of all frames, which means that there is almost no variation in the power variable. In addition, the pro camp only promoted a small number of arguments, i.e., 94% of the counts are zero counts, because most of the time no frame was promoted. The small number of cases reduces the significance. In the corporate tax reform, the effects of power are also somewhat limited: Powerful actors of the pro camp could not significantly decrease the absence of their frames, whereas power was significant for the contra camp at a level of 0.10 only. It is surprising that the power of the pro camp is not more significant, because the most powerful and resource-rich interest group, economiesuisse, was the leading house of the pro committee and was heavily involved in this campaign. There are three reasons that could explain this unexpected finding. First, economiesuisse was evaluated as the most powerful actor in the campaign. It gave the money, pulled the strings, and led the campaign. However, as we

Table 6.2 Zero-inflated negative binomial regression of media framing: ratios, robust standard errors, and p-levels

Asylum	Ratio	Robust s.e.	p	Naturalization	Ratio	Robust s.e.	p	Corporation Tax	Ratio	Robust s.e.	p
Count model (frequency)				Count model (frequency)				Count model (frequency)			
Media (t−1)	1.019	0.018	0.294	Media (t−1)	1.008	0.013	0.528	Media (t−1)	1.007	0.008	0.380
Contra input (t−1)	1.033	0.014	0.015	Contra (t−1)	1.032	0.006	0.000	Contra input (t−1)	1.082	0.017	0.000
Pro input (t−1)	1.010	0.097	0.916	Pro (t−1)	1.059	0.038	0.074	Pro input (t−1)	1.059	0.025	0.015
Minister (t−1)	2.043	1.062	0.169	Minister (t−1)	3.038	0.747	0.005	Minister (t−1)	4.290	1.345	0.000
Human. trad.	0.956	0.129	0.737	Rule-of-law	3.572	0.690	0.000	Tax equity	5.102	1.017	0.000
Rule-of-law	0.401	0.066	0.000	People-final-say	2.928	0.496	0.000	Tax loss	2.802	0.561	0.000
Abuse	0.931	0.114	0.563	Mass naturalization	2.421	0.412	0.000	SME	3.780	0.641	0.000
Efficacy	0.477	0.065	0.000					Competitiveness	3.875	0.596	0.000
Inflation model (absence)				Inflation model (absence)				Inflation model (absence)			
Media (t−1)	0.308	0.905	0.193	Media (t−1)	0.106	0.642	0.002	Media (t−1)	0.183	0.614	0.006
Power contra (t−1)	0.851	0.235	0.490	Power contra (t−1)	0.000	0.832	0.004	Power contra (t−1)	0.863	0.087	0.092
Power pro (t−1)	0.953	0.161	0.763	Power pro (t−1)	0.944	0.015	0.118	Power pro (t−1)	0.980	0.013	0.120
Constant	0.749	0.356	0.035	Constant	1.971	0.335	0.000	Constant	0.980	0.310	0.000
n total: 560, n zero obs.: 262				n total: 364, n zero obs.: 203				n total: 445, n zero obs.: 246			
Vuong: z=5.70, Pr > z=0.000				Vuong: z=6.14, Pr > z=0.000				Vuong: z=6.49, Pr > z=0.000			

have already observed, it preferred to stay in the background and turn the spotlight on the political parties with whom it formed a coalition. Its influence on the media is therefore underestimated because it was mainly an indirect one, via its political party allies. The model, however, does not account for indirect effects. If we re-estimate the model and try to take this indirect influence into account by assigning the power value of economiesuisse to the allied political parties or by lumping economiesuisse and its party allies together to form one single actor, the corresponding effect becomes significant at a level of 0.10. Second, economiesuisse and the ad hoc pro committee were no longer proactive with press releases and press conferences in the final six weeks. In this last phase, they had planned to concentrate on political advertisements. Moreover, with its three reactions to the press conferences of the Social Democrats, the ad hoc committee was unable to garner any attention.

Third, the argumentation of the Social Democrats—who were in charge of the contra committee during the campaign—resonated well with external events happening at the same time. The Social Democrats mainly argued that the tax cuts were an unfair privilege for the well-off and went against the principle of fair taxation (tax equity). Toward the end of the campaign, they linked their argumentation to the subprime crisis of UBS and to its President of the Board, Marcel Ospel, by claiming that rich managers such as Mr. Ospel would primarily benefit from the corporate tax reform. These events possibly gave support to the "tax equity" frame and, ultimately, may have convinced undecided voters and helped to explain why the vote unexpectedly (see Chapter 3) became so close. This case does not support the idea that power is more important in complex issues, indicating the need for further research.

Story Choices: Salience of Frames in Media Input and the Role of the Minister

Next, let us look at the upper part of Table 6.2, the count model (frequency). Overall, the lagged number of promoted frames and the lagged minister dummy indicator[5] significantly increase the daily frequency of the frame in the news media. The results are quite robust (sensitivity

---

[5] This is a binary indicator measuring whether the minister was promoting the frame the day before.

analyses, available upon request). There is variation between the camps with regard to the specific campaigns. In the *asylum law*, the contra camp significantly influenced the daily frequency of the news media frames, while the pro camp remained without influence. This makes sense for several reasons. First, the economic interest groups remained more or less uninvolved. Second, the center parties, which belonged to the pro camp, led a half-hearted campaign and preferred to stay invisible, whereas the right-wing party was more active with political advertisements (Chapter 5). Third, the pro camp was active indirectly through the responsible minister, who had been a member of the right-wing party. The minister officially wanted to keep a low-profile campaign. He refused, for instance, to participate in the most important TV debate on Swiss-German television. The influence of the minister is probably underestimated in this campaign because he was very active unofficially (not included in media input). He gave several speeches at public meetings of the right-wing party. Since these speeches were unofficial, we were unable to include them in our analysis and they are neither part of the minister dummy indicator nor part of the pro camp indicator. In the *naturalization* initiative, the number of promoted frames by the contra camp is significant, whereas the promoted frames of the pro camp are significant only at a level of 0.10. The pro camp invested a lot of money in political advertisements (Chapter 5) and was less active with media input. Finally, the minister dummy indicator is also significant at a level of 0.05 in this campaign. In the *corporate tax* reform, the number of promoted frames of both camps and the minister dummy indicator significantly increase the frequency of the news media frames on the next day. The regression results support the salience and the minister hypothesis, which state that the number of promoted frames is crucial and that the input by the minister is amplified by the news media. The results suggest that the minister plays a particularly important role in complex issues (most significant).

The disproportionate multiplication effect of the minister's frame is explored in Table 6.3. It is compared with the multiplication effect of the frames of the other actor types of both camps. The table shows the average number of arguments in the news media as a function of the input by different actor types on both sides on the previous day. For instance, in the asylum law campaign, the pro camp was reported 6.2 (top left number) times with the "humanitarian tradition" frame when the minister had promoted this frame on the previous day. By contrast,

Table 6.3 The media frames, with input by the different actor types on either side: average number of frames per day

Asylum	Core argument contra	2nd argument contra	Core argu- ment pro	2nd argu- ment pro
	Human. trad.	Rule-of-law	Abuse	Efficacy
Pro				
Minister	6.2	0.7	**8.3**	**3.5**
Pol. parties	1.5	0.3	**6.5**	**2.4**
Citizens' int. groups	2.5	–	**5.5**	–
Without input	1.1	0.5	**1.9**	**1.0**
Contra				
Ad hoc committees	**10.0**	**1.3**	6.6	3.3
Citizens' int. groups	**6.0**	**1.5**	3.7	4.0
Econ. int. groups	**5.0**	**1.5**	4.0	–
Pol. parties	**1.7**	**1.5**	2.0	0.7
Without input	**4.5**	**1.4**	2.4	1.1

Naturalization	Rule-of-law	People-final-say	Mass naturalization	
Pro				
Pol. parties	3.3	**4.3**	**4.1**	
Ad hoc committees	3.0	**2.0**	–	
Without input	1.9	**3.3**	**2.4**	
Contra				
Pol. parties	**18.6**	11.3	9.7	
Econ. int. groups	**18.8**	8.5	5.5	
Citizens' int. groups	**16.2**	7.2	4.8	
Minister	**14.9**	6.4	5.1	
Without input	**5.0**	1.9	1.2	

Corporation Tax	Tax equity	Tax loss	SME	Competitiveness
Pro				
Minister	8.3	7.0	**12.3**	**11.8**
Econ. int. groups	6.7	1.0	**10.4**	7.2
Pol. parties	6.8	6.0	**8.8**	5.7
Without input	1.4	0.9	**2.9**	2.8
Contra				
Pol. parties	**14.4**	3.2	3.0	1.3
Econ. int. groups	**12.5**	10.7	3.0	1.4
Citizens' int. groups	**4.5**	**2.0**	–	1.4
Without input	**4.5**	**1.4**	1.0	1.1

Note In the asylum law campaign, the economic interest groups of the pro camp are not shown because they were not very active with media input. The same is true for the ad hoc committee of the contra camp in the naturalization initiative the media offered the same frame only 1.5 times when the political parties of the pro camp had used it on the previous day or 2.5 times when the citizens' interest groups of the pro camp had done so. When none of the actor types of this camp had promoted the frame the day before, the media reported this frame 1.1 times. Compared to other actor types, Table 6.2 reveals that the *minister* meets with the largest response in the asylum law and in the corporate tax reform.[6] The multiplication effect of the minister is larger in the latter case than in the former. Both results are in line with the results of Table 6.2. They give support to the ideas that the media multiply the frames used by the minister the most and that the minister is especially influential in complex issues (see also Gerth et al. 2012). Compared to the other actor types, the input of the minister was less important in the naturalization initiative. In this campaign, all other actor types of the contra camp reached a higher multiplication effect than the minister. Possibly, the minister is less important in initiatives than in referenda since the initiatives occur at the beginning of the decision-making process, and the government and its administration are uninvolved in the policy proposal. Since we did not include other actor types in Table 6.2, we cannot compare the influence of different actor types based on the count model. Nevertheless, the power ratio of the contra camp in the inflation model indicates the same result: It is close to zero, which means that—although it is significant—it has almost no effect.

Compared to the number of arguments found in the media input ($n = 107$) and in the news media ($n = 733$) (see Table 6.1), the small multiplication effects of the pro camp in the naturalization initiative are surprising. We find more than 6 times as many arguments in the news media as in the media input. This is more than in all other cases, and, accordingly, the multiplication effect should have been highest in this case. More detailed analyses reveal four reasons for this finding: First, the initiative text often only consists of a sentence or two. It is sufficiently short that the media referred to it together with a short statement from the launching political actor without any media input from the initiator. Second, the hype surrounding the conflict between Blocher, the populist right-wing party (SVP), and Widmer-Schlumpf also provided the

---

[6] In contrast to Table 6.2, it was possible to include the informal speeches of the minister in the asylum law. Thus, it is not surprising that the minister is so important.

Table 6.4 Predicted change in the news media counts

Asylum	Naturalization	Corporation Tax	Change in …
3	7	6	Power contra $(t-1)$
1	0	1	Power pro $(t-1)$
29	83	65	Contra input $(t-1)$
1	9	30	Pro input $(t-1)$
6	16	19	Minister $(t-1)$
7	668	148	Cumulative effect: Minister $(t-1)$ + Contra input $(t-1)$/Pro input $(t-1)$

Note The predicted change is based on a change in the key factors from the minimum to the maximum value. The remaining variables were set at the mean or at zero (minister [$t-1$]), and the main frame of the respective camp was used

pro camp with media attention. New developments in the conflict were eagerly awaited by the journalists and gave the pro camp opportunities to speak about the initiative in the interviews. Third, there was the most important TV debate (Arena) in which Blocher and Widmer-Schlumpf participated and which was covered and discussed by the news media very prominently. Fourth, the pro camp also garnered media attention through other channels like letters to the editors or its aggressive poster, which are not part of the media input. According to the Swiss Commission against Racism, their poster was even racist.

Table 6.4 shows the predicted change in the news media counts depending on a change from the minimum to the maximum value in the key factors. We can see that the counts are most sensitive to the media input of the two camps and the minister's presence, whereas the predicted change based on a change of power is relatively small.

What cannot be detected in these statistical analyses is the insight based on a single case. As mentioned in Chapter 5, in the tax reform campaign a citizens' interest group of the contra camp produced a video about taxes representing the global and long-term perspective. They argued that Switzerland as a country of the first world should show solidarity with developing countries, be active in development politics and not be a country attractive for organizations aiming to optimize taxes. Such an argumentation was not newsworthy because it did not resonate with the main discourse in the country and was irrelevant for most people. It was not found in the news coverage. Here, the interest of journalists to sell their paper hinders the presentation of such a perspective.

Interpretation Choice

Next, we investigate whether journalists provide interpretation of, or control the information provided by, political actors. Generally, journalists rely on input by the political actors in institutionally driven debates. First and foremost, as journalists mentioned in interviews, they aim to produce comprehensible and reader-friendly texts, which reduce complexity in a meaningful way, or make interests transparent and links to challenges explicit—texts that illustrate the impact and reach the audience. For quality newspapers, an article should also deepen the knowledge and present many perspectives. However, the journalists do not rely exclusively on campaign inputs by political actors; they also turn the spotlight on experts. In the asylum and the naturalization initiative campaigns, the experts get a low standing[7] on the contra side (5 and 6%) whereas in the contra camp of the tax reform, the experts reach a high level of standing (20%) (not shown). Since the issue is complex, experts are used to debate it and to explain its meaning. However, for the quality of direct-democratic debates and the question of the manipulability of the outcome of direct-democratic votes, one has to ask why the experts are not obliged to declare their interests and why they are more visible on one side than the other. This can be problematic because experts enjoy a high level of legitimacy. A more detailed analysis reveals that the high standing of the experts on the contra side in the corporate tax reform was triggered by an article in a Sunday newspaper, the "NZZ am Sonntag": In the edition of January 13, 2008, a journalist reported on the experts who criticized the corporate tax reform. The newspapers from the German-speaking part of Switzerland were the first to react. For instance, on January 15, the "Tagesanzeiger" (a center-left regional newspaper) put the conflict between the experts and the responsible minister (Merz) on the front page and wrote that Merz had been let down by the experts. The "Tagesanzeiger" had already brought up the criticism of one professor (Waldburger) on November 26, 2007. However, it remained at a low level of standing, and the story in the "NZZ am Sonntag" was necessary to leverage the issue. The "NZZ" (a liberal quality paper and the weekday sister of the "NZZ am Sonntag") reacted differently. On January 16, it published an article by one of the experts. On the very same page, there was an article from the pro side in which the head of the

---

[7]By standing, I mean "having a voice in the media" (Ferree et al. 2002: 86).

most important economic interest group, economiesuisse, was also able to explain his opinion. A similar reaction can be found in the "St. Galler Tagblatt" (regional newspaper, belongs to NZZ publishing house, i.e., is liberal). This newspaper probably reacted due to its local proximity to the experts. It published an interview with the expert on January 18 but also covered the opposing view.

It is interesting to note that the pro camp was disappointed by the "NZZ am Sonntag". They were disappointed that this liberal newspaper reported critically on the tax reform several times. As a short telephone conversation with the responsible journalist (Heidi Gmür) revealed, the article in the "NZZ am Sonntag" was based on the curiosity and personal initiative of this journalist. After having heard several times the claim of professor Waldburger that the new law violated the constitution, she wondered what other professors thought about the issue. She found that, with one exception, all the professors she interviewed were against the new law. Only one of the professors interviewed stated that he believed in balance that the new law did not quite violate the constitution. However, this one professor was not familiar with the issue and stated that his opinion should not be reported. The journalist also had the required resources to write the story. She worked for a Sunday newspaper, and the issue was important. In addition, the information was relevant and interesting. The journalist did not expect her article to provoke such a reaction.

This illustration shows, first, that media bias is not the reason for the high standing of the experts on the contra side. Nevertheless, in the reaction of the "Tagesanzeiger", one can see an ideological imprint, whereas in the "NZZ" it seems important that both camps are able to give their opinion. Second, this case also shows that there are two public spaces—one in the French-speaking and one in the German-speaking part of Switzerland (Tresch 2009). With one exception, the newspapers in the French-speaking part did not react to the story in the "NZZ am Sonntag". Only the quality newspaper of the French-speaking part, "Le Temps", followed on January 28 with coverage of the experts' criticism. Crossing the language border clearly requires some time.

Table 6.5 investigates whether the standing of the experts in the tax reform is relevant for the content. The opponents of the corporate tax reform, together with the experts, mainly focused on matters of "*tax equity*". They argued that the tax cuts were an unfair privilege for the rich and went against the principle of fair taxation, and they claimed that the

Table 6.5 Shares devoted to the "Tax Equity" frame in the news media of the tax reform campaign: comparison between experts and rest

Corporation tax	Contra	Pro
Experts	63.6	58.6
Others	46.8	14.7
n	943	1123
Analysis of variance	$F=17.02$, $p=0.000$	$F=42.29$, $p=0.000$

reform was unconstitutional. This line of reasoning mainly applied to a controversial provision that included a reduction in tax rates on dividends for shareholders who held at least a 10% stake in a corporation. Compared to the other actors, the share of the "tax equity" frame is significantly higher among the experts. Thus, as a result of the increased standing of the experts, the "tax equity" frame became more important.

This is especially relevant for the pro side: The "*SME*" frame dominated the yes campaign. It stated that the small and medium-sized companies, which form the backbone of the Swiss economy, needed to benefit from a set of planned measures aimed at reducing financial and administrative burdens. In their media input, the "SME" frame was present at 38.4% (see Table 6.1). In the news media, the share reduced to only 30.2%. At the same time, the use of the "tax equity" frame by the pro camp increased from 7.7% in the media input to 15.0 in the news media. In other words, the "tax equity" frame introduced by the experts crowded out the "SME" frame to some extent.

Next, we investigate the role of regional newspapers in the tax reform campaign. The tax reform was framed as benefitting small and medium-sized enterprises. Since SMEs are typically an important part of the social life of regions and communities, it is especially important for regional media to cover issues that affect SMEs. They might do so by featuring people involved in individual SMEs that are affected by the result of the vote, by explaining consequences for the communities, and by citing regional political actors. Thus, the regional newspapers might have made an extra effort to focus on the "SME" aspect of the issue. Such an effort is in line with the interpretation function of journalists because it helps the reader to understand the complex issue. Table 6.6 shows that the regional newspapers gave significantly more standing to the regional political actors in the tax reform campaign.

Table 6.6 Standing of regional political actors in different media types and campaigns

Media type	Corporation tax
Regional	50.0
Elite	33.5
Tabloid	34.3
Free	0.0
TV	38.5
n	2066

Analysis of variance (regional vs. other media types): $F=44.27$, $p=0.000$

Table 6.7 Use of the "SME" frame in different media types

Frame	Corporation tax
Regional	22.6
Elite	21.2
Tabloid	19.1
Free	20.0
TV	16.7
Total	21.9
n	2066

Analysis of variance: $F=0.58$, $p=0.671$

Table 6.7 investigates whether the higher standing in the regional newspapers of the regional actors in the tax reform campaign is relevant for frame building. The regional newspapers might have emphasized the "SME" frame more because this frame addressed the needs of small and medium-sized companies. However, this is not the case, as Table 6.7 shows. There is only a negligible difference in the use of the "SME" frame between the different media types. Thus, the regional newspapers gave higher standing to regional actors without giving more emphasis to the "SME" frame.

Outcome: Dialogue

The degree of dialogue (convergence) in the different campaigns, types of media outlets, and media genres is shown in Table 6.8. In the asylum law campaign, we find a dialogue level of 70.1, in the naturalization campaign, it is 64.0, and in the corporation tax campaign, it is 55.3. With regard to differences between the campaigns, it can be noted that

Table 6.8 Level of dialogue by campaign, media type, and media genre

Campaigns	All media together	Media input
Asylum	70.1	69.9
Naturalization	64.0	69.3
Corporation Tax	55.3	41.5
All campaigns (mean)	63.1	60.2

Media type		All campaigns
Regional		64.6
Tabloid		63.6
TV		62.9
Elite		59.9
Free		28.3
Analysis of variance (free vs. other media types): $F=7.86$, $p=0.015$		

Media genre		All campaigns
Commentaries		65.5
Front Page		54.6
Analysis of variance (commentaries vs. front page): $F=0.89$, $p=0.402$		

the lowest level of dialogue is found in the most complex issue, the corporate tax reform (in line with the findings of Chapter 4), because *issue complexity* handicaps dialogue. In comparison with the level of dialogue in the media input (see last column in Table 6.8), we note that there is not substantially more dialogue in the news media. These findings are unexpected because the news media, with their mediation, are expected to increase dialogue. In light of the results, however, it becomes clear that political actors anticipate the mediating function and adapt to the media logic by increasing dialogue in the media input themselves. However, in the corporate tax reform, the news media converge on the main frames in 55% of their arguments, whereas in the media input, the two camps speak about the same frames in 41% of their main arguments. This result indicates that the contribution of journalists is particularly important in the complex issue. Furthermore, the convergence is not significantly different in tabloid newspapers and on TV news. I interpret this as a good sign for democracy. It seems that these media types do not simplify too much even though they are particularly prone to simplification and sensationalism. At the same time, convergence is significantly lower in free news media. The free press mediates less and provides a less coherent picture. These newspapers mainly reprint the information provided by the news agency. Compared to all other newspapers, they have fewest resources for coverage of direct-democratic campaigns. In addition, convergence is not significantly higher in the commentaries than on the front page, even though journalists want to attract the reader's attention with one message on the front page but could pick out one or two frames for a commentary in order to discuss them in more depth.

CONCLUSION

The results can be summarized based on the four choices. First, we find that the journalists tend to balance out the messages of each camp in all three campaigns ("Balancing Choice"). Second, the campaign-specific power of a political actor is important for the "Range of Views Choice" (frame absence/presence). It can be shown that power was not important in the case of the familiar issue (asylum law). Further research is needed to determine the relative importance of power in complex issues. Third, the number of promoted frames and the minister play an influential role for the daily frame *frequency* ("Story Choice"). The minister's influence was highest in the case of the complex issue (corporation tax) and was less important in the naturalization initiative. Possibly, the minister is less important in initiatives than in referenda since the initiatives occur at the beginning of the decision-making process, and the government and its administration are uninvolved in the policy proposal. Furthermore, a single case shows that journalists not only have an interest in balancing out the news, they are also interested in selling their newspaper, in this case at the cost of long-term and global perspectives. The profit orientation of journalists (and the organization behind them) can also be observed when journalists write about the breaking of a taboo. Luckily, this happens rarely. For instance, a poster showing three white sheep kicking a black sheep against a backdrop of the Swiss flag (in an initiative about the deportation of foreign criminals) was highly discussed in the news media or the proximity of some political actors to National Socialism in the EcoPop Initiative (a proposal to cut net immigration to no more than 0.2% of the population, which was rejected). In these campaigns, the thematic content was reduced. It is likely that political actors applied a distortion strategy and aimed to increase conflict in order to distract from content and to mobilize their community. In any case, the media focused on a controversial and value-wise sensitive aspect of a campaign and reduced the presence of other perspectives in these campaigns. Fourth, journalists investigate official claims by asking experts and help the reader to understand the topic in the complex issue ("Interpretation Choice").

With regard to dialogue, we generally do not find more dialogue in the news media than in the media input. The political actors anticipate the media logic and increase dialogue in the media input correspondingly. However, in the complex issue (corporation tax) the news media provide a higher level of dialogue, indicating that the contribution of the journalists is important. With regard to differences between media types, we find less dialogue in free news media. There are no significant differences between the other media types or media genres. The question is what do the results imply for the quality of direct-democratic debates and for the question of the manipulability of the outcome of direct-democratic votes. The level of dialogue found in the media is high in all three campaigns and gives rise to optimism. It is normatively desirable if the political actors already provide dialogue in the media input because it increases the chances of us finding dialogue in the media. In addition, the media increased dialogue in the complex issue where it was needed (corporation tax). In this way, the media offer dialogue in all three campaigns. Thus, the voters can evaluate the merits of alternative ways of framing an issue, and there is no single dominant perspective. Finally, even though the corporate tax reform campaign has been the most one-sidedly dominant campaign in terms of financial resources of all campaigns since the beginning of the 1980s, economiesuisse (the leading house of the pro side in this campaign) was not able to dominate with its frame in the public debate, despite all its money.

We also find that the minister (=Federal Councilor) plays an important role. The Swiss political elites are somewhat uneasy about this important role of the authorities in direct-democratic campaigns (Kriesi 2009): According to an informal, traditional conception, the minister is expected to exercise his or her campaigning role with a certain restraint. While entitled to provide the voters with a balanced diet of information, the authorities should leave the opinion formation in the general public primarily to civil society and the social and political forces of the country. This low-key approach of government is not confirmed in the study at hand. We find that the minister is very influential in the frame-building process in direct-democratic campaigns. In such campaigns, the minister can contribute to a high level of dialogue by offering an overview of different viewpoints including that of the government. Thus, the best way to offer dialogue is not to prevent the government from defending its position, but to guarantee that the competition of frames is not suppressed by the preponderance of any actor during the campaign—be it the government or some actor from civil society.

Interaction Between Context (Campaign Type, Country) and Frame Edition

The first choice ("Balancing Choice") probably depends on the type of campaign. In direct-democratic campaigns, the norm is to cover equally the contra and pro camps, while in elections, coverage is expected to be proportional to the chances of success, incumbency, or seats in the parliament. Comparing media coverage of a public debate with that of a referendum (on the same topic), Reinemann et al. (2012) find that the latter was more balanced than the former. However, coverage does not need to be balanced at all. In public debates (and particularly in scandals), but perhaps in election campaigns too, the media sometimes also step in and lead a campaign. If the media lead a public debate, the journalists do not aim for a balanced diet of information and we possibly find less dialogue. Instead, they might act as a major speaker themselves and advocate an opinion, or they might sharpen the message of one camp without being stopped or confronted by a campaign calling for another point of view. In Switzerland, the campaign against pit bulls and other fighting breeds of dog can be considered as an example of a public debate which was led by the media. The issue arose because several children were attacked or even killed by such dogs. Since 2000, the major Swiss tabloid paper "Blick" has set the issue at the top of its agenda several times and has supported the claim that these dogs should be banned. Another example is the media campaign against former Federal Councilor Samuel Schmid because of scandals and accidents in the Swiss military in summer 2008. In this case, a Sunday newspaper, "Sonntags Zeitung", started the campaign. Samuel Schmid made the mistake of not counter-arguing during the summer "silly season", preferring to sit the problem out. Furthermore, he was under intense political pressure from his former party, the Swiss People's Party, because he had accepted re-election when Blocher was replaced by Eveline Widmer-Schlumpf (at the end of 2007). Since Blocher was not re-elected, the Swiss People's Party wanted to go into opposition and wanted Samuel Schmid to resign from office as well. There was no party which counter-argued on his behalf and less dialogue in the news media. As a consequence, the media campaign had a large impact and Samuel Schmid had resigned from the Federal Council by the end of 2008. The second and third journalistic choices ("Range of Views Choice", "Story Choice") are less dependent on the campaign type. The fourth choice ("Interpretation Choice") depends on the type of campaign. In election campaigns, journalists might investigate more, for instance, about politicians' pasts and about scandals. This is also possible in public debates. In these cases, we find less dialogue.

Country characteristics seem to influence the frame edition process as well. The first, second, and final journalistic choices ("Balancing Choice", "Range of Views Choice" and "Interpretation Choice") are likely to be dependent on distance between media and political actors. Less distant journalists might balance the news less and might rely more on actors with a certain perspective and their interpretations. As a consequence, we might find less dialogue in the news media. In Western European democracies, journalistic norms include elite domination, proportionality, detachment, civility, and closure, whereas in the USA, norms such as endorsement of narrative and empowerment are prevalent (Ferree et al. 2002: 284). These choices also depend on the orientation of political communication. Dunaway and Lawrence (2015) show that media coverage is dependent on economic resources and probably would be less balanced, wide-ranging, and provided with contest in countries with dominant media logic. I expect the third choice ("Story Choice") to be dependent on the political and media system. In presidential systems, the president enjoys a high prestige and can be expected to be present very prominently in the news media. A focus on the president might also decrease dialogue, unless his or her position or actions are thoroughly discussed. Furthermore, the more dependent the media system is on advertising revenue, the more likely the story choice is influenced by how widely the article will be read. In this regard, Benson (2009, 2010) points to the importance of economic independence of the news media for a critical public debate. Finally, if the news media are not independent, the situation is quite different and can have serious consequences for the quality of democracy. For instance, if media organizations are (partly) owned by commercial corporations, the strong interweaving of media and business can lead to increased self-censorship (e.g., if media bosses are simultaneously active in the construction or energy sector). If media bosses (or their journalists) report negatively about the government, they can be left empty-handed when the next billion-dollar project is tendered. Thus, one has to expect that economic interests or the interests of a political leader are a dominant driving force in such a case and that this perspective will dominate the news. In such a case, there is no balancing norm established by journalists which gives political actors the incentive to enter into dialogue.

REFERENCES

Bennett, W. L. (1990). Taking the Public by Storm: Information, Cuing, and the Democratic Process in the Gulf Conflict. *Political Communication, 10,* 331–351.

Bennett, W. L., Pickard, V. W., Iozzi, D. P., Schroeder, C. L., Lagos, T., & Caswell, E. C. (2004). Managing the Public Sphere: Journalistic Construction of the Great Globalization Debate. *International Communication Association, 54*(3), 437–455.

Benson, R. (2009). What Makes News More Multiperspectival? A Field Analysis. *Poetics, 37*(5–6), 402–418.

Benson, R. (2010). What Makes for a Critical Press? A Case Study of French and U.S. Immigration News Coverage. *International Journal of Press/Politics, 15*(1), 3–24.

Bernhard, L. (2012). *Campaign Strategy in Direct Democracy.* Hampshire: Palgrave Macmillan.

Blumler, J. G., & Gurevitch, M. (1995 [1975]). Towards a Comparative Framework for Political Communication Research. In J. G. Blumler & M. Gurevitch (Eds.), *The Crisis of Public Communication* (pp. 59–72). London: Routledge.

Blumler, J. G., & Kavanagh, D. (1999). The Third Age of Political Communication: Influences and Features. *Political Communication, 16,* 209–230.

Danielian, L. H., & Page, B. I. (1994). The Heavenly Chorus: Interest Group Voices on TV News. *American Journal of Political Science, 38*(4), 1056–1078.

Dunaway, J., & Lawrence, R. G. (2015). What Predicts the Game Frame? Media Ownership, Electoral Context, and Campaign News. *Political Communication, 32*(1), 43–60.

Entman, R. M. (2007). Framing Bias: Media in the Distribution of Power. *Journal of Communication, 57,* 167–176.

Ferree, M., Gamson, W. A., Gerhards, J., & Rucht, D. (2002). *Shaping Abortion Discourse Democracy and the Public Sphere in Germany and the United States.* Cambridge: Cambridge University Press.

Galtung, J., & Ruge, M. H. (1965). The Structure of Foreign News. *Journal of Peace Research, 2*(1), 64–91.

Gans, H. J. (1979). *Deciding What's News: A Study of CBS Evening News, NBC Nightly News, Newsweek, and Time.* New York: Pantheon Books.

Gerth, M., Dahinden, U., & Siegert, G. (2012). Coverage of the Campaigns in the Media. In H. Kriesi (Ed.), *Political Communication in Direct-Democratic Campaigns: Enlightening or Manipulating?* (pp. 108–124). Hampshire: Palgrave Macmillan.

Greene, W. H. (2000). *Econometric Analysis.* Upper Saddle River, NJ: Prentice-Hall.

Hackett, R. A. (1985). A Hierarchy of Access: Aspects of Source Bias on Canadian TV News. *Journalism Quarterly, 62,* 256–265.

Hallin, D. C., & Mancini, P. (2004). *Comparing Media Systems Three Models of Media and Politics.* Cambridge: Cambridge University Press.

Höglinger, D. (2008). Verschafft die direkte Demokratie den Benachteiligten mehr Gehör? Der Einfluss institutioneller Rahmenbedingungen auf die mediale Präsenz politsicher Akteure. *Swiss Political Science Review, 14*(2), 207–243.

Kiousis, S., Mitrook, M., Wu, X., & Seltzer, T. (2006). First- and Second-Level Agenda-Building and Agenda-Setting Effects: Exploring the Linkages Among Candidate News Releases, Media Coverage, and Public Opinion During the 2002 Florida Gubernatorial Election. *Journal of Public Relations Research, 18*(3), 265–285.

Kriesi, H. (2009). The Role of the Government and of the Federal Administration in Direct-Democratic Campaigns. In H. Kriesi (Ed.), *Festschrift für Peter Knöpfel.* Lausanne: IDHEAP.

Kriesi, H., Adam, S., & Jochum, M. (2006). Comparative Analysis of Policy Networks in Western Europe. *Journal of European Public Policy, 13*(3), 341–361.

Kriesi, H., & Trechsel, A. H. (2008). *The Politics of Switzerland.* Cambridge: Cambridge University Press.

Lawrence, R. (2000). *The Politics of Force: Media and the Construction of Police Brutality.* Berkeley: University of California Press.

Livingston, S., & Bennett, L. W. (2003). Gatekeeping, Indexing, and Live-Event News: Is Technology Altering the Construction of News? *Political Communication, 20,* 363–380.

Long, S. J., & Freese, J. (2006). *Regression Models for Categorical Dependent Variables Using Stata.* College Station, TX: Stata Press.

Mazzoleni, G., & Schulz, W. (1999). *"Mediatization" of Politics: A Challenge for Democracy?* (Vol. 16, pp. 247–261). London: Routledge.

McQuail, D. (1992). *Media Performance: Mass Communication and the Public Interest.* London: Sage.

Price, V., & Tewksbury, D. (1997). News Values and Public Opinion: A Theoretical Account of Media Priming and Framing. In G. A. Barnett & F. J. Boster (Eds.), *Progress in Communication Sciences: Advances in Persuasion* (Vol. 13, pp. 173–212). Greenwich, CT: Ablex.

Reinemann, C., Fawzi, N., & Röder, P. (2012). Mehr Beteiligung = bessere Berichterstattung? Ein Vergleich der Presseberichterstattung überdie parlamentarische Entscheidung und den Volksentscheid zum Nichtraucherschutzgesetz in Bayern. *Studies in Communication/Media, 1*(3–4), S. 351–380.

Schudson, M. (1998). *The Good Citizen: A History of American Civic Life.* Cambridge: Harvard University Press.

Schudson, M. (2000, Spring). Overcoming Voter Isolation: Citizenship Beyond the Polls. *The Responsive Community,* 38–45.

Schulz, W. (1976). *Die Konstruktion von Realität in den Nachrichtenmedien.* Freiburg and München: Verlag Karl Alber.

Seymour-Ure, C. (1974). *The Political Impact of Mass Media.* London: Constable.

Shoemaker, P. J., & Reese, S. D. (1996). *Mediating the Message: Theories of Influences on Mass Media Content* (2nd ed.). White Plains, NY: Longman.

Steenbergen, M. (2008). *Count Models.* Bern: University Bern (Unpublished document).

Strömbäck, J., & Nord, L. W. (2006). Do Politicians Lead the Tango? A Study of the Relationship Between Swedish Journalists and Their Political Sources in the Context of Election Campaigns. *European Journal of Communication, 21*(2), 147–164.

Tresch, A. (2009). Politicians in the Media: Determinants of Legislators' Prominence in Swiss Newspaper. *The International Journal of Press/Politics, 14*(1), 67–90.

Vuong, Q. H. (1989). Likelihood Ratio Tests for Model Selection and Non-nested Hypotheses. *Econometrica, 57,* 307–333.

Weaver, D. H., & Wilhoit, C. G. (1991). *The American Journalist: A Portrait of U.S. News People and Their Work* (2nd ed.). Bloomington: Indiana University Press.

Wolfsfeld, G. (1997). *Media and Political Conflict: News from the Middle East* (Reprint ed.). Cambridge, MA: Cambridge University Press.

CHAPTER 7

Flow of Frames

Introduction[1]

The topic of this chapter is the flow of frames. First, we investigate the direction of the flow of frames: Whether the relationship between political actors and journalists is reciprocal or unidirectional. This step allows us to test the causal order claimed in the frame-building model (causal order hypothesis). Second, we look at the flow in the different communication channels and investigate from which channel the news frames mainly come (channel hypothesis). Finally, it is of interest whether and when the frames flow. For this step, we look at media attention and present descriptive information about *how much* media attention direct-democratic campaigns receive and *when* they are covered (effort and timing routines). These three aspects complete our insights into the origin of dialogue in the news media.

Who Is the Driving Force?

As introduced in Chapter 2, my general approach for conceptualizing the relationship between political actors and the mass media is an actor-oriented political process model (Wolfsfeld 1997). The relationship

---

[1] Part of this chapter has been previously published in Hänggli (2012a, b) and Hänggli and Kriesi (2010).

R. Hänggli, *The Origin of Dialogue in the News Media*,
Challenges to Democracy in the 21st Century,
https://doi.org/10.1007/978-3-030-26582-3_7

between the campaigners in the public debate and the mass media is one of mutual dependence, but as Gans (1979) and Wolfsfeld stressed, this relationship is likely to be an asymmetrical one with the political process as the driving force. This is in line with Sigal's idea (1973) that by releasing news, political actors take the first step toward making news. It is also in the tradition of Baerns' "Determinationsthese" (1991), a thesis well-known among Swiss and German communication scientists. It says that news coverage is based on contributions from political actors more than 60% of the time. In particular, Baerns states that political actors influence the content of news coverage (1991: 98). Strömbäck and Nord (2006), however, disagree with Sigal, Gans, and Baerns and conclude that journalists, not politicians, lead the tango. They assert that journalists have the *ultimate* power and control over the framing of news stories. Nevertheless, they also state that, with the exception of one main national television program, between 65 and 77% of the news stories in the four main newspapers and the two main television news programs in Sweden are based on media input from political actors. They agree that the political actors are frequently used as sources in the news stories. Thus, the *political actors* are expected to lead the frame-building process by providing the frames (causal order hypothesis). It is in this context that we refer to Bentele et al.'s (1997) term "Induktion", i.e., a communicative input which has an impact on the news. By framing the issue strategically, we argue (see Chapter 4) that political actors face at least three strategic choices. The journalists contribute to the debate by clarifying the opposing positions (which Bennett et al. 2004 call "recognition") and by eliciting mutual reactions from the opposing political actors (which they call "responsiveness"). With regard to the second and third choices involved in strategic framing ("Oppositional Emphasis Choice" and "Contest Emphasis Choice"), I expect that moderate market competition, as we have in Switzerland, slightly increases the journalists' preferences for contest frames. By increasing conflict, the news media increase news value and therefore their competitive performance. There is no expectation regarding offensive or defensive use of opponents' frames.

WHICH COMMUNICATION CHANNEL IS IMPORTANT?

I expect that *media input* is the most important communication channel in the frame-building process because the media releases and conferences are, obviously, directed toward the news media and sent or organized several times during the campaign phase. I call this the *channel* hypothesis. Posters and political advertisements (see Chapter 2 for an overview of the different communication channels) are not suitable for introducing new frames because they can only transport short messages. Instead, they are used for mobilization, and on rare occasions also for provocation. Posters might be able to strengthen and support a frame promoted in the media input, on the emotional level as well. *Provocative* posters or advertisements can be used to trigger a heated public debate or a debate about a certain framing. Such a heated debate occurs only rarely and none of our campaigns represented such a case. Letters to the editor are also not expected to be the main source for news coverage. As mentioned in Chapter 5, they can be seen as an open forum for public debate and are not primarily aimed at influencing news coverage.

Effort: How Much Media Attention?

Market orientation poses a challenge to resource-intensive ways of covering politics (Baker 2002). As a consequence of the market orientation, the media are under a permanent pressure of cost competition. Over the last 20 years, this pressure has increased as the number of readers of the press has declined and the number of media outlets has shrunk. Thus, the expensive and ethical coverage of political matters is increasingly challenged, and overall, the effort of the media in covering politics is called into question (Baker 2007). Resource-intensive journalistic formats such as in-depth commentary or reportage could be replaced by emotionalized, personalized and provocative "horse race" coverage, or by simple reprints of political actors' press releases. Nevertheless, in Switzerland, as in other countries of consensus democracy, the press is the dominant type of media and still earns more in advertising revenue than other types of media (Künzler 2005): The newspapers enjoy constitutional protection and are part of everyday life for the majority of Swiss citizens (Marcinkowski 2006). In the year 2000, there were 453 newspapers sold for every 1000 Swiss adults (Hallin and Mancini 2004: 23). Such a comparatively high rate of newspaper readership is only topped by Scandinavian countries. The high subscription rates build the financial foundation of the press, while advertising provides another 60–80% of subscription newspaper revenue (Meier 2004: 251). These two resources give the press a sound financial basis (Marcinkowski 2006). In addition, direct-democratic campaigns are newsworthy because they are important (Schulz 1997). Importance is measured in terms of lives affected. Direct-democratic campaigns affect the general public and are thus important.

As a consequence, the media are expected to make an effort in all direct-democratic campaigns and to "provide the public with the campaign information needed for voting on the campaign issue" (Gerth et al. 2009: 85). Direct-democratic campaigns take place several times a year and it is clear that the news media are expected to cover them. Although the media routinely report on the issues at stake in these campaigns, they cover issues of greater public interest more extensively. However, we chose the most important vote of the day in all three campaigns. Thus, all three proposals are relevant and I expect to find no variation between the campaigns. By contrast, I do expect to find differences between the media types. In this regard, I distinguish between the following types of media: high-quality elite newspapers ("elite"), regional newspapers ("regional"), tabloid newspapers ("tabloid"), free newspapers ("free"), and Public Service TV news ("TV"). Elite newspapers are particularly expected to invest resources in accurate, independent, and objective campaign coverage because they primarily aim at providing high-quality news. Regional newspapers are also expected to make an effort in reporting about direct-democratic campaigns because the process of concentration has strengthened the leading regional papers: Fewer titles are producing an increasing level of circulation (Lucht and Udris 2008). Tabloid newspapers are not expected to make an extra effort in direct-democratic campaigns because they want to deliver soft news stories with emotionalized and easy-to-understand messages. The free newspapers want to have the latest news headlines, and direct-democratic campaigns only rarely provide such latest news. Thus, it is probable that the free newspapers do not often report on direct-democratic campaigns. Even though the effort of TV cannot be directly compared to the effort of newspapers, it seems interesting to include TV in the analysis too. The Swiss public broadcasting organization (SRG) still operates as a non-profit enterprise. It is constitutionally bound to produce television programming for the entire country (Meier 2004: 253), meaning that the TV programming also has to provide information about the political issues of the country. Thus, I expect the media to make an effort in all campaigns. More specifically, elite newspapers might make the greatest effort, whereas free newspapers might make the least.

TIMING: WHEN DO THE MEDIA COVER DIRECT-DEMOCRATIC CAMPAIGNS?

The media are expected to cover direct-democratic campaigns mainly from 6 weeks to 3 weeks before the voting day. This may not be an obvious assumption, as in Switzerland political actors are allowed to publicly debate right up to the day of the vote. However, it can be explained by the information routine of the authorities and the voting behavior of the Swiss citizens and is in line with the idea that political institutions appear to influence the timing of the news coverage in ordinary politics (Baerns 1991: 98). Since 1978, the government and parliament have presented their views on a referendum or initiative in a ballot pamphlet, which is sent to each citizen. The pamphlet presents the government's position first and in more detail, followed by the challengers' points of view. This mailing is sent to the citizens three to four weeks before the vote. The majority of citizens wait until they receive the pamphlet and subsequently send their ballot by mail. Thus, the "critical period" of information processing is situated just before and during this mailing of the ballots. I do not expect to discern any differences between the media types. I expect to find earlier media coverage in the asylum law campaign since in this instance the political actors started their campaign earlier.

METHOD

We pursue a dual strategy for data analysis and treat the campaign agenda both as an aggregate and a daily phenomenon. The purpose of such a dual strategy is to find mutually reinforcing results. In the analysis of daily effects, we use a zero-inflated negative binomial regression model (see Appendix for details). For the estimation of the model, we use a stacked file, with five (four in the naturalization campaign) cases for each day, one for each of the main frame categories, plus one for the residual category. We introduce a dummy variable for each of the main frames in order to control for their variable salience. In order to control for contemporaneous correlation, we cluster the standard errors over time (=robust s.e.).[2] We also lag the dependent variable by one day so as to control for the autoregressive effect.

---

[2] This correction was designed for linear models, and it is not completely clear whether it works as well for this kind of model. However, the results are also robust without the clustering (Sensitivity analyses [model s2], not shown here).

In the first time-series analysis of daily effects (Table 7.2), we study the lagged effect of the framing of political actors on the framing of the media and vice versa. In order to do so, we can make use of the fact that political actors and the media do not communicate simultaneously, but in a stable morning-evening sequence in which the publication of (morning) newspapers precedes events produced by the political actors during the day, which are in turn consistently followed by the broadcast of (evening) news bulletins and by the press of the next day. Lagging the independent framing of the political actors of the two camps (contra and pro) by one day $(t-1)$ provides the relevant input for the framing of the press, while the framing of the political actors of the same day (t) provides the input for TV. Conversely, the independent framing of the newspapers and of the TV lagged by one day $(t-1)$ provides the input for the political actors on the next day (t). The arguments from the newspapers and from TV were combined in the media variable.[3]

RESULTS

The Lead of the Political Actors

Figure 7.1 compares the percentage shares of the frames in the media input with those in the media's news reporting. There are two graphs for each campaign—one with the shares of the contra camp (on the left) and one with the shares of the pro camp (on the right). The overall impression is that, in general, the *news media* rather faithfully reproduce the framing of the two camps. Thus, the percentage shares of the frames in the news media are generally similar to the shares found in the media input (cf. "Substantive Emphasis Choice"). The media tended to respect frame ownership and reported accordingly. There are two instances (the "abuse" frame of the pro camp in the asylum campaign and the "mass

---

[3] I will use the following abbreviations for the variables: Media $(t-1)$ is the number of arguments reported in the media on day $t-1$. Contra input $(t-1)$ and pro input $(t-1)$ is the number of arguments presented as input material by the contra and pro camps, respectively, on day $(t-1)$. Contra ads $(t-1)$ and pro ads $(t-1)$ are the number of arguments presented in the political advertisements of the contra or pro camps on day $t-1$. Contra LtE $(t-1)$ and Pro LtE $(t-1)$ are the lagged number of arguments in the letters to the editor. Human, trad, and the remaining variables in the count model are dummy indicators for the four (three in the naturalization campaign) main framing categories, with the residual category ("others") forming the reference category.

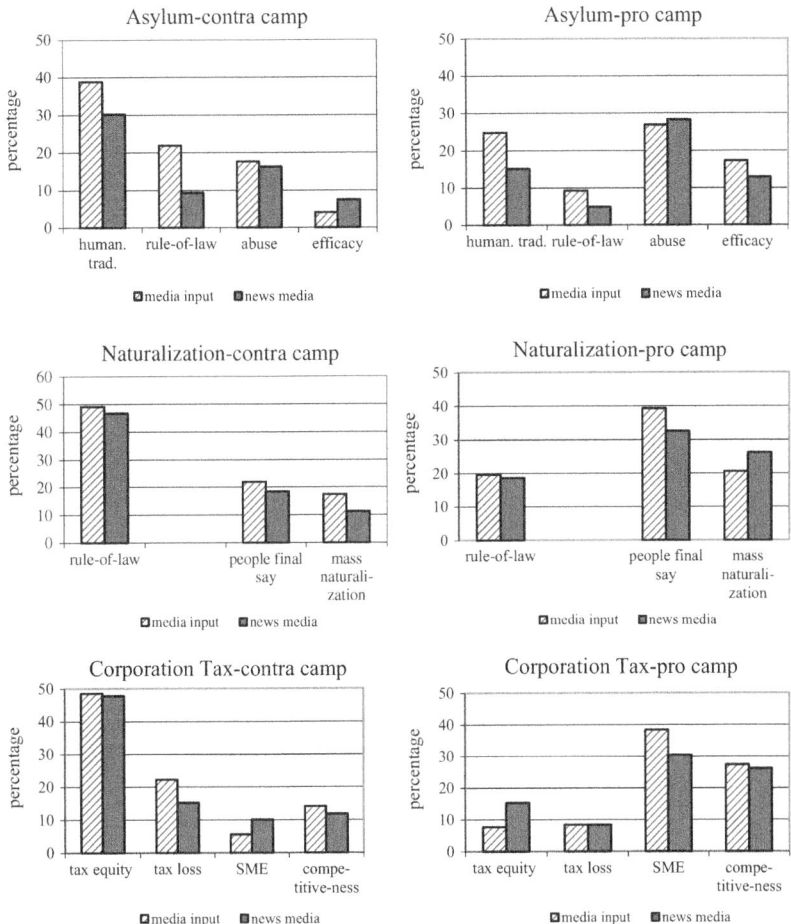

Fig. 7.1 Comparison between the percentage shares of the frames in the media input and in the news media

naturalization" frame of the pro camp in the naturalization campaign) in which the news media increased the share of the *main* frames compared to the media input. This finding is probably due to the advertisements: In both cases, the pro camp was very active with advertisements and focused on the respective frames in the ads (Chapter 5).

We saw in Chapter 4 that while the political actors did indeed focus predominantly on their own frames, they did not do so exclusively, but rather referred to their adversaries' frames as well. The journalists also reported on both camps with their adversaries' frames but in the corporate tax reform they doubled the share of the pro camp's "tax equity" counter-frame and increased the share of the contra camp's "SME" counter-frame and in the asylum campaign they increased the share of the contra camp's "efficacy" counter-frame. The findings go back to the level of dialogue and the "Story Choice" discussed in Chapter 6. In the corporate tax reform, the level of dialogue found in the media input was lowest, and the reliance on the framing of both camps for the story of an article ("Story Choice") was crucial. In the other campaigns, the level of dialogue was already high in the media input, and if journalists were to primarily emphasize the framing input of one camp, the degree of dialogue would still be high. Therefore, it was most necessary in the corporation tax campaign that the framing of both sides was used. Thus, by giving importance to the framing input of both sides, journalists increased the share of the counter-frames (tax equity and SME) and in so doing also increased the level of dialogue.

Table 7.1 provides a more detailed overview of the frames in the media input and in the news media of the three campaigns. Compared to Fig. 7.1, it adds the distinction between the offensive and defensive use of the frames and reports the "others" and the "contest" frames. The media input corresponds to what was shown in Chapter 4 (Table 4.1). Compared to the media input, there are just a few additional differences in the media's news reporting. First, in the case of the asylum law, the media framing is more diverse than the political actors' input, since the "other" thematic frames account for roughly a quarter of the media frames on either side, while they make up only one-seventh (contra camp) or one-fifth (pro camp) of the input material produced for the media. The use of this residual type of frame can be interpreted as a sign of the independence of the newspapers from the government's position, since the most important quality paper of Switzerland—the NZZ—contributed substantively to this category. In the other two campaigns, the media made no special effort with their own or other frames. Thus, the media do not show more frame-building power in the case of the unfamiliar issue, the corporate tax reform. Second, as one might also have expected on the basis of the American and British experiences, and as already reported in Chapter 6, the media rely more heavily on

Table 7.1 Substantive (Offensive and Defensive Use) and contest frames of the two camps in the media input and the news media: percentages

Asylum

Substantive	Frame	Media input Contra	Media input Pro	News media Contra	News media Pro
Offensive	Human. trad.	38.7	4.5	30.2	2.5
	Rule-of-law	21.5	0.0	9.3	0.3
	Abuse	0.0	26.9	0.0	27.8
	Efficacy	0.0	17.3	0.0	12.8
	Others	13.9	16.1	23.8	22.1
	All offensive	74.1	64.8	63.4	65.6
Defensive	Human. trad.	0.1	20.3	0.0	12.6
	Rule-of-law	0.4	9.3	0.0	4.5
	Abuse	17.6	0.0	16.2	0.5
	Efficacy	4.0	0.0	7.5	0.1
	Others	0.0	0.0	0.0	0.5
	All defensive	22.2	29.6	23.8	18.3
Contest		4.1	5.7	12.8	16.2
Total (%)		100	100	100	100
n		726	335	1528	927

Naturalization

	Frame	Media input Contra	Media input Pro	News media Contra	News media Pro
Offensive	Rule-of-law	48.9	0.0	46.0	0.0
	People final say	0.0	39.3	0.1	31.5
	Mass naturalization	0.4	20.6	0.1	24.8
	Others	4.9	7.5	7.2	5.8
	All offensive	52.6	65.5	53.3	62.1
Defensive	Rule-of-law	0.2	19.6	0.0	18.5
	People final say	21.9	0.0	18.5	0.0
	Mass naturalization	17.0	0.0	11.1	0.0
	Others	0.2	0.0	0.0	0.0
	All defensive	40.6	19.6	29.6	18.5
Contest		6.5	13.1	17.0	19.0
Total (%)		100	100	100	100
n		675	107	1176	733

Corporation tax

	Frame	Media input Contra	Media input Pro	News media Contra	News media Pro
Offensive	Tax equity	48.5	0.0	47.8	0.3
	Tax loss	22.3	0.0	15.2	0.2
	SME	0.0	38.4	0.3	30.2
	Competitiveness	0.0	27.3	0.0	25.9
	Others	4.3	11.3	2.5	4.5
	All offensive	75.1	76.9	65.8	61.0
Defensive	Tax equity	0.0	7.7	0.0	15.0
	Tax loss	0.0	8.4	0.0	8.2
	SME	5.6	0.0	9.7	0.2
	Competitiveness	14.1	0.0	11.8	0.0
	Others	0.0	0.0	0.0	0.0
	All defensive	19.7	16.2	21.6	23.5
Contest		5.2	6.9	12.7	15.5
Total (%)		100	100	100	100
n		462	594	943	1123

contest frames in their news reporting (cf. "Contest Emphasis Choice"). However, even in their case, substantive frames largely predominate. Thus, we can state that in Swiss direct-democratic campaigns, framing is primarily conducted in substantive terms. Third, there is also not a great deal of trespassing (=offensive use of the opponents' frame) in the media either. If the opponents' frames are used, they are used defensively (cf. "Oppositional Emphasis Choice").

Having established the predominance of substantive framing and having shown the rare use of trespassing, we now focus exclusively on the substantive frames, i.e., on the arguments and combine the offensive and defensive use of them. Table 7.2 presents the regression results for the three campaigns. On the left-hand side of each table, the media's framing constitutes the dependent variable; on the right-hand side, it is the framing by the two camps which constitutes the dependent variables.

Let us first look at the left-hand side of the tables for the three campaigns, where the news media frames are the dependent variable. In the inflation model (absence), the ratios of both camps (contra [t−1] and pro [t−1]) are smaller than one, which means that the input of the political actors decreases the probability of a frame's absence in the media. Two of the corresponding six effects reach conventional levels of significance, and one is significant at the 10% level. In the count model (frequency), the ratios are larger than one. This means that the input of the political actors increases the frequency of an argument in the news media. With two exceptions, the effects are significant at the 5% level. One is significant at the 10% level.

As is shown in the right-hand side of the three tables, the reverse does not apply: The framing by the media on the previous day (media [t−1]) has a decreasing or no effect on the framing by political actors. In the inflation model (absence), the ratios are smaller than one, but only the ratios of the corporate tax reform are significant at the 5% level. Moreover, in the count model (frequency), the ratio is smaller than one, which means that if a camp has succeeded in getting into the media on a given day, it will reduce its effort to get into the media on the following day. With two exceptions, these negative effects are significant at the 5% level. In summary, the results of Table 7.2 strongly suggest that the frames promoted by the politicians influenced the media frames, whereas the opposite is less likely. Thus, we feel comfortable in considering the political actors as the driving force in the frame-building process.

Table 7.2 Who is driving whom? Results of zero-inflated negative binomial regression of media framing on lagged framing by the two camps, and vice versa: Ratio, robust standard errors, and p-levels

Dependent variable: news media				Dependent variable: media input						
News media	Ratio	Robust s.e.	p	Contra camp	Ratio	Robust s.e.	p	Pro camp	Ratio	Robust s.e.	p
Asylum											
Count model (frequency)				*Count model (frequency)*				*Count model (frequency)*			
Media (t−1)	1.021	0.015	0.168	**Media (t−1)**	**0.928**	**0.021**	**0.001**	**Media (t−1)**	**0.917**	**0.036**	**0.028**
Contra input (t−1)	**1.032**	**0.013**	**0.015**	Contra input (t−1)	0.984	0.009	0.078	Contra input (t−1)	1.060	0.055	0.259
Pro input (t−1)	**1.066**	**0.069**	**0.320**	Pro input (t−1)	2.173	0.404	0.000	Pro input (t−1)	1.668	0.470	0.069
Human. trad.	0.955	0.126	0.725	Human. trad.	1.554	0.367	0.062	Human. trad.	0.524	0.194	0.081
Rule-of-law	0.415	0.048	0.000	Rule-of-law	1.803	0.522	0.042	Rule-of-law	1.865	0.360	0.001
Abuse	0.904	0.109	0.401	Abuse	0.408	0.096	0.000	Abuse	0.941	0.139	0.678
Efficacy	0.492	0.065	0.000	Efficacy				Efficacy			
Inflation model (absence)				*Inflation model (absence)*				*Inflation model (absence)*			
Media (t−1)	0.289	0.633	0.050	Media (t−1)	0.983	0.033	0.609	**Media (t−1)**	**0.999**	**0.053**	**0.978**
Contra input (t−1)	**0.287**	**1.668**	**0.454**	Contra input (t−1)	0.943	0.027	0.031	Contra input (t−1)			
Pro input (t−1)	**0.000**	**2.327**	**0.000**	Pro input (t−1)				Pro input (t−1)	0.984	0.123	0.897
Constant	0.602	0.327	0.065	Constant	1.731	0.659	0.009	Constant	1.602	0.315	0.000
n total: 560, *n* zero obs.: 262				*n* total: 560, *n* zero obs.: 501				*n* total: 560, *n* zero obs.: 488			
Vuong: z=5.37, Pr>z=0.000				Vuong: z=1.4, Pr>z=0.081				Vuong: z=1.88, Pr>z=0.030			

(continued)

Table 7.2 (continued)

	Dependent variable: news media			*Dependent variable: media input*					
				Contra camp			*Pro camp*		
News media	Ratio	Robust s.e.	p	Ratio	Robust s.e.	p	Ratio	Robust s.e.	p
Naturalization									
Count model (frequency)									
Media (t−1)	1.008	0.012	0.515	0.961	0.014	**0.008**	0.908	0.047	**0.061**
Contra (t−1)	**1.044**	**0.013**	**0.001**	0.987	0.011	0.276	0.865	0.166	0.450
Pro (t−1)	**1.054**	**0.034**	**0.095**						
Rule-of-law	3.010	0.656	0.000	8.010	3.093	0.000	2.626	0.638	0.000
People final say	2.541	0.495	0.000	3.351	1.084	0.000	7.684	2.299	0.000
Mass naturalization	2.187	0.428	0.000	3.653	0.877	0.000	1.804	0.496	0.032
Inflation model (absence)									
Media (t−1)	0.115	0.998	0.032	0.982	0.021	0.397	0.631	0.555	0.407
Contra (t−1)	**0.003**	**22.091**	**0.789**	0.950	0.080	0.516	0.000	1.338	0.000
Pro (t−1)	**0.226**	**0.732**	**0.042**						
Constant	1.774	0.298	0.000	1.712	0.574	0.001	1.865	0.976	0.056

n total: 364, *n* zero obs.: 203
Vuong: z=6.87, Pr>z=0.000

n total: 364, *n* zero obs.: 308
Vuong: z=2.12, Pr>z=0.017

n total: 364, *n* zero obs.: 343
Vuong: z=2.13, Pr>z=0.017

(continued)

Table 7.2 (continued)

Dependent variable: news media				Dependent variable: media input							
News media	Ratio	Robust s.e.	p	Contra camp	Ratio	Robust s.e.	p	Pro camp	Ratio	Robust s.e.	p
Corporation Tax											
Count model (frequency)				*Count model (frequency)*				*Count model (frequency)*			
Media (t−1)	1.010	0.009	0.271	**Media (t−1)**	**0.981**	**0.009**	**0.040**	**Media (t−1)**	**0.981**	**0.016**	0.258
Contra input (t−1)	**1.095**	**0.025**	**0.000**	**Contra input (t−1)**	0.781	0.066	0.003	Contra input (t−1)	0.603	0.061	0.000
Pro input (t−1)	**1.083**	**0.036**	**0.015**	Pro input (t−1)				Pro input (t−1)	0.815	0.273	0.541
Tax equity	4.931	0.981	0.000	Tax equity	4.872	2.619	0.003	Tax equity	0.537	0.195	0.088
Tax loss	2.789	0.521	0.000	Tax loss	2.631	1.489	0.087	Tax loss	3.188	0.468	0.000
SME	3.525	0.635	0.000	SME	0.652	0.410	0.497	SME	1.467	0.230	0.015
Competitiveness	3.816	0.558	0.000	Competitiveness	0.986	0.616	0.983	Competitiveness			
Inflation model (absence)				*Inflation model (absence)*				*Inflation model (absence)*			
Media (t−1)	0.166	0.529	0.001	Media (t−1)	**0.288**	**0.455**	**0.006**	**Media (t−1)**	**0.932**	**0.030**	**0.018**
Contra input (t−1)	**0.712**	**0.237**	0.152	Contra input (t−1)	0.866	0.275	0.599	Contra input (t−1)	0.605	0.683	0.462
Pro input (t−1)	**0.891**	**0.067**	0.082	Pro input (t−1)				Pro input (t−1)	1.734	0.683	0.000
Constant	1.044	0.287	0.000	Constant	2.102	0.667	0.002	Constant			

n total: 445, *n* zero obs.: 246
Vuong: z=5.92, Pr>z=0.000

n total:445, *n* zero obs.: 395
Vuong: z=3.5, Pr>z=0.000

n total: 445, *n* zero obs.: 380
Vuong: z=2.61, Pr>z=0.000

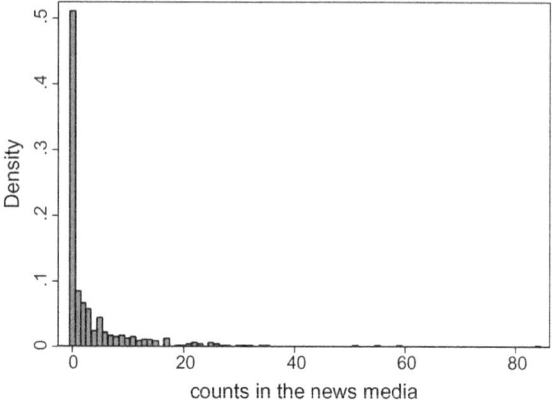

Fig. 7.2   Histogram of the news media counts in the corporate tax reform

However, in the corporate tax reform, there are hints that it might also have worked the other way round, i.e., that the media frames have an influence on the promoted frames in the media input: The two ratios (0.288, 0.932) in the inflation model (absence) on the right-hand side of Table 7.2 are significant. In the following, we investigate these two cases. For the examination, only the smaller counts in the news media are relevant, since 90% of the counts in the news media are smaller than or equal to 11 (Fig. 7.2).

Figures 7.3 and 7.4 reveal that the frames in the news media probably influenced the media input frames by the *contra* camp, whereas in the case of the *pro* camp the influence of the news media was not important. The line shows the probabilities of a zero count in the media input dependent on the number of frames in the news media. For each frame, a graph is presented. Figure 7.4 investigates the effect on the frame counts of the *contra* camp. The graphs show that a small number of news media frames bring about a remarkable drop in the probability of a zero count in the media input. This means that the news media significantly and strikingly increase the probability that a frame is used in the media input on the next day. As the upper left graph shows, this is most valid for the "tax equity" frame, where the corresponding probability increases by more than 0.3. In the tax reform campaign, the argumentation of the Social Democrats—who were in charge of the contra committee during the campaign—resonated well with external events happening at the same

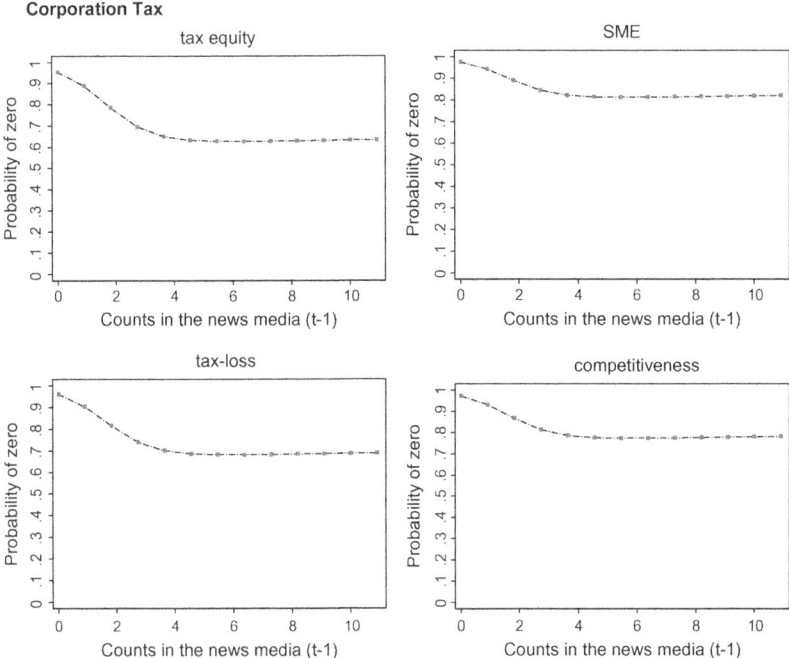

Fig. 7.3   Probability of zero counts in the media input (t) of the contra camp

time. As introduced in Chapter 5, the Social Democrats reacted to the UBS subprime crisis and presented individuals who would profit from the reform. On February 14th, they claimed that stockholders with controlling shares, such as Ospel, would also benefit from the tax reform (tax equity). In other words, the drop in the upper left graph in Fig. 7.3 shows that the presence of the "tax equity" frame in the news media (because of the UBS subprime crisis) decreased the chance of no such frames in the press releases of the contra camp (in this case the Social Democrats).

Figure 7.4 examines the effect on the promoted frames of the pro camp. There is no similar drop. In the case of the pro camp, the predicted decrease in the zero probability is only around 0.1. In summary, the data support the idea that the promoted frames in the media input influence the news media frames, whereas the news media influenced the promoted frames only in the exceptional case of the contra camp in the corporate tax reform.

Corporation Tax

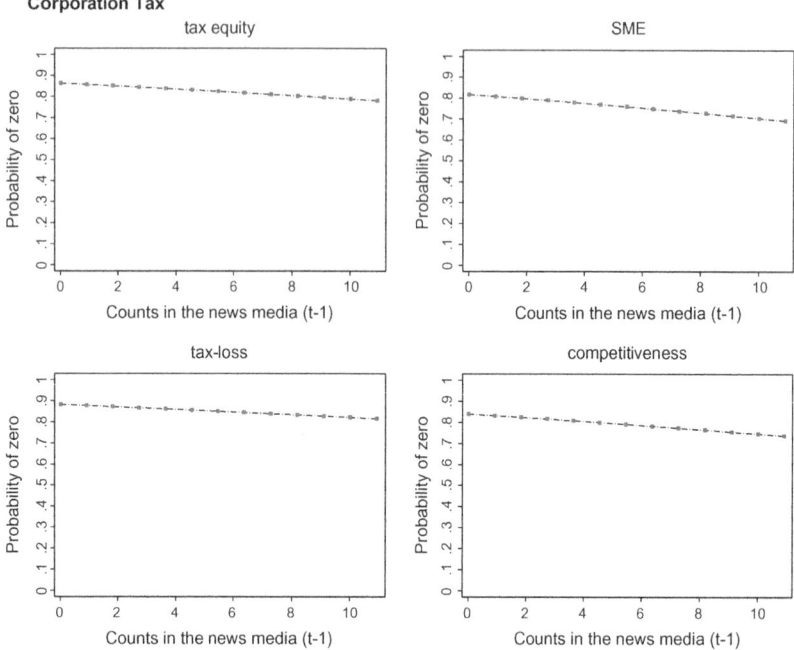

Fig. 7.4   Probability of zero counts in the media input (t) of the pro camp

In both the count and the inflation model, the lagged dependent variable (media [t−1]) controls for serial correlation. The significant ratio in the inflation model (absence) is smaller than one, which means that the frames in the news media reduce the probability of a zero count on the following day. In other words, the media also writes about the campaign independently of the explicit input of the two camps. They carry out interviews with politicians, discuss the consequences of a proposal or provide background information. In times of concern around fake news, being independent also means that the media guarantee objective information and stay credible. In direct democracy, the media does so because it has *established its own routines* for dealing with a direct-democratic campaign. As is shown by the panels in Fig. 7.5, which present the daily development of the media coverage of the two camps, these routines imply that there is a "critical period" of press coverage toward the end

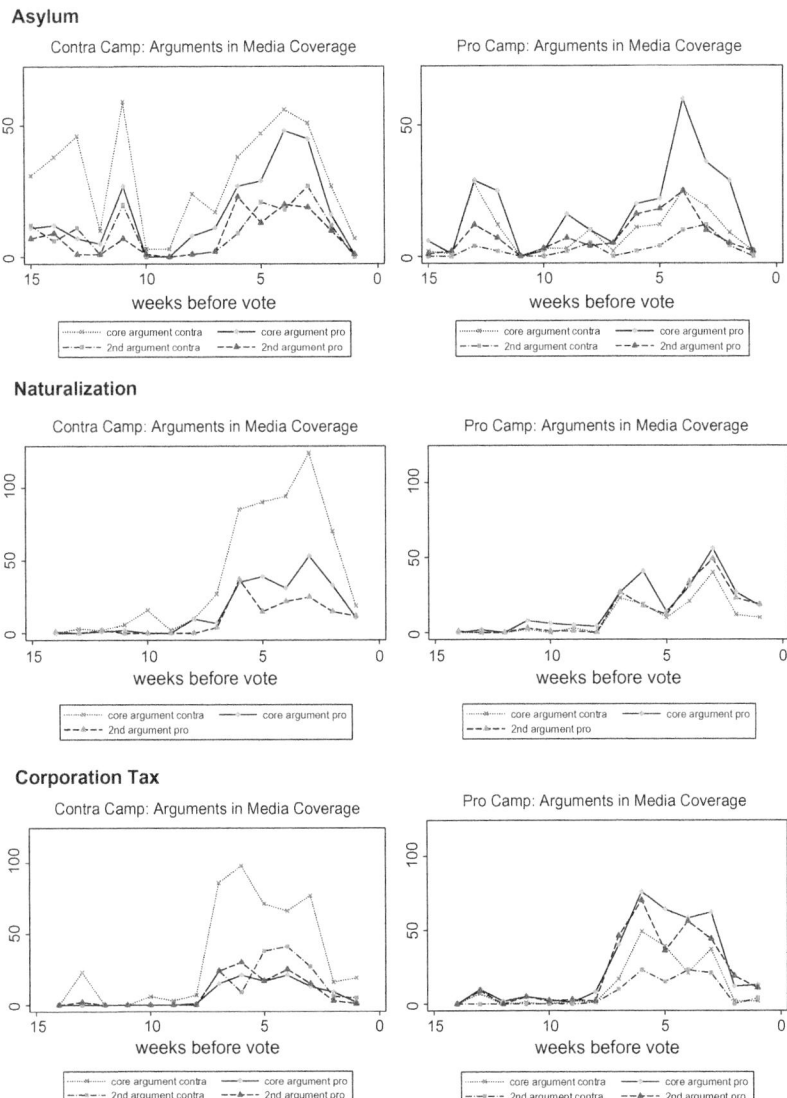

Fig. 7.5 The development of the campaign on a weekly basis—by camp and campaign: absolute counts of substantive frames

of the campaign, when the citizens have received their voting material and are casting their votes (mainly by mail). For the asylum law, and to a lesser extent for the tax reform, there is also a first "critical period" at the beginning, when the Swiss media presents the basic issues of the campaign and the contrasting positions of the two camps. Furthermore, *external events* structure the debate. In the asylum law campaign, summer holidays brought a reduction of media coverage in the middle of the campaign (weeks 9–6). In the naturalization initiative, the first 100 days of Eveline Widmer-Schlumpf in office as a minister clearly structured the campaign. She wanted some time to settle into her new job and become familiar with the role. The schedule of news coverage obviously followed this time plan. Only when these first 100 days had passed, in the 8th week before the vote, did the campaign and media coverage on this issue begin. In the case of the corporate tax reform, the campaign did not begin until after the Christmas break.

Before we look at the importance of communication channel, we examine the influence of opinion polls. Table 7.3 shows the percentage of organizations that adapted their campaign based on opinion poll(s). On average, 10% of organizations changed their campaign in this way. In the asylum law, opinion polls predicted correctly a yes vote. In the first poll, a majority of 54% was predicted, whereas the second opinion poll predicted a solid majority of 61%. One organization of the contra camp organized an additional media conference and two organizations placed additional advertisements because they hoped to counteract this second result. In the naturalization initiative, the first poll suggested that the outcome was open. As a reaction, the contra camp became more active. The second poll rendered the contra camp more optimistic by predicting

Table 7.3 Percentage of organizations that adapted their campaign based on opinion poll(s)

	Contra	Pro	Week
Asylum	6.0	0.0	5 and 2
Naturalization (1st opinion poll)	28.0	0.0	6
Naturalization (2nd opinion poll)	8.0	25.0	2
Tax Reform	7.7	11.8	3

Note (a) There were two opinion polls in the asylum law and in the tax reform campaign. In the asylum law, we asked about both opinion polls together (b) Week refers to week before the vote when the opinion poll was released a no vote of 56%. The pro camp placed more ads (partly planned but also some additional) to mobilize people and bring out the vote. In this case, they also changed their argumentation, switching their emphasis to the second frame.

In the corporate tax reform, the poll predicted an open result with 46% in favor, 31% against the law and 23% of voters undecided. On both sides, some of the organizations were motivated to become more active. To summarize, I note that most organizations did not adapt their activities based on the opinion polls. If political actors adapted their campaign, they became more active. With one exception (pro camp in the naturalization initiative), they stayed on message.

Media Input as the Most Important Communication Channel

Table 7.4 investigates whether the political advertisements and letters to the editor have an influence on the news media frames the next day. In the inflation part, the coefficients of the advertisements and the letters to the editor are insignificant and, moreover, not all of them have the expected signs, i.e., are larger than one. Thus, the ads were not helpful in introducing frames into the news the following day. There is one exception: In the naturalization initiative, the frames of the pro camp in the letters to the editor were also covered in the news. In this campaign, the pro camp was passive with media input and did not put out any in the final four weeks of the campaign. By contrast, they became active with letters to the editor and ads (see Chapter 5, Fig. 5.1). The populist right-wing party (SVP) led the pro camp campaign and organized an orchestrated letter-writing action. Since there was no longer any media input, the letters became significant. The ads did not influence the news because they served to mobilize people or to directly target people toward the end.

In the count part, the advertisements and letters to the editor also remain largely insignificant. Again, there are exceptions. We see that the pro camp successfully increased the number of their frames in the news with the help of letters to the editor in the naturalization initiative (only significant at the 10% level) for the same reason as just mentioned. In the corporate tax reform, the advertisements of the pro camp and the letters of the contra camp significantly increased the emphasis on their frames in the news. The pro camp was successful with the ads because they released some of their ads early (more than 10 weeks before the vote).

Table 7.4 Which channel is influential? Results of zero-inflated negative binomial regression of media framing on lagged framing by the media input, political advertisements, and letters to the editor of the two camps: Ratios, robust standard errors, and p-levels

Asylum

News media	IRR	Robust s.e.	p
Count model			
Media (t−1)	1.020	0.015	0.171
Contra (t−1)	1.031	0.013	0.015
Pro (t−1)	1.072	0.067	0.270
Contra ads (t−1)	**1.021**	**0.031**	**0.501**
Pro Ads (t−1)	**1.004**	**0.010**	**0.701**
Contra LtE (t−1)	**0.985**	**0.061**	**0.803**
Pro LtE (t−1)	**0.937**	**0.066**	**0.356**
Human. trad.	0.913	0.149	0.577
Rule-of-law	0.411	0.060	0.000
Abuse	0.871	0.122	0.326
Efficacy	0.496	0.069	0.000
Inflation model			
Media (t−1)	0.277	0.572	0.025
Contra (t−1)	0.264	1.061	0.210
Pro (t−1)	0.000	1.787	0.000
Contra ads (t−1)	**0.813**	**0.149**	**0.166**
Pro ads (t−1)	**0.984**	**0.025**	**0.537**
Contra LtE (t−1)	**0.691**	**0.225**	**0.101**
Pro LtE (t−1)	**0.860**	**0.311**	**0.629**
Constant	1.078	0.312	0.001

n total: 560, n zero obs.: 262
Vuong: z=4.85, Pr>z=0.000

Naturalization

News media	IRR	Robust s.e.	p
Count model			
Media (t−1)	1.008	0.011	0.454
Contra (t−1)	1.040	0.015	0.007
Pro (t−1)	1.047	0.039	0.221
Contra ads (t−1)	**1.034**	**0.066**	**0.603**
Pro Ads (t−1)	**1.002**	**0.007**	**0.793**
Contra LtE (t−1)	**1.023**	**0.030**	**0.433**
Pro LtE (t−1)	**1.056**	**0.033**	**0.082**
Rule-of-law	2.506	0.581	0.000
People final say	2.146	0.456	0.000
Mass naturalization	1.988	0.414	0.001
Inflation model			
Media (t−1)	0.138	0.788	0.012
Contra (t−1)	0.521	0.340	0.055
Pro (t−1)	0.376	0.469	0.037
Contra ads (t−1)	**0.975**	**0.227**	**0.913**
Pro ads (t−1)	**0.980**	**0.025**	**0.406**
Contra LtE (t−1)	**1.075**	**0.073**	**0.321**
Pro LtE (t−1)	**0.575**	**0.281**	**0.048**
Constant	1.995	0.305	0.000

n total: 364, n zero obs.: 203
Vuong: z=4.95, Pr>z=0.000

Corporation Tax

News media	IRR	Robust s.e.	p
Count model			
Media (t−1)	1.004	0.008	0.607
Contra (t−1)	1.085	0.017	0.000
Pro (t−1)	1.082	0.029	0.003
Contra ads (t−1)	**1.012**	**0.075**	**0.871**
Pro Ads (t−1)	**1.034**	**0.013**	**0.007**
Contra LtE (t−1)	**1.056**	**0.025**	**0.021**
Pro LtE (t−1)	**1.042**	**0.028**	**0.128**
Tax equity	3.901	0.859	0.000
Tax loss	2.484	0.470	0.000
SME	2.632	0.644	0.000
Competitiveness	2.366	0.542	0.000
Inflation model			
Media (t−1)	0.158	0.530	0.000
Contra (t−1)	0.747	0.219	0.182
Pro (t−1)	0.896	0.055	0.047
Contra ads (t−1)	**1.156**	**0.254**	**0.569**
Pro ads (t−1)	**0.995**	**0.030**	**0.861**
Contra LtE (t−1)	**0.819**	**0.123**	**0.819**
Pro LtE (t−1)	**0.899**	**0.074**	**0.148**
Constant	1.168	0.289	0.000

n total: 445, n zero obs.: 246
Vuong: z=6.03, Pr>z=0.000

The letters of the contra camp were influential because the contra camp actively used this channel toward the end. In Table 7.1, we saw that the ads influenced the media coverage in the naturalization initiative and in the corporate tax reform. It is plausible that we do not find support for this idea here because our model tests the influence of sponsored frames on the media coverage the next day (the same is the case for other lags). I would not, however, exclude the possibility that ads can increase the attention toward a frame more generally. Such an effect cannot be covered with a similar model.

Effort: How Much Media Attention?

Table 7.5 shows the average number of articles produced by a media type in each campaign. At the bottom, the total numbers of articles in each campaign are listed. These numbers show first of all that the media were involved in all three campaigns. With regard to the media types, we find the highest average number of articles in elite and regional newspapers. Not surprisingly, we find the lowest number in the free media. Across the campaigns, we observe the highest numbers in the familiar and easy issue (asylum law), whereas we discern the lowest in the unfamiliar and complex issue (corporation tax). The early involvement in the asylum law might have increased the number of articles, whereas the late start of the naturalization initiative probably reduced the number of

Table 7.5 Effort: Average number of articles/TV reports produced by media type

Media type	Asylum	Naturalization	Corporation tax	Number of outlets
Elite	58	41	28	4 (2)[a]
Regional	44	29	28	9 (1)
Tabloid	14	12	11	3 (1)
TV	11	3	5	2
Free	6	7	1	2
Total	559	380	327	20
Analysis of variance	$F = 3.96$, $p = 0.028$	$F = 2.60$, $p = 0.081$	$F = 2.23$, $p = 0.118$	

[a]The number in brackets shows the number of Sunday newspapers. For the mean, the Sunday newspapers were counted as 1/6 according to the proportion of weekdays for which they produce an issue. For instance, we arrive at 2.33 outlets in the elite media type. The elite newspapers together produced 136 articles in the asylum law campaign. Divided by 2.33, this is 58

articles produced. In addition, it is possible that the complexity of the issue in the corporation tax reduced the number of articles produced by journalists. However, further studies are needed to show whether this finding can be generalized.

One of the regional newspapers (St. Galler Tagblatt) was remarkably active in the asylum law and the corporate tax reform. It produced 81 articles on the former and 51 on the latter. Proximity has been shown to be one of the news factors (Galtung and Ruge 1965; Schulz 1976; Price and Tewksbury 1997), and this finding might be explained by the fact that, in both cases, prominent figures with local ties were involved. In the asylum law, one of the ad hoc committees (BK) opposed to the reform proposal was led by a member of the business elite (Markus Rauh), who had grown up and lived in the area. In addition, a minis-ter (Regierungsrat) of St. Gallen, Peter Schönenberger, also joined his committee. In the pro camp, another minister (Regierungsrat) of the canton of St. Gallen, Karin Keller-Sutter, was also active. In the corporate tax reform, a professor (Waldburger) from the University of St. Gallen was an important expert on the issue and criticized the reform from early in the campaign. It is possible that the involvement of these locally tied figures increased the news value and triggered more articles. A short telephone conversation with the responsible editor from this newspaper (Stefan Schmid) confirmed this suggestion; when presented with the finding, he proposed the very same explanation. In addition, he confirmed that the journalists were also personally interested in both issues, which might also contribute to explaining this finding.

Timing: Most Media Coverage Six to Three Weeks Before the Vote Takes Place

Figure 7.6 shows the intensity of the three campaigns based on the num-ber of arguments, aggregated over the weeks. Firstly, we see that the campaigns—after being covered on a lower level for some weeks—only started in earnest seven weeks (for the corporate tax reform) or six weeks (for the asylum law and the naturalization campaign) before the day of the vote. The media coverage of the asylum law campaign started earlier due to some highly involved political actors of the contra camp who began early. Secondly, in the third week before the vote, the debate in the news media peaked. As suggested above, this is related to the mail-ing of the information bulletin three to four weeks before voting day.

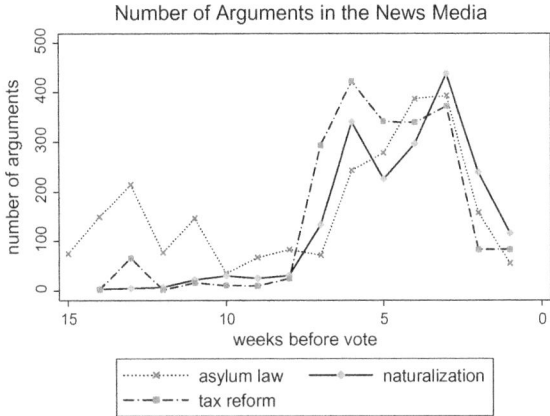

Fig. 7.6 Coverage in the news media over time

Finally, the debate was covered on a significantly lower level in the final two weeks of the campaign. This result corresponds to findings from previous research on referendum campaigns (De Vreese and Semetko 2004; Marquis et al. 2011). The timing of the media coverage in the three campaigns correlates highly at around 0.8.[4] There are no significant differences between the media types.

Nevertheless, the media can introduce certain accents during a campaign. Firstly, TV, in its role as a public service organization, is responsible for one or two public opinion polls during campaigns. In the asylum law campaign, the first of the two public opinion polls predicted a close result, encouraging the contra camp to increase its efforts—without success as we know. In the naturalization initiative, the first of the two polls revealed a surprisingly high number of "yes" voters (48% of the respondents). Again, this prompted the contra camp to increase its efforts, which resulted in a successful campaign. In both instances, the second poll did not have a comparable effect. In addition, the other camp remained more or less unaffected by the poll. Secondly, the media organized the Swiss TV debate show (Arena), which, in the case of the naturalization

[4]The weekly argument counts of the asylum law and the naturalization campaign correlate at 0.78 (0.89 for the last 10 weeks), those of the asylum law and corporate tax reform at 0.73 (0.79 for the last 10 weeks), and the corporation tax and naturalization campaign correlate at 0.88 (0.84 for the last 10 weeks).

initiative, attracted a record number of viewers (810,000) and triggered news coverage over the following days. This was an extraordinary event that can be explained by the showdown the program presented between the new Justice Minister (Eveline Widmer-Schlumpf) and the former Justice Minister (Christoph Blocher). Normally, "Arena" is less important, attracting an average of 234,000 viewers.[5] The timing of this event is important because it can affect the effort a political actor puts forth or the content of a public debate.

Conclusion

My analysis confirms that the input of the political actors plays a decisive role in Swiss direct-democratic campaigns. It is the political actors who introduce the most important frames into the public discourse. The causal order of my frame-building model is mainly confirmed. The channel hypothesis investigated whether the frames stem mainly from media input (press releases and media conferences). This hypothesis tends to be supported but is not fully confirmed. If other channels (letters to the editor or advertisement) become influential, it is because political actors no longer issue media input or become more active on other channels. When looking at how much attention the media pay to direct-democratic campaigns, we find that the media make an effort in all three campaigns (effort routine). Elite newspapers make the greatest effort, while free newspapers exert the least. In addition, the media make more effort in longer campaigns than in shorter ones. One of the regional newspapers made a remarkably high effort in two campaigns because representative figures with local ties were involved and the journalists were interested in the issue. Finally, journalists cover direct-democratic campaigns mainly between the sixth and the third week before the vote takes place following the institutional routine of the political authorities and actors (timing routine). Nevertheless, the media introduced accents in the campaign by conducting public opinion polls. In the naturalization initiative, the TV show "Arena" intensified the debate, and the journalists increased their use of contest frames toward the end of the campaign. Overall, this chapter shows that there is a relatively clear order

[5] http://www.nzz.ch/nachrichten/politik/schweiz/streit_um_neue_arena_nach_der_rekord-sendung_1.736781.html, March 2019.

in the flow of information, and in the effort and timing of campaigns. This clarity and job division seems to be supportive of dialogue.

Interaction Between Context (Campaign Type, Country) and Flow of Frame

In other debates or other contexts, the pattern can look different. Particularly in relation to scandals, but also occasionally in elections, the news media (watchdog journalism) can take the lead and be the ones who construct and promote frames, too. With regard to channels, social media can also be crucial in these debates: A comment on social media can trigger an issue and can shape a debate (e.g., #MeToo). Effort and timing can also vary considerably depending on debate and context.

References

Baerns, B. (1991). *Öffentlichkeitsarbeit oder Journalismus: Zum Einfluss im Mediensystem* (2nd ed.). Köln: Wissenschaft und Politik.

Baker, E. C. (2002). *Media, Markets, and Democracy*. Cambridge: Cambridge University Press.

Baker, E. C. (2007). *Media Concentration and Democracy: Why Ownership Matters*. Cambridge: Cambridge University Press.

Bennett, W. L., Pickard, V. W., Iozzi, D. P., Schroeder, C. L., Lagos, T., & Caswell, E. C. (2004). Managing the Public Sphere: Journalistic Construction of the Great Globalization Debate. *International Communication Association, 54*(3), 437–455.

Bentele, G., Liebert, T., & Seeling, S. (1997). Von der Determination zur Intereffikation. Ein integriertes Modell zum Verhältnis von Public Relations und Journalismus. In G. Bentele & M. Haller (Eds.), *Aktuelle Entstehung von Öffentlichkeit. Akteure-Strukturen-Veränderungen* (pp. 225–250). Konstanz: UVK.

De Vreese, C. H., & Semetko, H. A. (2004). News Matters: Influences on the Vote in a Referendum Campaign. *European Journal of Political Research, 43*(5), 701–724.

Galtung, J., & Ruge, M. H. (1965). The Structure of Foreign News. *Journal of Peace Research, 2*(1), 64–91.

Gans, H. J. (1979). *Deciding What's News: A Study of CBS Evening News, NBC Nightly News, Newsweek, and Time*. New York: Pantheon Books.

Gerth, M., Rademacher, P., Pühringer, K., Dahinden, U., & Siegert, G. (2009). Challenges to Political Campaigns in the Media: Commercialization, Framing, and Personalization. *Studies in Communication Studies, 9*(1), 69–89.

Hallin, D. C., & Mancini, P. (2004). *Comparing Media Systems Three Models of Media and Politics*. Cambridge: Cambridge University Press.

Hänggli, R. (2012a). Key Factors in Frame Building—Model Specification. *American Behavioral Scientist*, Special Issue, 300–317.

Hänggli, R. (2012b). Key Factors in Frame-Building. In H. Kriesi (Ed.), *Political Communication in Direct Democratic Campaigns: Enlightening or Manipulating?* (pp. 125–142). Hampshire: Palgrave Macmillan.

Hänggli, R., & Kriesi, H. (2010). Political Framing Strategies and Their Impact on Media Framing in a Swiss Direct-Democratic Campaign. *Political Communication, 27*(2), 141–157.

Künzler, M. (2005). *Das schweizerische Mediensystem im Wandel: Herausforderungen, Chancen, Zukunftsperspektiven*. Bern: Haupt.

Lucht, J., & Udris, L. (2008). *Democracy in the Media Society: Changing Media Structures—Changing Political Communication?* Zurich: University of Zurich, Forschungsbereiche Öffentlichkeit und Gesellschaft (fög).

Marcinkowski, F. (2006). Mediensystem und politische Kommunikation. In U. Klöti, P. Knöpfel, H. Kriesi, W. Linder, Y. Papadopoulos, & P. Sciarini (Eds.), *Handbuch der Schweizer Politik* (4th ed., pp. 394–424). Zürich: NZZ-Verlag.

Marquis, L., Schaub, H.-P., & Gerber, M. (2011). The Fairness of Media Coverage in Question: An Analysis of Referendum Campaigns on Welfare State Issues in Switzerland. *Swiss Political Science Review, 17*(2), 128–163.

Meier, W. A. (2004). Switzerland. In M. Kelly, G. Mazzoleni, & D. McQuail (Eds.), *The Media in Europe* (pp. 248–260). London: Sage.

Price, V., & Tewksbury, D. (1997). News Values and Public Opinion: A Theoretical Account of Media Priming and Framing. In G. A. Barnett & F. J. Boster (Eds.), *Progress in Communication Sciences: Advances in Persuasion* (Vol. 13, pp. 173–212). Greenwich, CT: Ablex.

Schulz, W. (1976). *Die Konstruktion von Realität in den Nachrichtenmedien*. Freiburg and München: Verlag Karl Alber.

Schulz, W. (1997). *Politische Kommunikation theoretische Ansätze und Ergebnisse empirischer Forschung zur Rolle der Massenmedien in der Politik*. Opladen: Westdeutscher Verlag.

Sigal, L. (1973). *Reporters and Officials*. Lexington, MA: D.C. Heath.

Strömbäck, J., & Nord, L. W. (2006). Do Politicians Lead the Tango? A Study of the Relationship Between Swedish Journalists and Their Political Sources in the Context of Election Campaigns. *European Journal of Communication, 21*(2), 147–164.

Wolfsfeld, G. (1997). *Media and Political Conflict: News from the Middle East* (Reprint ed.). Cambridge, MA: Cambridge University Press.

CHAPTER 8

Role of Dialogue in Public Opinion Formation

INTRODUCTION

In this chapter, I show that the frames present in the news media are indeed present in the public opinion formation process of citizens. The extent to which a frame is used by other elites is defined as the strength of a frame in communication, whereas the strength of a frame in thought is measured through its relevance to the vote decision. The question that arises is whether the same frames are strong in both communication and in thought and whether the strong frames in communication cause the frames in thought to become strong? One purpose of this chapter is to answer these questions. The other is to look at the relative importance of the frames in thought for the vote decision in comparison with the partisan heuristic. I will be able to show that frames present in the news media are relevant for opinion formation. The same frames are strong in both communication and thought. In the asylum law and in the corporate tax reform, the core frames in communication even caused the frames in thought to become stronger over time (framing effect). Furthermore, frames in thought are also important when controlling for the partisan-based path of opinion formation. However, in the crucial case of ambivalence or low issue importance, partisan heuristics can be more influential.

© The Author(s) 2020
R. Hänggli, *The Origin of Dialogue in the News Media*,
Challenges to Democracy in the 21st Century,
https://doi.org/10.1007/978-3-030-26582-3_8

Strength of Frames in Communication

I have defined a *strong* frame in communication as a frame that *provokes a defensive reaction* by the opponents and/or that resonates in the media (Chapter 2). Credibility of source and cultural congruence of frame content (Chong and Druckman 2007a: 100) are preconditions for strong frames in communication. Indeed, political actors only promote frames with which they or their organizations have credibility and which are convincing, comprehensible, and culturally embedded (Chapter 4). Beyond these factors (with little variance in our cases), what others might be crucial to make a frame strong in communication? The strength of frames in communication might vary depending on the issue. I suggest that the complexity of an issue might weaken a frame, since complexity handicaps campaign dialogue. Political actors might have to explain further what the issue at stake is about before they can discuss each other's frames. Additionally, the numbers of main frames discussed per issue probably also affects the strength of the frames in communication. The more frames that are discussed, the weaker each of them is.

Strength of Frames in Thought

Traditionally, a strong frame when applied to frames in thought has been defined as one that is persuasive or *applicable* (Druckman 2009: 25). "Strong frames are those that emerge from public discussion as the best rationales for contending positions on the issue" (Chong and Druckman 2007b: 116). Frames in thought, also called *individual frames*, are "internal structures of the mind" (Kinder and Sanders 1990: 74). A person who reads a media frame might add some personal experience, forge links that are not explicitly made in the text or use another individual cognitive device to make sense of the political news. In other words, a frame in thought is the individual's cognitive understanding of a given situation (Goffman 1974). The precondition for a frame in thought to become strong (=applicable) is that it is *accessible* (=one is exposed to this frame) and *available* (=understandable) (Druckman 2009). Accessibility implies conscious information processing.

Ultimately, frame dialogue in the media is only relevant when it has an impact on opinion formation. In direct-democratic campaigns, it is probable that the strong frames in communication achieve the preconditions for strong frames in thought: The frames of direct-democratic campaigns are expected to be accessible because they are highly present in the media and to be available since they are strategically chosen by the campaigners. The campaigners are experienced and have a good understanding of the citizens' cognitive capacity and choose the frames accordingly. In addition, the media are not interested in transporting messages which cannot be understood by their readers. I also suggest that strong frames in communication do not merely reach the preconditions of a strong frame in thought, but really become applicable. My first hypothesis (H1) is therefore as follows: In direct-democratic campaigns, strong frames in communication are also strong frames in thought.

Framing Effects

I wish to ascertain whether the link between frames in communication and in thought is causal. When a frame in communication affects an individual's frame in thought, i.e., their cognitive understanding of a given situation and/or their opinion, it is called a *framing effect* (Druckman 2001). In direct-democratic campaigns, I expect the frames in communication to have a causal effect on the frames in thought (H2). The campaigns allow causal inferences to be drawn about direct-democratic campaign effects because they imply the intensification of information flow. A number of studies identify moderator variables of framing effects such as frame dialogue, predispositions, citizen deliberation, political information, and source credibility (Druckman 2001: 241). The first two factors seem to be the most relevant: Framing dialogue because the public debate among political elites is the "key engine driving the citizens' voting choices" (Kriesi 2005: 202), and predispositions because they are conceived as the "clearest limit on framing effects" (Chong and Druckman 2007b: 111). I will thus include these moderating factors as control variables in my analyses.

First, I will control for dialogue between different frames. Sniderman and Theriault (2004) find that people exposed to several frames are less prone to a framing effect (see also Chong and Druckman 2007a). Second, predispositions are also controlled for in the model. Voters might compare the information contained in a frame with their own predispositions and reject frames which contradict their predispositions (e.g., Shen and Edwards 2005). There are general (partisan) and issue-specific predispositions. General predispositions are partisan preferences, while the *issue-specific* predisposition is an issue-specific value, attitude, or policy core belief. This predisposition is linked to the substantive content of the specific choice at hand, such as the xenophobic predisposition in immigration issues or ideological commitments to the market economy (for the corporate tax reform). In order to take account of conflicting predispositions, I also take ambivalence into account in my analyses. In addition, I include a variable controlling for initially undecided voters. They have higher demands for information than voters who decide rather quickly (Eagly and Chaiken 1993) and might behave differently.

Partisan Heuristic Versus Systematic Processing

According to the dual-process theories in social psychology (Chaiken and Trop 1999; Eagly and Chaiken 1993), the general predisposition, i.e., the partisan preference, is very important. This approach distinguishes between two paths of individual opinion formation process: the frame-based (=systematic) path and the heuristic path. The main distinction between the two is based on the role played by frames. In systematic opinion formation, frames are important for the voting decision. It also entails conscious thinking and personal involvement (i.e., motivation and ability), both of them increasing the usage of the frame-based path (Druckman and Nelson 2003; Slothuus 2008). Frame-based voting has been shown to be reinforced by two key campaign characteristics—intense campaigns preceding the vote and familiar projects (Kriesi 2005). Intense campaigns increase frame-based voting because they reduce information hurdles for the voters (accessibility) and motivate voters to assess conflicting arguments (i.e., assess their applicability) (see Chong and Druckman 2007a). The familiarity of an issue increases the use of the frame-based path because it makes arguments easier to comprehend (availability). Since we are dealing with intense campaigns in all three cases, we expect differences only based on familiarity.

In contrast to the frame-based path of opinion formation, heuristic opinion formation is based on heuristic shortcuts. In this regard, partisan heuristic is a very important shortcut in general (e.g., Campbell et al. 1960), in elections (e.g., Lodge and Hamill 1986; Rahn 1993) and in direct-democratic campaigns (Kriesi 2005: 168; Selb et al. 2009; Colombo and Kriesi 2017; Boudreau and MacKenzie 2014; Bowler and Donovan 1998). It means that voters rely on recommendations made by partisan elites without necessarily paying attention to frames; it is their partisan preference (e.g., Slothuus 2010) or their social identity more generally (Achen and Bartels 2016; Mettler 2018) which influences their voting choice. Rahn (1993) and Cohen (2003) have shown how over-whelming the influence of party cues can be. Indeed, voters might even change their voting position and bring it in line with their favorite par-ty's position in order to be consistent. Several terms are used to describe this behavior, such as rationalization (Jacoby 1988), projection (Iyengar and Kinder 1987), persuasion (Brody and Page 1972), following (Lenz 2012), and issue opinion change (Lenz 2009). In all of these behaviors, the heuristic path dominates the frame-based (=systematic) path.

Overall, however, this is not the dominant way of forming opinions in direct-democratic campaigns. Kriesi (2005: 222), Boudreau and MacKenzie (2014), and Bullock (2011) claim that in situations where citizens meet a prepared debate, they also rely on the frame-based path. In these situations, people are provided with detailed information and with a pre-structured choice (pro or contra). In accordance with their findings, I expect the frame-based path to be important in direct-dem-ocratic votes, even when controlling for the partisan-based path (H3). Furthermore, I expect the importance of the frame-based path to vary depending on issue importance (H4). People interested in a topic are interested in arguments and more motivated to think about that topic. They are open to changing their issue position based on a change in argument position. In other words, they are persuadable (Lenz 2012). By contrast, people not interested in a topic rely more on the cue of their preferred party (as long as they know it) and either do not rely on arguments or rationalize (i.e., bring their voting positions in line with the position of their party). Other heuristics are the status quo heuris-tic, trust heuristic, and emotional heuristic. In the first, one wants to maintain the status quo, in the second, one relies on people who appear trustworthy (like a minister or an expert on a topic), while emotions are decisive in the third. Partisan heuristic is the most important heuristic in the case of direct-democratic campaigns.

Typically, partisan and issue-specific orientations tend to be consist-ently aligned in the individual's mind, but this is not always the case. To the extent that voters are aware of a mismatch between their parti-san and their issue-specific orientations, they are likely to be ambivalent with respect to their voting choice (Alvarez and Brehm 1995, 2002; Rudolph 2005; Steenbergen and Brewer 2004; Selb et al. 2009). In this case, the voter has some grounds to favor the policy and other grounds to oppose it. As Steenbergen and Brewer (2004) point out, most people probably do not care about conflicting predispositions, until they realize that they imply different meanings for their position on a particular policy. Campaigns, being rich in information, are likely to draw people's attention to such conflicting predispositions and open the possibility for exploiting them. Thus, it is important to control for ambivalence. Since I generally expect different effects for the initially undecided voters, I will also include control variables for these voters.

In the following, I will discuss methods and then investigate the strength of the frames in communication and in thought. I will first present the results for strength of frames in communication. Second, I shall compare it to the commonly used measure of a strong frame, i.e., the strength of frames in thought. Third, I will investigate the extent to which the strength of frames in thought increase over time (framing effect). In order to gauge the strength of frames and the framing effects, I will control for dialogue among the frames, partisan orientation (i.e., the voters' general predisposition), issue-specific orientation (i.e., the voters' predisposition linked to the substantive content of the specific choice at hand), ambivalence, and indecision. Fourth, I will explore the relative importance of the frame-based (=systematic) path of opinion formation process in comparison with the partisan-based (=heuristic) path.

OPERATIONALIZATION AND METHODS

The strength of the frames in communication is operationalized by the opponents' defensive reactions with respect to a given frame, i.e., by the shares of the opponents' counter-arguments, averaged across the frames in the media input and the media frames (Hänggli and Kriesi 2010). To provide an example for the calculation: The pro camp in the asylum law counter-framed (=defensive use of the argument) the "humanitarian tradition" frame with a share of 20.3% in the media input and attained a news media share of 12.6% with it. The average of the two numbers is 16.5%, i.e., the strength of this frame (Table 8.1). The maximum is 100%, which would indicate that the actor defensively speaks only about his or her opponents' frame, while the minimum is 0%. The importance of the frames as assessed by the campaigners will be used to evaluate the measure for the strength of frames in communication. In the interviews, all campaigners were asked to name the three least important arguments

Table 8.1 Strength of the frames in communication

		Asylum		*Naturalization*		*Corporation tax*	
Contra	Core frame	Human. trad.	16.5	Rule-of-law	19.1	Tax equity	11.4
	2nd frame	Rule-of-law	6.9			Tax loss	8.3
Pro	Core frame	Abuse	16.9	People final say	20.2	SME	7.7
	2nd frame	Efficacy	5.8	Mass naturalization	14.1	Competitiveness	13.0

Note Strength of frames in communication is operationalized by the *opponents'* defensive reactions with respect to a given frame, i.e., by the shares of the opponents' counter-frames, averaged over the frames in the media input and the frames in the news media

from a list of ten arguments.[1] Mentions as "unimportant" are coded as "0," while all other mentions are coded as "1" (=important). For each argument, a summary indicator reflects the number of times it was mentioned by the other respondents as important. Since the campaigners normally consider their own arguments as more important, this low threshold of importance is used here.

Empirically, the strength of frames in thought is established by asking individuals to rate the persuasiveness of various frames in communication, on a particular issue. Since this measure is not at my disposal, I will use reasons mentioned spontaneously by citizens for their vote choice in the official voting analysis (VOX) conducted in the two weeks after the vote. Additionally, I will use the respondents' positions[2] on the different frames and measure the impact those positions have on the voting choice. The stronger the corresponding effect, the more important the frame, i.e., the stronger the corresponding frame in thought. The strength of frames in thought is measured at a certain point in time, at the end of the campaign. To analyze framing effects, I use the same model but look at differences over time. I will speak of a framing effect to signify the *significant increase* in the impact of a frame over time. The variable to be explained in the model predicting vote choice corresponds to the vote intention prior to the vote and the vote choice after the vote,

---

[1] The exact question was: "Which of the ten arguments from the list (shown to the campaigner) do you conceive as the three most important, as the single most important, and the three least important?" I do not use the evaluation of the most and the three most important arguments here.

[2] The specific questionnaire item reads as follows (for the humanitarian tradition frame, for example): "On a scale from 0 (completely disagree) to 5 (completely agree), how much do you agree with the argument: The humanitarian tradition must be maintained?"

respectively (I will refer to both simply as vote choice in the following). This variable distinguishes the supporters of the propositions (coded as 1) from both their opponents and the undecided voters (coded as 0).[3] For the group of the initially undecided voters, a dummy variable is introduced that takes into account the effects attributable to this group. It takes the value of 1 for those who were undecided at the beginning of the campaign and 0 otherwise. The voting choice will be estimated based on the position of the different frames. The model makes full use of the panel structure of the data.

The model controls for frame dialogue, partisan and issue preference, ambivalence, and indecision. Frame dialogue is controlled by using different frames at the same time. There are three variables in the model (β_1, β_2, and β_3) based on predispositions: one each for the two key predispositions and one for ambivalence. It is important to note that the two predispositions were measured only once, at the beginning of the campaign. Following Tillie (1995) and Van der Eijk et al. (2006), the partisan predispositions are operationalized on the basis of propensity scores, i.e., a set of questions asking the respondents to indicate how likely it is that they will ever vote for each of the five major Swiss parties. The responses range from "will never vote for this party" (score 0) to "will certainly vote for this party at some time in the future" (score 10). Based on this information, both parties and voters were mapped onto a single latent continuum using a non-parametric multiple unidimensional unfolding technique (see Coombs 1964; Van Schuur 1993). Using voters' preference orderings among parties, non-parametric unfolding models rank both parties and voters on a latent dimension.[4] Subsequently, the party ordering can be tested against the null hypothesis that the parties are not represented along the latent scale in terms of their rank in the unfoldable order. The unfolding model unveils a rank ordering of

---

[3] For the vote intentions, the specific questionnaire item reads as follows: "If there were a ballot tomorrow, would you be strongly in favor, rather in favor, rather against or strongly against the toughening of the asylum law?" Being (strongly or rather) in favor of the proposition is coded as 1, and being undecided or (rather or strongly) against as 0. For the vote choice, the questionnaire item reads: "How did you vote? Did you agree with or reject the asylum law?" Again, agreement is coded as 1 and non-decision and rejection as 0.

[4] Respondents who do not attribute a utility higher than five to any of the six parties, plus the (very few) respondents who attribute equal preference to all of the parties, are considered not to have any particular partisan predisposition and, accordingly, are dropped from the analysis. I have used MUDFOLD 4.0 for my analysis (see, Van Schuur and Post 1998).

the five parties from left to right, which matches conventional agreement (GPS, SPS, CVP, FDP, and SVP) and corresponds to the assumption of unidimensionality for all three campaigns.

The measure for the issue-specific predisposition depends on the type of proposition. Xenophobia, the issue-specific predisposition for the asylum and naturalization campaigns, is measured by a set of questions about the perception of threats caused by foreigners.[5] For the corporation tax, the issue-specific predisposition score is intended to measure the individual's stakes in the market economy.[6] The ambivalence measure is the product of a respondent's score on the partisan predisposition scale and the negatively signed issue-specific predisposition scale.[7] Thus, ambivalent voters (e.g., xenophobic voters on the left or non-xenophobic voters on the right) receive high scores on the ambivalence measure. These voters observe a mismatch between their predispositions and are cross-pressured with regard to their vote choice. They resolve their ambivalence by following their partisan predisposition or by sticking to their issue-specific orientation. How they resolve their ambivalence depends on the issue. If the issue is central to a party, party loyalty is critical. By contrast, if the issue touches the core of the voter's specific predisposition, issue-specific preferences are more important.

---

[5] The five statements concerned individual safety threat ("I am afraid of increasing violence and vandalism in my neighborhood by foreigners"), individual economic threat ("I am afraid that my economic prospects will get worse because of foreigners"), collective safety threat ("I am afraid of increasing violence and vandalism in Swiss society by foreigners"), collective cultural threat ("These days, I am afraid that the Swiss culture is threatened by foreigners"), and collective economic threat ("I am afraid that the economic prospects of Swiss society will get worse because of foreigners"). With regard to partisan predispositions, these questions were only asked once, at the beginning of the campaign, since my aim is to determine the extent to which voters converge on their pre-campaign issue-specific predispositions.

[6] The questions were part of a battery that asked for the kind of country the respondents preferred. Each item asked the recipient to choose between polar contrasts: "Please tell me what kind of Switzerland you prefer: a Switzerland… a) …with more state interventions in the economy, or with more market competition; b)…that places more emphasis on solidarity, or on individual responsibility; c)…with large income differences, or small income differences?" Each item was measured on a five-point scale, ranging from strong agreement with the first part to strong agreement with the second part of the item.

[7] The most common measures used for ambivalence are the multiplicative measure used here (see Keele and Wolak 2008: 680), and Griffin's ambivalence index (or a modified version of this index) (see Steenbergen and Brewer 2004: 103f.).

The framing coefficients (β_4 and β_5, see below) refer to the effects of the frames on the vote at different points in time. Since I have a binary dependent variable and the responses of voters in a panel are not independent of each other (Rabe-Hesketh and Skrondal 2005: 247), I use a random intercept probit model, which takes the following form:

$$\text{vote}_{it} = (\alpha + u_i) + \beta_1 \text{ip}_i + \beta_2 \text{pp}_i + \beta_3 \text{amb}_i + \sum_j (\alpha_j + \beta_{4j}\text{fc}_{ij} + \beta_{5j}\text{fp}_i)$$
$$+ \sum_k (\alpha_k + \beta_{6k}\text{ip}_i + \beta_{7k}\text{pp}_i + \beta_{8k}\text{amb}_i) + \beta_9 \text{un}_i$$
$$+ \sum_k \text{un}_i * (\beta_{10k}\text{ip}_i + \beta_{11k}\text{pp}_i + \beta_{12k}\text{amb}_i) + v_i$$

where "vote" is a dichotomous indicator, either the vote intention or vote at time t, "ip" is the respondent's issue-specific predisposition, "pp" his or her partisan predisposition, "amb" stands for ambivalence, "fc" the respondent's position on the contra frames (one or two frames), "fp" the respondent's position on the pro frames (two frames), and "un" for undecided. The index j refers to all-time points in the campaign, whereas the index k refers only to later time points in the campaign—the midpoint (only in the case of the asylum law—in the other two campaigns we conducted only a two-panel wave) and the endpoints. The index i refers to respondent i.

To analyze further the importance of the frame-based path (Tables 8.4 and 8.5), I rely on the persuasion test by Lenz (2012: 253f.). Persuasion refers to a change in argument position, that is a change in x, that causes, all things being equal, a change in the vote intention, y. We can apply this test only in panels with at least three waves. The asylum case meets this criterion. We examine whether persuasion between the first two interviews leads to changes in vote intention between the second and the third waves. I apply this model (y: vote intention, x: argument position, ip: Issue predisposition, s: sex, edu: education, pi: party identification (SVP, FDP/LPS, CVP, SP, Greens):

$$y_{w3} = \rho_{w1} y_{w1} + \Delta_{y21}(y_{w2} - y_{w1}) + a\text{ip}_{w1} + b s_{w1} + c \text{edu}_{w1}$$
$$+ d\text{pi}_{w1} + \Delta_{x21}(x_{w2} - x_{w1}) + e_{w1} x_{w1} + \mu_{w3}$$

The key test is whether prior changes in argument positions $x_{w2}-x_{w1}$, lead to change in vote intentions y_{w3}. If they do, Δ_{x21} will be different from zero. If it is, we can assume that argument positions matter. Since I expect the persuasion effect to depend on how important the issue is for a person and whether she or he knows the partisan position, I select the observations based on these criteria.

RESULTS

Strength of Frames in Communication

We know from Chapter 4 that the strategic actors search for a frame that they believe has the capacity to become a strong substantive frame. Are the frames most promoted indeed strong frames? I address this aspect next. The strength of frames in communication in the three campaigns is presented in Table 8.1. As this measure shows, in the asylum law campaign, the "humanitarian tradition" frame, which is the most important frame of the contra camp, turns out to have been more or less equally strong as the core frame of the pro camp—the "abuse" frame. Both frames were counter-attacked by the other camp in one in six arguments. The other frames of the two camps, i.e., "rule-of-law" and "efficacy," still provoked a defensive reaction in the opponent's camp, but to a much more limited extent. In the naturalization campaign, the "rule-of-law" frame proved to be more or less equally strong as the "people final say" frame, which was the main frame of the pro camp. The second frame of the pro camp, "mass naturalization," is also relatively strong. This might go back to the strategic framing change of the pro camp. In the political *advertisements*, the pro camp changed the strategy (Chapter 5). Instead of the "people final say" frame, they relied on the "mass naturalization" frame toward the end of the campaign because the campaigners received feedback from their activists indicating that the "people final say" frame was not convincing. In the corporate tax reform, the "competitiveness" frame is the strongest, despite the fact that it is only the second most important frame of the pro camp. The main frame of the pro camp, the "SME" (small and medium enterprises) frame, is found to be the weakest frame in communication (not in thought) of the whole campaign. This is a result of the fact that, as a valence argument connecting to positive emotions, it remained less controversial during the debate. Almost everyone agrees that SMEs are a good thing, so in a complex issue, other frames are more controversial and therefore stronger in communication. As we saw in Chapter 4, one organization avoided the SME argumentation line altogether. I argued that valence arguments referring to positive emotions are counter-framed less because they are more difficult to successfully rebut. The strength of a frame in communication measures its potential to have a cognitive effect on frames in thought. It does not, however, include the non-cognitive effects like the direct effect of emotions on vote choice. I will discuss below how positive emotions had a direct effect

Table 8.2 Share of political actors who assessed their opponents' arguments as important

		Asylum		Naturalization		Corporation tax	
Contra	Core frame	Human. trad.	91.7	Rule-of-law	62.5	Tax equity	52.9
	2nd frame	Rule-of-law	33.3			Tax loss	58.8
Pro	Core frame	Abuse	78.8	People final say	83.3	SME	76.9
	2nd frame	Efficacy	72.7	Mass naturalization	50.0	Competitiveness	76.9

in this campaign (Wirth et al. 2010). The second strongest frame was the core frame of the contra camp ("tax equity"). Comparing the three cases, we generally see that the frames in the naturalization campaign were the strongest, while the frames in the corporate tax reform campaign were the weakest. This is in line with my idea that both the number of main frames and the complexity of an issue reduce the strength of a frame: In the asylum law and in the corporate tax reform, there were four main frames, whereas in the other case, I found three main frames (Chapter 4). The corporate tax reform was the most complex issue.

Table 8.2 shows the share of the political actors who evaluated their opponents' frames as important. This assessment by the campaigners lends support to my measure of strength: First, the core frames are considered to be stronger than the second main frame, with 52–91% of the political actors perceiving their opponents' core frame as important and only 33–76% evaluating their opponents' second frame as important for the campaign. Second, the "SME" frame is also not evaluated as stronger than the "competitiveness" frame. Contrary to the strength measure, the "tax loss" frame is moderately stronger than the "tax equity" frame. We will return to this aspect below. In contrast to the strength measure showed in Table 8.1, there is no variation between the campaigns in the evaluation by the campaigners.

The analyses conducted so far provide a tool for the strength of frames in communication. Based on my measure, it can be noted that in direct-democratic campaigns, the strongest and second main frames together elicit a defensive reaction by other elites in every fourth argument.

Strength of Frames in Thought

To assess the strength of frames in thought, I will begin by exploring whether the frames in communication were accessible to the citizens.

This is a precondition for frames to become strong in thought. In the interviews, participants were asked whether they had heard of ten different arguments.[8] It might be argued that the way this question was asked (only passive agreement needed) makes the frames inherently accessible for the respondents. While this criticism cannot be completely denied, as 90% of the Swiss electorate considers direct-democratic campaigns as important or very important (Kriesi and Trechsel 2008: 66), the results do not seem implausible. Figure 8.1 shows the proportion of respondents who stated they had heard of the respective frames. There are two graphs for each campaign. On the left-hand side, the graphs show the proportion of *contra* voters who had access to the frame. On the right-hand side of the figure, the graphs illustrate the share of *pro* voters who were exposed to it. The graphs show that, first of all, more than 85% of the respondents in the asylum law and naturalization campaigns had heard of the frames at the end of the campaign (panel wave = 3), whereas in the corporate tax reform, only a little more than 70% had heard of them by the end of the campaign. The graphs also show that in the asylum campaign, around 80% of the respondents had already heard the arguments at the beginning of the campaign (panel wave = 1), whereas the campaign effect is stronger in the other two campaigns. It is important to note that access to the arguments does not seem to be influenced by the position of the voter. The same arguments are most accessible for contra and pro voters in all three campaigns, followed by the other core argument.

The graph shows that the precondition of accessibility is fulfilled. For those voters who did not have access to the core arguments, it can already be stated that the framing effects, which I will discuss later, are insignificant (not shown). This lends support to Nelson et al.'s (1997) and Druckman's (2009) idea that accessibility is a precondition for applicability. As I do not have data for the availability of the frames, I will turn to applicability next.

I investigate applicability in two ways. On the one hand, I look at reasons for vote decisions, and on the other hand, the influences of frame positions on vote decisions are presented when controlling for other factors. Table 8.3 lists reasons for vote choice. It shows, first of all, that

---

[8]The exact question was (example for the humanitarian tradition frame): "There have been different opinions with regard to the asylum law. In the following, I will read aloud some arguments. Could you please indicate with 'yes', 'no', or 'don't know' whether you have ever heard of them in the current debate: 'The humanitarian tradition must be maintained'?"

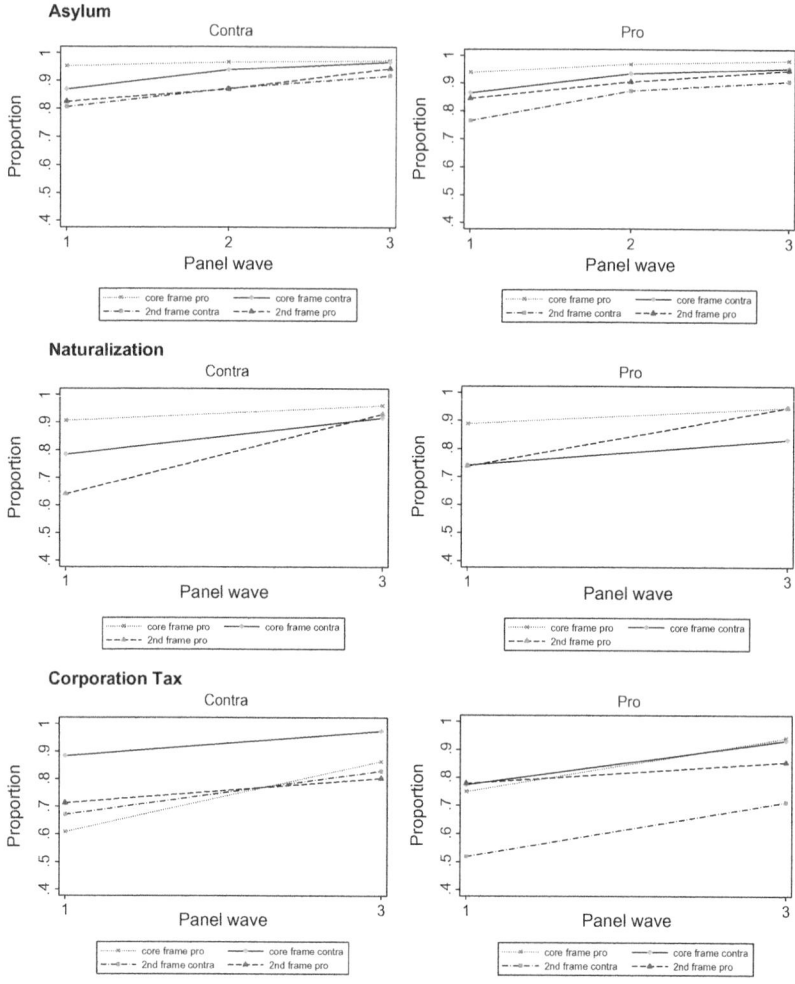

Fig. 8.1 Accessibility of frames in thought

the frames promoted by political actors and presented in the news media are also the important frames for the voting choice! For each campaign and camp, the frame most promoted is the reason most frequently mentioned. In the asylum law campaign, the second frame of the contra camp (rule-of-law) is absent. In this case, the frame did not become strong in thought. In the corporate tax reform, in line with the strategy of the

Table 8.3 Reasons for vote decision

Reasons (arguments)	Reasons (frame)	Percentage
Asylum Law		
Reasons for No		
Human dignity/human rights/ principle of humanity in danger	Humanitarian tradition	44
Taking a harder line on tackling the problems in the asylum system is ineffective	Abuse defensive	34
Other (diverse other arguments) and affected by law	Others and heuristic (emotions)	17
General negative statements	Heuristic (emotions)	11
Politically motivated	Heuristic (partisan)	5
Recommendation (e.g., party)	Heuristic (partisan)	4
Reasons for Yes		
The abuse of asylum policy must be stopped	Abuse	62
Application/implementation pro arguments in general	Efficacy	11
Other (diverse other arguments)	Other	13
Recommendation (e.g., party)	Heuristic (partisan)	6
Naturalization		
Reasons for No		
This initiative brings discriminatory and arbitrary naturalization decisions	Rule-of-law	85
Politically motivated	Heuristic (partisan)	31
General statements (initiative is negative, system of today works well)	Heuristic (emotions and status quo)	29
This poll damages the image of Switzerland	Other—image frame	8
Other reasons	Other	5
Reasons for Yes		
Each municipality should decide by itself which authority is responsible for naturalization	People final say	61
Mass naturalization has to be stopped	Mass naturalization	46
General statement (initiative is positive)	Heuristic (emotions)	21
Court appeals against naturalization decisions should be forbidden	Rule-of-law defensive	19
Recommendation (party, others)	Heuristic (partisan)	15
Corporation Tax		
Reasons for No		
A tax relief for major shareholders is unfair	Tax equity	42
General reasons (is a bad proposal)	Heuristic (emotion)	22
This reform addresses the wrong point: The companies not the shareholders should be given tax relief	Competitiveness defensive	20
No SME promotion	SME defensive	17

(continued)

Table 8.3   (continued)

Reasons (arguments)	Reasons (frame)	Percentage
Personally not affected by law, I will not profit from this law	Heuristic (emotions)	17
This reform brings unacceptable tax losses for Federal government or cantons, and other tax loss arguments	Tax loss	11
Reasons for Yes		
This tax reform advances SMEs	SME and heuristic (emotions)	74
This reform addresses the correct point, namely reduction of taxes for shareholders	Competitiveness	29
General (good proposal)	Heuristic (emotions)	26
Double taxation (as profit for companies and as dividend income for shareholders) is unfair/should be reduced	Tax equity defensive	17
Personally affected by law	Heuristic (emotions)	14
Recommendation of federal council/minister	Heuristic (partisan)	7

Note Multiple answers possible. Open question asking for vote choice. *Source* Vox Analysis

pro camp, the SME (core pro) frame was the most important frame for yes voters. In the case of the tax loss frame, the pro camp tried strategically to keep this frame out of the debate. It seems that this strategy was quite successful, as the tax loss frame remained rather a weak frame in thought for the no voters. Furthermore, in all the campaigns, we see counter-frames (defensive frames) as reasons for vote decisions. This shows that campaigners riposte successfully. For yes voters in the asylum law and for no voters in the naturalization initiative, no counter-frames appear as reasons for their vote decision. In the asylum law, the pro camp successfully integrated the "humanitarian tradition" in the "abuse" frame. It seems that the "humanitarian tradition" frame was not a strong frame in thought for the yes voters. Future research must analyze whether successful trespassing is a means to refute an argument. In the naturalization initiative, no voters voted strategically (politically motivated).

Second, the partisan heuristic played a role in all campaigns but was particularly important in the naturalization initiative. Almost a third of citizens were politically motivated to vote no. Their no vote is a reaction against the right-wing party (SVP) and its campaign, not necessarily a statement against the initiative (Engeli et al. 2008). Among the yes voters, political motivation was no factor. However, the partisan heuristic was also present. Almost every sixth voter relied on the recommendation of her or his preferred party. To a minor extent, we find politically motivated people also among no voters in the asylum law. They wanted to support left parties and to criticize the right-wing party (SVP) and its minister and leading figure Christoph Blocher, independently of the proposal.

Third, *general* agreement or disagreement with the proposal and people who *feel* (not) *affected* by the law play a role in the naturalization initiative and the corporate tax reform. I summarize these types of reasons as emotional heuristics. It is a heuristic way of making sense of the information available to citizens. In the naturalization initiative, a general (dis)agreement is linked to the partisan heuristic. Some people abstained from systematic information processing because of the conflict among the SVP and the new minister Eveline Widmer-Schlumpf. In the corporate tax reform, it is linked to emotions directly regarding the taxation policy in question. When looking at partisan heuristics below (Fig. 8.4), we will come back to this aspect.

In order to further analyze the strength of frames in thought, the predicted vote is modeled dependent on the framing position and controlling for frame dialogue, partisan preference, issue preference, ambivalence, and indecision. The relevant framing coefficients are presented in Table 8.4 (for result of full model, see Appendix Table A.6). The results show the following: The effects of all the arguments are significant at the 5% level. The coefficients show the effect of the respondents' position on the vote intention. The relationship is as expected: The more a voter holds a contra position, the more he or she is inclined to vote "no," whereas the opposite is true for the pro arguments. Thus, the results support the idea that the frames present in the news media are strong in thought. The significant frame coefficients show that frames are important in direct-democratic campaigns and the voters are "largely capable of handling the task of direct-democratic voting. It may be that they do not use the best arguments one could use for the task at hand; they still make systematic use of the most important arguments provided by the political elites for their voting choice" (Kriesi 2005: 223). The effects are strongest in the asylum law, whereas they are weakest in the naturalization initiative. The conflict among the parties reduced the importance of frames in the naturalization campaign. We see below that the coefficients in the corporate tax reform are weaker than in the asylum law, possibly because heuristics are involved. All other things being equal, the effect of the SME frame (core frame pro) is smaller in Table 8.4 than the percentage shown in Table 8.3 would indicate. Obviously, when analyzing different influence factors at the same time, the SME frame becomes weaker. It is still strong but not

Table 8.4   Influence of frame position on vote intention as measure for frames in thought

	Asylum			Naturalization			Corporation tax		
	Coef.	s.e.	P > z	Coef.	s.e.	P > z	Coef.	s.e.	P > z
Core frame contra t3	−0.451	0.100	***	−0.232	0.066	***	−0.229	0.057	***
2nd frame contra t3	−0.353	0.103	**				−0.331	0.057	***
Core frame pro t3	0.521	0.095	***	0.351	0.068	***	0.465	0.066	***
2nd frame pro t3	0.511	0.095	***	0.233	0.068	***	0.507	0.073	***

Note The whole model is presented in Table A.6. Coefficients at the end of the campaign (t3)

dominatingly strong. The result here is more similar to the measure of strength of frames in communication than the result in Table 8.3. I will come back to this when discussing Fig. 8.4. Interestingly, pro frames have a bigger impact on the vote intention than contra frames, particularly in the economic issue. Pro arguments may have been more influential as they addressed immediate (e.g., the advancement of investments and creation of new jobs in the corporation tax) instead of alleged long-term (e.g., potential negative long-term effects for the social insurance system in the corporation tax) consequences of the reform (see also Kühne et al. 2011).

Framing Effects

The development of frame strength is addressed next in Fig. 8.2.[9] The predicted vote is shown in relation to the framing position and controlling for partisan preference, issue preference, ambivalence, and, where necessary, also undecidedness (see Appendix Table A.6). There is one graph for each frame. The impact of a frame should become stronger over time in the case of a framing effect. In the asylum law, the effects do indeed become stronger over time. With the exception of the "rule-of-law" (2nd contra) frame, the difference in frame strength between wave one and wave two/three is significant.[10] This means that the frames

[9] These illustrations are based on the model used for Table A.6. I used the variables relevant for the specific time point and set the other variables at their means.

[10] The point estimates for the linear combination for the difference in frame strength between two time points provide the following results:

Human. trad. frame: (t2)−(t1): $z=-3.24$, $P>z=0.001$, (t3)−(t1): $z=-3.72$, $P>z=0.000$, (t3)−(t2): $z=-0.98$, $P>z=0.329$.

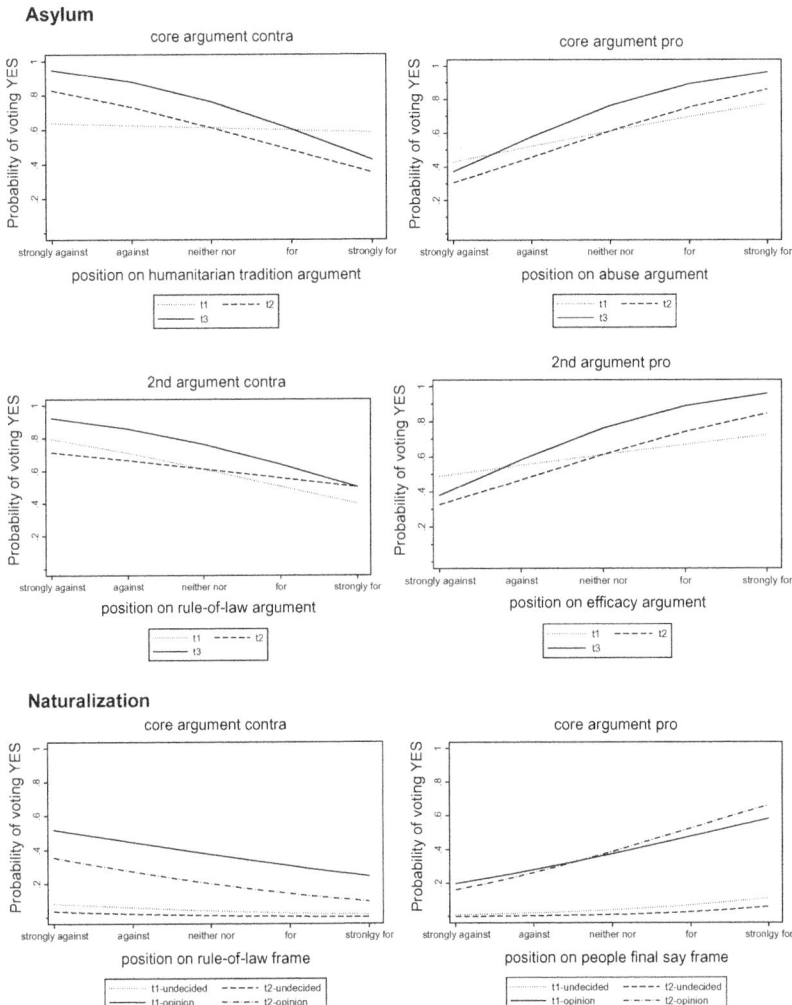

Fig. 8.2 Framing effects: graphical representation of the impact of frame position on the voting choice and its variation over time

Abuse frame: (t2)–(t1): $z = 1.76$, $P > z = 0.078$, (t3)–(t1): $z = 2.64$, $P > z = 0.008$, (t3)–(t2): 1.03, $P > z = 0.301$.

Efficacy frame: (t2)–(t1): 2.38, $P > z = 0.017$, (t3)–(t1): $z = 3.32$, $P > z = 0.001$, (t3)–(t2): 1.24, $P > z = 0.215$.

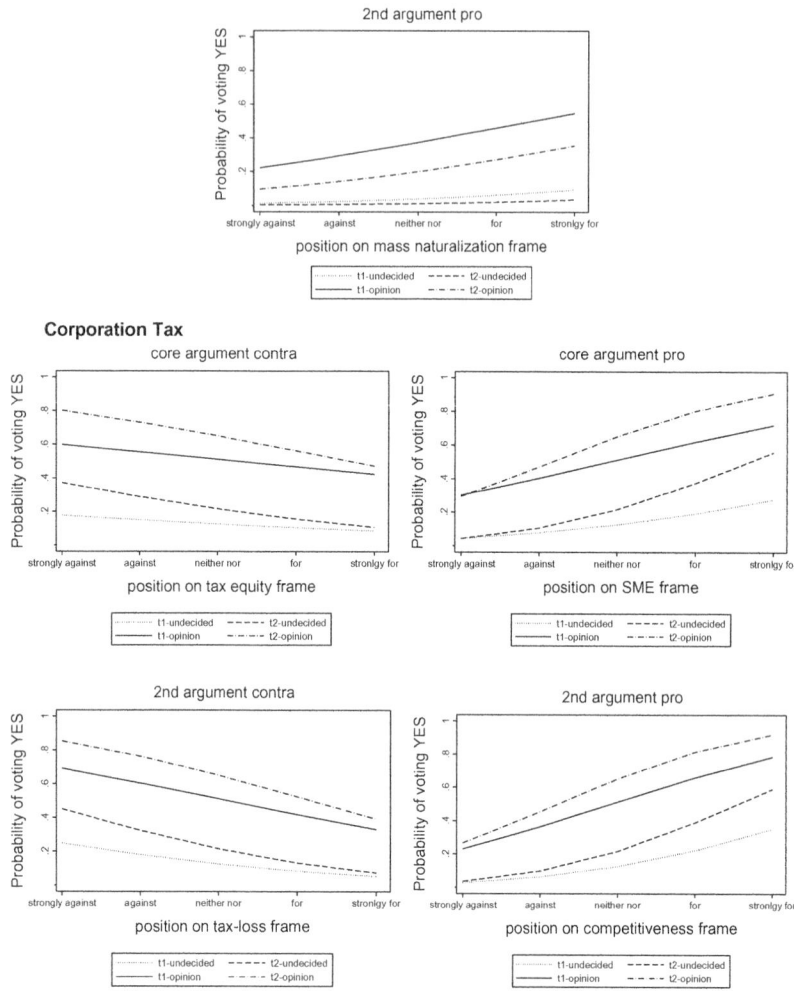

Fig. 8.2 (continued)

in communication caused the frames in thought to become stronger. We see a framing effect between the first and the second/third waves. Furthermore, it also shows that the framing effect did not increase between the second and the third waves.

In the naturalization initiative, however, the frame strength does not grow over time. Therefore, in this campaign we cannot speak of a framing effect. It is plausible that the conflict about the new justice minister (Eveline Widmer-Schlumpf) distracted voters from the substance of the debate. Nevertheless, decided voters in favor of the pro frame were still more inclined to vote "yes," whereas decided voters who were in favor of the contra frame rather voted "no." Undecided voters were uninfluenced by the frames. Even though there is no framing effect, we can see a campaign effect in the graphs of the core frame contra and the second frame pro. We see that the curves for the decided voters drop from t1 to t3. At the beginning, the respondents were more inclined to vote "yes" than at the end; this is a campaign effect and can be explained through the late start of the campaign. At the beginning, a third of voters were unfamiliar with the issue and the partisan preferences were unknown. In addition, the initiative was called "for democratic naturalizations," which may have been misleading and skewed initial inclinations. The positive title of the initiative probably increased the share of voters favoring the proposal at the beginning. With regard to the strategy of the pro camp emphasizing a different frame toward the end of the campaign, we note no impact. The change of main frame did not make a difference. This is not surprising when voters did not rely on frames that much anyway.

In the corporate tax reform, the strength of frames again increases over time. However, the framing effect is only significant for the SME frame.[11] The effect of the tax equity frame (core contra) is underestimated because of the undecided voters. This can be demonstrated by a model (shown in the Appendix Table A.7) that includes interaction terms between undecided voters and the framing positions. Figure 8.3 shows the results graphically. First, we can see that the tax equity frame becomes much stronger in t3 than it was previously. The respective coefficient in t3 in this model is -0.542 and the difference to t1 is very significant.[12] Thus, with the interaction term, the framing effect of the tax equity frame is very strong and very significant. Indeed, it is now stronger than the second frame. This result shows a campaign effect: The left-wing party successfully claimed that the tax cuts were an unfair privilege for the well-off and went against the principle of fair taxation (tax equity frame). Second, the undecided voters (t3) *in favor of the tax*

[11] SME frame: $(t2)-(t1)$: $z = 2.3$, $P > z = 0.022$.
[12] Tax equity frame: $(t2)-(t1)$: $z = 4.35$, $P > z = 0.000$.

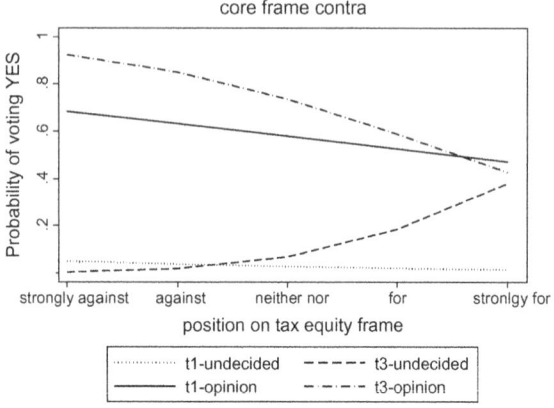

Fig. 8.3 Corporation tax: impact of core contra frame (tax equity) on the vote decision, in consideration of the interaction effect between undecided voters and frame position

equity frame were more inclined to vote "yes" than those with the contra position on this frame. The coefficient is positive (0.994) and very significant. This goes back to the argument of the pro camp claiming that double taxation is unfair.

I would like finally to address a note of concern: With only one exception, the frames in thought have been shown to be already influential at the beginning of the campaigns (coefficients at t1, Table A.6). Respondents might have known the frames from preliminary phases of signature collection or from the parliamentary process. However, it cannot be denied that this finding goes back to a method artifact stemming from the way we collected it. In order to measure strength of frames in thought, we rely on argument positions. Many people are able to position themselves on an argument, before they are able to link arguments and issue. If we were to ask them about their vote intention and then ask about their reason(s) openly, we would see more growth in influence of frames over time. As a consequence, actual changes in terms of framing effects are more limited over time due to our measurement. In the same way, accessibility is also rather easy to achieve. It was asked in a closed form by reading out loud the argument and asking people whether they have heard of the argument. If people were asked to actively state the arguments, accessibility would be much lower.

Partisan Heuristic Versus Systematic Processing

Figure 8.4 presents the voting choice for different partisan preferences and positions on the frames. For the sake of simplicity, all frames were combined into one factor on each side: a pro frames factor and a contra frames factor.[13] This figure allows us to gauge the importance of the frame-based path in comparison with the partisan path: The slope of a curve shows the importance of the frame-based path, whereas the width between the three curves is relevant for the importance of the partisan path.[14] The general impression provided by this figure is that both frames and partisan heuristics are important in determining the voting choice (the curves are not flat, nor do they converge on one curve). The third hypothesis is confirmed: The frame-based path is important in direct-democratic votes, even when controlling for and in comparison with the partisan-based path. The relative importance varies between pro and contra frame and between the campaigns.

In the asylum law campaign, the partisan logic played a role for both sides. For the supporters of the contra frames, the partisan logic was more important than the frames. For instance, a voter attached to right-wing parties who strongly agreed on the contra frames was inclined to vote "yes" with a probability of 0.63.[15] This finding is attributable to the successful strategy of the pro camp, which made use of a double-edged argument by endorsing the concern advanced by their adversaries. In a first step, they pointed out that they were strongly in favor of the humanitarian tradition of Switzerland. In a second step, they maintained that the revised law would strengthen this claim because it would help fight against abuse, thereby helping those asylum seekers who really deserved protection. We see a different pattern on the other side. The supporters of the pro frames voted yes independently of their partisan preferences. For this group of voters, the frame-based path was clearly more important than the heuristic path—in such a way that even a voter from the left, favoring the pro frames, had a predicted probability of

---

[13] All campaign arguments were jointly included in one factor analysis.

[14] Based on the partisan predisposition scores, I coded left as including Green and Social Democrat voters, moderate right as in-between voters favoring Christian Democrats and Liberals, and conservative right as including voters favoring the People's Party.

[15] The predicted probabilities are calculated for decided voters at the end of the campaign with mean values on remaining variables.

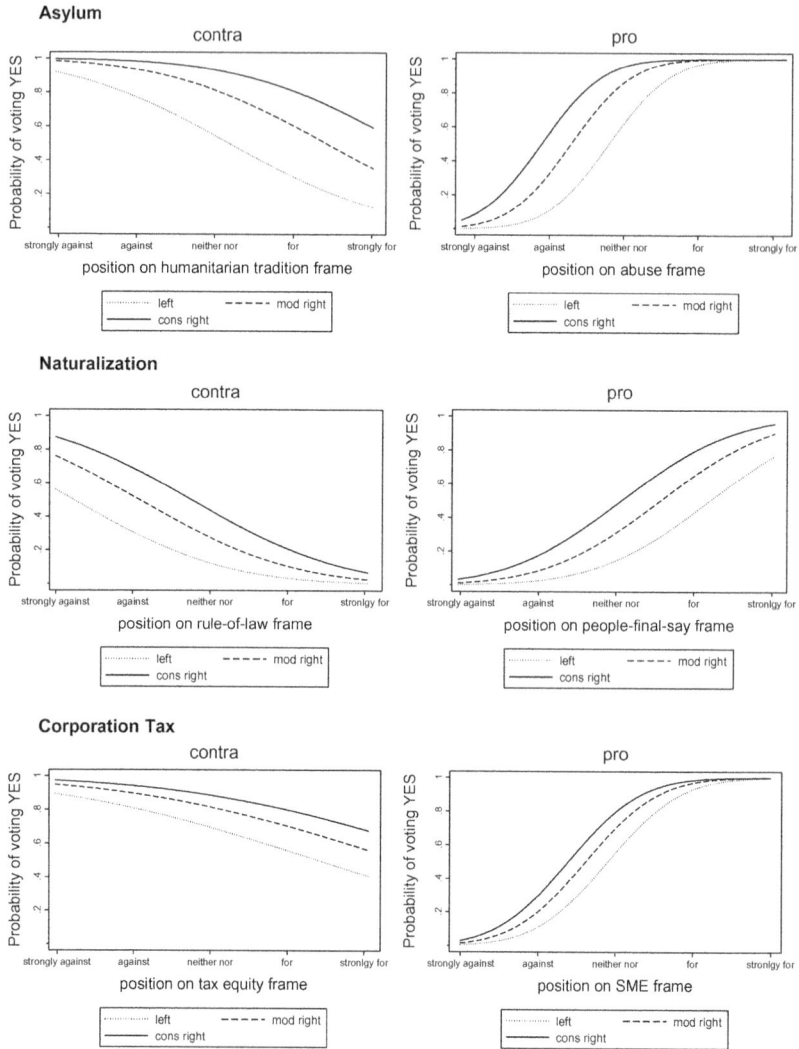

Fig. 8.4 The combined impact of frame-based and partisan-based paths: vote choice (t=end of the campaign) for different political preferences for decided voters

voting yes of 0.99. This result derives from the strength of the "abuse" frame. Moreover, issue familiarity might also have increased the relevance of the frame-based path. In the naturalization campaign, frame-based choice and partisan path were both important. For instance, a left voter who was strongly in favor of the pro frames was inclined to vote "yes" with a probability of 0.71. If he or she did not strongly favor the pro frames, but still favored them nevertheless, the probability decreased to 0.39. If he or she was a right-wing voter who strongly favored the pro frames, the probability increased to 0.95.

In the corporate tax reform, the pro frames were almost as strong as in the asylum law. Surprisingly, however, the partisan heuristic path is present but weaker than in the other two campaigns. This is unexpected because one might expect the partisan logic to be more important in unfamiliar issues since citizens are less motivated for systematic information processing. Let me illustrate the effect: a voter who was strongly in favor of the contra frames and close to a conservative right party voted yes with a probability of 0.69. If he or she was close to the left and strongly favored the contra frames, the probability decreased to 0.45. This effect is in line with the expectations. However, it could be stronger (the expected probability could be closer to 0). Some voters who held a strongly favoring position on the contra frames ignored not only their framing position but also their partisan predisposition by voting yes! In other words, there must be an additional force which causes some of these citizens to vote yes. The influence of the sentimental-based path in the opinion formation process probably explains this finding. Wirth et al. (2010) showed that positive emotions also had a direct effect in the corporate tax reform (only in this case, not in the other campaigns) and that 10% of the variance of the vote intentions could be explained by the impact of emotions. Thus, in the corporate tax reform emotions played a role as an additional heuristic route. The findings in Table 8.3 also point in this direction. The argument "this tax reform advances SMEs" includes an emotional element (SMEs) and thus needs to be interpreted as combining both frame-based and emotional elements of opinion formation. In addition, general reasons (the proposal is good or bad) or personal concerns were reason enough to vote yes (26% and 14%) or no (22%). The opinion poll conducted after the vote also supports this finding. It showed that those who are in favor of the free market economy generally agreed to the reform (Vox analysis by Hirter and Linder 2008: 20).

Table 8.5 gives support for the fourth hypothesis in the case of the asylum law. The importance of the frame-based path depends on issue importance. First, we find a persuasion effect for the group of people who think the issue is important to them and who have knowledge about their preferred party's position. At the same time, their partisan identification and issue predisposition do not matter for their vote choice. Obviously, these people rely least on their partisan identification. For some of these people, the core argument contra (humanitarian tradition) was enough to persuade them to vote against the proposal. They concluded that the new law would endanger the humanitarian tradition of Switzerland and voted against it. The efficiency argument (second argument pro) also played some role, even though it is below the 5% significance level. Interestingly, arguments on both sides stand out. This suggests that these people weighed the pros and cons of the issue. By contrast, people with no issue interest and knowledge about partisan positions (third group) rely most on partisan identification and issue predisposition. For these people, the abuse argument (core argument pro) was important, either independently or as a persuasion effect. They did not really care about the issue but followed their party in arguing why they voted against the proposal—in other words we are dealing with rationalizing here. Next, the left and right pole parties (Greens and SVP) are still decisive for the vote choice of people with no knowledge of partisan positions at the first wave (second and fourth groups). Probably, these voters learned the position of their preferred party during the campaign and voted accordingly. It seems as the more oppositional character of these two parties help these parties to find followers. Those with high issue importance (second group) probably answered based at least partly on social desirability. It is unlikely that people would have a high interest in the issue and not know where their preferred party stands. Thus, they were afraid to say that they have no or little interest in the topic. With one exception, we also see no persuasion effect here. This additionally indicates no deep thinking about the topic. For the fourth group, the adjusted R2 drops below 0.5. Their behavior is least predictable. It seems that they care most for efficiency (second argument pro) and rely on parties at the poles of the spectrum.

Finally, I apply the same model as above *for the cross-pressured people* in the asylum law issue: people with a xenophobic issue predisposition and a moderate partisan orientation (independent of issue importance). The results (Table 8.6) show no persuasion effect but do show a

Table 8.5 Prior persuasion test for vote intention on t3

Issue importance	Important						Unimportant					
Knowledge about preferred party position	Yes			No			Yes			No		
	Coef.	s.e.	P > z	Coef.	s.e.	P > z	Coef.	s.e.	P > z	Coef.	s.e.	P > z
votl t1	0.406	0.088	***	0.641	0.103	***	0.446	0.052	***	0.358	0.064	***
Δ votl t2t1	0.277	0.075	***	0.32	0.073	***	0.252	0.043	***	0.276	0.046	***
Issue pred	0.011	0.025	*	0.054	0.028	°	0.065	0.018	***	0.072	0.019	***
Sex	−0.084	0.039		−0.051	0.048		−0.015	0.022		0.005	0.028	
Age	0	0.001		−0.001	0.001		0	0.001		−0.001	0.001	
Education	−0.004	0.013		0.005	0.013		0	0.006		0.002	0.009	
Partisan orientations												
SVP	0.104	0.086		0.195	0.084	*	0.152	0.045	**	0.125	0.054	
LPS_FDP	0.007	0.082		0.059	0.084		0.156	0.055	**	−0.017	0.061	
CVP	0.107	0.071		0.036	0.077		−0.111	0.046	*	0.057	0.054	
SP	−0.099	0.105		0.056	0.094		0.055	0.052		−0.047	0.062	
Greens	−0.116	0.1	*	−0.201	0.084	*	−0.125	0.054	*	−0.236	0.065	***
Persuasion effects												
Delta (t2−t1) core argument contra	0.051	0.021	*	0.008	0.023		0.019	0.012		0.005	0.016	
Delta (t2−t1) 2nd argument contra	0.031	0.022		0.005	0.022		0.012	0.012		0.018	0.017	
Delta (t2−t1) core argument pro	0.026	0.024		0.031	0.024		0.032	0.013	*	0.016	0.017	

(continued)

Table 8.5 (continued)

Issue importance	Important						Unimportant					
Knowledge about preferred party position	Yes			No			Yes			No		
	Coef.	s.e.	P>z	Coef.	s.e.	P>z	Coef.	s.e.	P>z	Coef.	s.e.	P>z
Delta (t2 −t1) 2nd argument pro	0.045	0.023	°	−0.011	0.028		0.014	0.013		0.044	0.016	**
Argument positions t1												
Core argument contra	−0.025	0.026		0.026	0.026		0.004	0.014		−0.043	0.017	*
2nd argument contra	−0.016	0.024		−0.077	0.027	**	−0.010	0.016		−0.022	0.02	
Core argument pro	0.06	0.027	*	0.045	0.036		0.07	0.016	***	0.028	0.021	
2nd argument pro	0.032	0.027		0.007	0.034		0.025	0.016		0.06	0.02	**
Adj R2	0.66			0.671			0.702			0.498		
n	160			133			404			375		

$°p<0.1$; $*p<0.05$, $**p<0.01$; $***p<0.001$, n total: 1072

Table 8.6 Persuasion test for cross-pressured people

Asylum	Coef.	s.e.	P > z
votI t1	0.326	0.093	**
Δ votI t2t1	0.186	0.084	*
Issue pref	−0.027	0.045	
Sex	0.047	0.037	
Age	−0.001	0.001	
Education	0.007	0.013	
Partisan orientations			
SVP	0.201	0.075	**
LPS_FDP	−0.170	0.086	°
CVP	0.112	0.077	
SP	0.000	0.088	
Greens	−0.081	0.094	
Persuasion effects			
Delta (t2−t1) core argument contra	−0.012	0.019	
Delta (t2−t1) 2nd argument contra	0.007	0.017	
Delta (t2−t1) core argument pro	−0.011	0.029	
Delta (t2−t1) 2nd argument pro	0.014	0.028	
Argument positions t1			
core argument contra	−0.006	0.021	
2nd argument contra	−0.024	0.020	
core argument pro	0.050	0.035	
2nd argument pro	0.064	0.032	°
Adj R2	0.306		
n	152		

$°p<0.1; *p<0.05; **p<0.01$

"Markus Rauh" effect. Even though the effect of the Liberal parties (LPS, FDP) is significant only below the 5% level, we can make sense of it by referring to a liberal ad hoc committee (Bürgerliches Komitee) who opposed the proposal. Markus Rauh, a member of the business elite, was the figurehead of this committee and present in the news media (Chapter 7). The results indicate that he reached cross-pressured citizens with a liberal partisan orientation and a xenophobic predisposition. This is plausible. Rauh is a charismatic person who is credible to speak for liberal values. In one of his public statement, for instance, he argued that the new proposal does not help to fight against abuse (a core concern of xenophobic people) but that it introduces arbitrariness and costs a lot. Rauh illustrated his argumentation with a well-known example of a family who was deported erroneously and rather brutally.

Conclusion

In this chapter, I have explored the strength of frames in communication and strength of frames in thought. In the case of frames in communication, the campaigners' counterattacks are a measure for the relevancy of a frame. In the case of frames in thought, I rely on two measures: Whether and to what extent a frame is mentioned as reason for the individuals' vote decision and the importance of a frame position in the individuals' opinion formation process (controlling for other factors). Ultimately, frame dialogue is only important when frames evolving from the construction, promotion, and edition processes have an effect on opinion formation. The overall result of this chapter is that the frames present in the dialogue in the news media are indeed highly relevant for the vote decision. In other words, frame building is very important, and dialogue in the news media matters for public opinion formation.

The results clearly suggest that the main frames on either side were strong frames in communication, since they could not be ignored but rather elicited strong defensive reactions from the opponents' side in the media input and the news media. However, in three cases we see differences between promoted frames, strength of frames in communication, and strength of frames in thought. First, in the asylum law campaign the second frame of the contra camp (rule-of-law) was of minor importance in the opinion formation process of citizens. The discussion was dominated by the other frames. Thus, not all promoted frames are used in the opinion formation process. Second, the pro camp's strategic change from the "people final say" frame to the "mass naturalization" frame in the naturalization initiative did not cause the "mass naturalization" frame to be stronger than the "people final say" frame. However, it was clearly recognizable as the second strongest frame in communication and in thought of the pro camp. Thus, even though the strategic change came late and did not help the frame to break through, it may have made the "mass naturalization" frame stronger. In addition, the analysis indicates that taking sides was important in this campaign, reducing the effects of frames. Third, in the corporate tax reform, the core frame of the pro camp (SME) was only second strongest in communication because it remained less controversial. However, it was still a strong frame in thought. This case shows that my measure of frames in communication detected this relevant frame but underestimated its impact for opinion formation. Thus, frames discussed less controversially, frames which are accepted by many, or those not so vulnerable to rebuttal can appear as not so strong in communication but still become strong in thought. Thus, my measure for strength of frame in communication identifies as strong those arguments which are strong in the cognitive processing of information. If the core frames are not the strongest frames in communication, we need to check for other influences (like direct influence of emotions on the vote decision). Depending on the research interest, the measure for the strength of frames in communication can also be extended by including frames from opinion leaders or friends, or in more general terms, by including other channels relevant for the overall flow of communication. The measure of strength of frames in communication identifies as relevant the same frames as the commonly used measure, the strength of frames in thought. Thus, the first hypothesis is confirmed: In direct-democratic campaigns, strong frames in communication are also strong frames in thought. The precondition of accessibility was also fulfilled. The strong frames in communication might help "to anticipate which frames are likely to emerge as being the most applicable on an issue" (Chong and Druckman 2007b: 117).

This chapter also shows that there is a framing effect from the frames in communication on the frames in thought in two of the three direct-democratic campaigns. Hypothesis two is confirmed: In two campaigns, there is a link from the frames in communication to the frames in thought. Even if not completely, we can still show evidence of growth in influence of frames over time embedded in *actual* campaigns. The strongest framing effect was discovered in the asylum law. Three of four main frames in thought became significantly stronger over time. In the corporate tax reform, both core frames in communication caused the frames in thought to become significantly stronger (when the behavior of the undecided voter was taken into consideration). Additionally, emotions independent of partisan orientation and argument positions probably played a role in the corporate tax reform. Golder (2016) shows that emotions might mobilize (bring more citizens to vote) but the vote generally is in line with predispositions. More problematic are complex proposals (like the corporate tax reform), especially when not intensively discussed. Since the corporate tax reform was intensively discussed, I expect the biasing effect to be larger in cases of complex but low intensity campaigns. In the naturalization initiative, the strength of frames in thought did not become stronger over time. Thus, there was no framing effect in this campaign. The conflict about the new justice minister (Eveline Widmer-Schlumpf) potentially distracted voters from the substance of the debate. Finally, the frames remain important for the vote decision, when controlling for and in comparison with partisan heuristic. Therefore, hypothesis three can be confirmed. Hypothesis four is also confirmed. Based on the analysis of the asylum law, we can state that the importance of the frame-based path depends on issue importance. Since the asylum law is the familiar case with low complexity, we assume that in the other cases we would find the same result or even a stronger partisan orientation. Partisan orientation was more important in the polarized case (naturalization initiative), because of the conflict between the SVP and BDP, and in the corporate tax reform because of its complexity. Thus, we are dealing with the most likely case for detecting no persuasion effects in the asylum law campaign, and yet we see a persuasion effect for a small number of voters. Those with no interest in the topic or cross-pressured people seem to rely more on partisan identification. In this regard, the book gives empirical support to the realistic theory of democracy (Achen and Bartels 2016). Social identities (partisan identities in our cases) are relevant for voters' choices, particularly in the case of ambivalence, low issue importance, polarization, or issue complexity.

INTERACTION BETWEEN CONTEXT (CAMPAIGN TYPE, COUNTRY) AND FRAMING EFFECTS

Research shows that topic salience is good for the opinion formation process also in public debates: High levels of media attention can motivate people to scrutinize arguments and not rely only on heuristics (Ciuk and Yost 2016). Indeed, even voters with lower awareness are able to make meaningful political choices if the topic is highly salient (Seeberg et al. 2017). Generalizing to elections or other situations with a lower level of dialogue in the news media, we expect partisan identity to play a more important role. Lenz (2012: 3f.) showed that it is policy performance that matters in elections not policy positions. He finds that voters often first pick a politician, then adopt his or her view. Policies or policy congruence seems to matter less, whereas the good performance of politicians is rewarded. As mentioned above, our book gives empirical support to the idea that social identities (partisan identities in our cases) are relevant for voters' choices (Achen and Bartels 2016). Lupia (2016) describes how voters can be lead to transform information into knowledge, but it becomes clear that this process does not happen by itself. In elections, it (transformation of information into knowledge) is more unlikely to happen than in direct-democratic campaigns because elections are less substantive. In particular, in election campaigns, closer races are characterized by a higher use of contest frames (Dunaway and Lawrence 2015). For voters in these cases, there is a trade-off between more election news coverage and the crowding out of substantive information. When looking at country differences, opinion formation processes work in a similar way. In direct democracy in California, many voters also rely on arguments highly present in the campaigns for their vote decision (Bowler 2015). The same is true for referendums on the European Constitutional Treaty in France and the Netherlands (Hobolt and Brouard 2011; Maatsch 2007), and for the Brexit vote in the UK (Hobolt 2016).

References

Achen, C. H. & Bartels, L. M. (2016). *Democracy for Realists. Why Elections do not Produce Responsive Government*. Oxford: Oxford University Press.

Alvarez, R. M., & Brehm, J. (1995). American Ambivalence Towards Abortion Policy: Development of a Heteroscedastic Probit Model of Competing Values. *American Journal of Political Science, 39*, 1055–1082.

Alvarez, R. M., & Brehm, J. (2002). *Hard Chopices, Easy Answers*. Princeton, NJ: Princeton University Press.

Boudreau, C., & MacKenzie, S. A. (2014). Informing the Electorate? How Party Cues and Policy Information Affect Public Opinion About Initiatives. *American Journal of Political Science, 58*(1), 48–62.

Bowler, S. (2015). Information Availability and Information Use in Ballot Proposition Contests: Are Voters Over-Burdened?*. *Electoral Studies, 38*, 183–191.

Bowler, S., & Donovan, T. (1998). *Demanding Choices: Opinion, Voting, and Direct Democracy*. Ann Arbor: University of Michigan Press.

Brody, R. A., & Page, B. I. (1972). Comment-Assessment of Policy Voting. *American Journal of Political Science, 66*(2), 450–458.

Bullock, J. G. (2011). Elite Influence on Public Opinion in an Informed Electorate. *American Political Science Review, 105*(August), 496–515.

Campbell, A., Converse, P., Miller, W., & Stokes, D. (1960). *The American Voter*. New York: Wiley.

Chaiken, S., & Trop, Y. (1999). *Dual-Process Theories in Social Psychology*. New York: Guildford Press.

Chong, D., & Druckman, J. N. (2007a). A Theory of Framing and Opinion Formation in Competitive Elite Environments. *Journal of Communication, 57*(1), 99–118.

Chong, D., & Druckman, J. N. (2007b). Framing Theory. *Annual Review of Political Science, 10,* 103–126.

Ciuk, D. J., & Yost, B. A. (2016). The Effects of Issue Salience, Elite Influence, and Policy Content on Public Opinion. *Political Communication, 33*(2), 328–345.

Cohen, G. L. (2003). Party Over Policy: The Dominating Impact of Group Influence on Political Beliefs. *Journal of Personality and Social Psychology, 85*(5), 808–822.

Colombo, C., & Kriesi, H. (2017). Party, Policy – or Both? Partisan Biased Processing of Policy Arguments in Direct Democracy. *Journal of Elections, Public Opinion and Parties, 27*(3), 235–253.

Coombs, C. H. (1964). *A Theory of Data*. New York: Wiley.

Druckman, J. N. (2001). The Implications of Framing Effects for Citizen Competence. *Political Behavior, 23,* 225–256.

Druckman, J. N. (2009). What's It All About? Framing in Political Science. In G. Keren (Ed.), *Perspectives on Framing*. New York: Psychology Press.

Druckman, J. N., & Nelson, K. R. (2003). Framing and Deliberation: How Citizens' Conversations Limit Elite Influence. *American Journal of Political Science, 47*(4), 729–745.

Dunaway, J., & Lawrence, R. G. (2015). What Predicts the Game Frame? Media Ownership, Electoral Context, and Campaign News. *Political Communication, 32*(1), 43–60.

Eagly, A. H., & Chaiken, S. (1993). *The Psychology of Attitudes*. New York: Harcourt Brace.

Engeli, I., Anouk, L., & Nai, A. (2008). Analysis of the Federal Votes of June 1, 2008 (Analyse der eidgenössischen Abstimmungen vom 1. Juni 2008). *Vox Analysis.*

Goffman, E. (1974). *Frame Analysis*. Cambridge: Harvard University Press.

Golder, L. (2016). *Keine Angst vor Emotionen: in der direkten Demokratie überwiegen Argumente*. Bern: Gfs Bern. http://www.gfsbern.ch/de-ch/Detail/keine-angst-vor-emotionen-in-der-direkten-demokratie-ueberwiegen-argumente. September 2017.

Hänggli, R., & Kriesi, H. (2010). Political Framing Strategies and Their Impact on Media Framing in a Swiss Direct-Democratic Campaign. *Political Communication, 27*(2), 141–157.

Hirter, H., & Linder, W. (2008). Analysis of the Federal Votes of February 24, 2008 (Analyse der eidgenössischen Abstimmungen vom 24. Februar 2008). *Vox Analysis*. Berne: University of Berne.

Hobolt, S. B. (2016). The Brexit Vote: A Divided Nation, a Divided Continent. *Journal of European Public Policy, 23*(9), 1259–1277.

Hobolt, S., & Brouard, S. (2011). Contesting the European Union? Why the Dutch and the French Rejected the European Constitution. *Political Research Quarterly, 64*(2), 309–322.

Iyengar, S., & Kinder, D. R. (1987). *News That Matters: Television and American Opinion*. Chicago: University of Chicago Press.

Jacoby, W. G. (1988). The Impact of Party Identification on Issue Attitudes. *American Journal of Political Science, 32*(3), 643–661.

Keele, L., & Wolak, J. (2008). Contextual Sources of Ambivalence. *Political Psychology, 29*(5), 653–673.

Kinder, D. R., & Sanders, L. M. (1990). Mimicking Political Debate with Survey Questions: The Case of White Opinion on Affirmative Action for Blacks. *Social Cognition, 8*, 73–103.

Kriesi, H. (2005). *Direct Democratic Choice: The Swiss Experience*. Lanham, MD: Lexington Books.

Kriesi, H., & Trechsel, A. H. (2008). *The Politics of Switzerland*. Cambridge: Cambridge University Press.

Kühne, R., Schemer, C., Matthes, J., & Wirth, W. (2011). Affective Priming in Political Campaigns: How Campaign-Induced Emotions Prime Political Opinions. *International Journal of Public Opinion Research, 23*(4), 485–507.

Lenz, G. S. (2009). Learning and Opinion Change, Not Priming: Reconsidering the Priming Hypothesis. *American Journal of Political Science, 53*(4), 821–837.

Lenz, G. (2012). *Follow the Leader?* Cambridge: Cambridge University Press.

Lodge, M., & Hamill, R. (1986). A Partisan Schema for Political Information Processing. *The American Political Science Review, 80*(2), 505–520.

Lupia, A. (2016). *Uninformed*. Cambridge: Cambridge University Press.

Maatsch, S. (2007). The Struggle to Control Meanings: The French Debate on the European Constitution in the Mass Media. *Perspectives on European Politics and Society, 8*(3), 261–280.

Mettler, S. (2018). *The Government-Citizen Disconnect*. Russell Sage Foundation.

Nelson, T. E., Oxley, Z. M., & Clawson, R. A. (1997). Toward a Psychology of Framing Effects. *Political Behavior, 19*(3), 221–246.

Rabe-Hesketh, S., & Skrondal, A. (2005). *Multilevel and Longitudinal Modeling Using Stata* (2nd ed.). College Station, TX: Stata Press.

Rahn, W. M. (1993). The Role of Partisan Stereotypes in Information Processing About Political Candidates. *American Journal of Political Science, 37*, 472–496.

Rudolph, T. J. (2005). Group Attachment and the Reduction of Value-Driven Ambivalence. *Political Psychology, 26*, 905–928.

Seeberg, H. B., Slothuus, R., & Stubager, R. (2017). Do Voters Learn? Evidence that Voters Respond Accurately to Changes in Political Parties' Policy Positions. *West European Politics, 40*(2), 336–356.

222   R. HÄNGGLI

Selb, P., Kriesi, H., Hänggli, R., & Marr, M. (2009). Partisan Choices in a Direct-Democratic Campaign. *European Political Science Review, 1*(1), 155–172.

Shen, F., & Edwards, H. H. (2005). Economic Individualism, Humanitarianism, and Welfare Reform: A Value-Based Account of Framing Effects. *Journal of Communication, 55*(4), 795–809.

Slothuus, R. (2008). More Than Weighting Cognitive Importance: A Dual-Process Model of Issue Framing Effects. *Political Psychology, 29*(1), 1–28.

Slothuus, R. (2010). When Can Political Parties Lead Public Opinion? Evidence from a Natural Experiment. *Political Communication, 27*(2), 158–177.

Sniderman, P. M., & Theriault, S. M. (2004). The Structure of Political Argument and the Logic of Issue Framing. In P. M. Sniderman & S. M. Theriault (Eds.), *Studies in Public Opinion: Attitudes, Nonattitudes, Measurement Error and Change* (pp. 133–165). Princeton, NJ: Princeton University Press.

Steenbergen, M., & Brewer, P. R. (2004). The Not-So-Ambivalent Public: Policy Attitudes in the Political Culture of Ambivalence. In W. E. Saris & P. M. Sniderman (Eds.), *Studies in Public Opinion. Attitudes, Nonattitudes, Measurement Errors, and Change* (pp. 93–132). Princeton, NJ: Princeton University Press.

Tillie, J. (1995). *Party Utility and Voting Behavior*. Amsterdam: Het Spinhuis.

Van der Eijk, C., Van der Brug, W. W., Kroh, M., & Franklin, M. (2006). Rethinking the Dependent Variable in Voting Behavior: On the Measurement and Analysis of Electoral Utilities. *Electoral Studies, 25*(3), 424–447.

Van Schuur, W. H. (1993). Nonparametric Unfolding Models for Multicategory Data. *Political Analysis, 4,* 41–74.

Van Schuur, W. H., & Post, W. J. (1998). *MUDFOLD: A Program for Multiple Unidimensional Unfolding*. Version 4.0 [Software manual]. Groningen: ProGAMMA.

Wirth, W., Schemer, C., Kühne, R., & Matthes, J. (2010). The Impact of Positive and Negative Affects in Direct-Democratic Campaigns. In H. Kriesi (Ed.), *Manipulation or Deliberation*. Zurich: Unpublished Manuscript.

PART III

Conclusion

CHAPTER 9

Conclusion

As Schattschneider (1988 [1960]) pointed out almost 60 years ago, the competitive way of discussing alternatives is of key importance for democracy. The media have long played a vital role in conveying information from the political scene to the public (Lippmann 1947 [1922]), and in our diverse modern society, citizens still get an important share of their information from the news media, with around 76% of the Swiss resident population regularly reading a regional or quality newspaper (WEMF 2017). As a consequence, this is where the competitive way of discussing alternatives should be found. Thus, I looked at the news media and asked: *Under what conditions will we see dialogue in the news media? What are the driving mechanisms? What is the role of dialogue in the Public Opinion formation process?* In Swiss direct democracy, we have seen that contestation is the result of competition among different types of self-interested political actors in a mediatized context. As introduced in the first chapter, dialogue means that competing political actors talk about each other's interpretations. The framing concept served as the analytical tool for the analysis. Framing is the process by which political actors and journalists define the issue for the public (e.g., Nelson et al. 1997a, b). By analyzing which processes and factors influence the creation or changes of frames applied by journalists (frames in news media or media frames), i.e., *"frame building"* (Scheufele 1999), I found out more about the conditions for dialogue.

© The Author(s) 2020   225
R. Hänggli, *The Origin of Dialogue in the News Media*,
Challenges to Democracy in the 21st Century,
https://doi.org/10.1007/978-3-030-26582-3_9

FRAME BUILDING

For analyzing frame building, I proposed a distinction between the frame construction, frame promotion, and frame edition processes. In the construction of frames, political actors decide on the three strategic framing choices: First, they have to choose one or more substantive frames capable of attracting the attention of the media and the public to their own cause and steering it away from the cause of their opponents ("Substantive Emphasis Choice"). In the "Oppositional Emphasis Choice", the political actors determine how much attention to devote to their opponents' substantive frame(s) as compared to their own frames, as well as whether they want to use their opponents' frames offensively (=trespassing) or defensively (=counter-framing). The third strategic question concerns the decision of whether to focus on the contest (=personal attacks and conflicts) or the substantive content of the debate—on politics or on policy ("Contest Emphasis Choice"). In the frame promotion process, they decide on how to vary these choices in the different communication channels and over time. I have distinguished between mediated (media input and letters to the editor), unmediated (political advertisements and direct mails), and internal (information for members) channels. Both mediated and unmediated channels target the general public, while the internal channel is aimed at members and supporters. In the frame edition process, the contribution of journalists is analyzed.

THE THREE STRATEGIC FRAMING CHOICES

With regard to the "Substantive Emphasis Choice", we find that political actors emphasize one or two strong frames in the media input (Chapter 4). They generally also use these mainframes in channels other than the media input and stay on their frames (Chapter 5). In the unmediated channels, the political actors focus most on their core frame, i.e., in around half of all arguments. By contrast, they focus on this least in the internal communication, in which the core frame is used in every fourth argument. With regard to variation over time, it can be concluded that the political actors stay on their frame, except for the pro camp in the naturalization initiative. In this case, the pro camp changed their strategy and switched—in particular in their ads—from the "people final say" frame to the "mass naturalization" frame toward the end of the campaign because the "people final say" frame was not convincing. In order to garner media attention during the whole campaign, the political actors rely mainly on routine staged events for media input such as media conferences and media releases. In addition, political actors are careful not to organize too many media conferences because they are afraid that if they do so journalists will no longer attend (anticipation effect of media logic). By comparing media input with news media, we find that the percentage shares of the frames in the news media are generally similar to the shares found in the media input. The news media tend to respect frame ownership and report accordingly. The framing input of the political actors is decisive here (Chapter 7).

With the "Oppositional Emphasis Choice", political actors do not revert exclusively to their own mainframes, but rather also discuss their opponents' frames, i.e., enter into dialogue (Chapter 4). We find that the political actors pay more attention to their opponents' frames in the mediated channels than in the unmediated and internal channels (anticipation effect of media logic) (Chapter 5). Mediation obviously motivates the political actors to enter into dialogue with each other. In the mediated channels, it is rational for them to counter-frame because all the arguments are present in the news. In fact, counter-framing is a key strategy! The political actors counter-frame because they want to win the vote. By rebutting their opponents' arguments, they try to reduce their impact. By contrast, with the unmediated channels the political actors primarily want to mobilize citizens to vote, whereas the internal channels should inform the members. With regard to variation over time, we can state that campaign dialogue does not disappear over the course of the campaign. Furthermore, issue complexity and inequality of financial resources reduce dialogue. We show that the frames owned by opponents are largely addressed defensively rather than offensively, that is, by means of counter-framing rather than trespassing. Trespassing was virtually absent, both in the different communication channels and over time. The journalists also reported on both camps with their adversaries' frames and attributed a slightly more offensive stance to both camps (Chapter 7).

As far as the third strategic question, "Contest Emphasis Choice", is concerned, we show that the political actors rely mainly on substantive framing. We find that actors with more extreme partisan positions use more contest frames and that the dispute between Christoph Blocher, the SVP, and Eveline Widmer-Schlumpf caused the quarrelling political actors to rely significantly more on contest frames in the naturalization campaign (Chapter 4). Concerning the different communication channels (Chapter 5), we find that in direct-democratic campaigns, the political actors often refrain from using contest frames in their ads and in direct mail. By contrast, they use more contest frames in the letters to the editor and in the communication with members than in the media input. Toward the end of the campaigns, we find more contest frames only in the media input and in the news media. In the other channels, the use of contest frames is not increased. The substantive frames also dominate in the media. However, the journalists gave slightly more emphasis to contest frames than the political actors (Chapter 7).

Contribution of the Journalists (Frame Edition)

Direct democracy is not only the well-institutionalized interaction between government, parliament, parties, and the public (Linder et al. 2008: 214). It also requires the contribution of the media. I call this frame edition. First, we find that the journalists tend to balance out the messages of each camp in all three campaigns ("Balancing Choice"). Whereas political actors want to win the vote, journalists want to write an objective article. Second, for the "Range of Views Choice" (frame absence/presence), the campaign-specific power of a political actor is important. It can be shown that power was not important in the case of the familiar issue (asylum law), but further research is needed to determine the relative importance of power in complex issues. The political actors anticipate this behavior of journalists. Thus, weak political actors campaign together with and join forces with more powerful actors (anticipatory effect of media). Third, the number of promoted frames and the minister play an influential role for the daily frame *frequency* ("Story Choice"). The minister's influence is highest in the case of the complex issue (corporation tax). This choice also reveals the economic interest of journalists (or the media organization behind them). Limited resources can hinder journalists' ability to put the discussion into political, economic, or cultural context and to focus on substance. Indeed, the yearbook "Quality of the Media", which examines Swiss media standards, shows that quality journalism is increasingly challenged by news focusing on contest (fög/Universität Zürich 2013–2018). In our study, the economic limitations of the media can be detected in the free (non-paid for) press. They edit least and on the whole do not put debates into context. In addition, economic constraints can be detected if the long-term, global perspective, which does not sell easily, cannot make it into the debate, or if journalists (not in the cases under investigation but in other campaigns) examine discussions about value-wise sensitive aspects in a contest-oriented way. Fourth, journalists investigate official claims by asking experts and help the reader to understand the topic in complex issues ("Interpretation Choice"). Overall, the degree of campaign dialogue in the news is about as high as in the media input: The political actors anticipate the media logic and prepare for it by increasing campaign dialogue in the media input. In the complex issue (corporation tax), where dialogue in the press releases was somewhat lower, the news media increased the level of dialogue.

Flow of Frames and Role of Dialogue in Public Opinion Formation

We are able to show that the political actors and the journalists dance the tango well together, as they are familiar with both their dance partners and the music. My analysis shows that it is the political actors who introduce the most important frames into the public discourse in direct-democratic campaigns. In such campaigns, the political actors take the lead by framing the issue strategically (causal order hypothesis). The three strategic framing choices and the promotion activities, particularly in the media input (channel hypothesis), influence the creation, or changes of frames applied by journalists. The journalists generally respect the lead of the powerful political actors and contribute to the debate by clarifying the opposing positions (which Bennett et al. 2004 call "recognition") and by eliciting mutual reactions from the opposing political actors (which they call "responsiveness"). News media report on direct-democratic campaigns and start to provide information about three months prior to a vote (effort and timing).

The frames present in the dialogue in the news media are highly relevant for the vote decision. The mainframes on either side were strong frames in communication and in thought, also when controlling for and in comparison with partisan heuristic. Among our sample of cases, we analyzed one of the most complex objects (corporate tax reform) that has ever been submitted to the voters. Since the issue was very complex, emotions could have disturbed the opinion formation process to some extent (Wirth et al. 2010; Kühne et al. 2011). Indeed, complexity and campaign intensity have been shown to play a crucial role in the individual's opinion formation process (Kriesi 2005). In general, highly complex issues of low intensity suffer the highest likelihood of a biased opinion formation process, even more so if they come to vote at the same day as emotional campaigns of high salience (Golder 2016). Low intensity does not apply to the cases examined here, as all of the cases we looked at were highly intense. The opinion formation process in highly salient but low complexity cases generally is not biased. This insight gives me confidence for low complexity cases, even in times of post-factual politics, which are typically characterized by appeals to emotions but also by high intensity. The corporate tax reform was highly intense but also extraordinarily complex. Thus, I am convinced that the opinion formation process in this case was more biased than normal. In the naturalization initiative, people took sides because of a situational conflict and became less informed than in other campaigns. However, in this case we do not see that their vote intention was biased in the sense that a notable share of votes was not in line with voters' preferences. On average, around a third of Swiss people in votes are well-informed, a third averagely informed and a third poorly informed (Gruner and Hertig 1983; Bütschi 1993; Kriesi 2005; Milic et al. 2014: 276). Similarly, Colombo (2018) shows that 70% of voters are able to provide a content-related justification for their vote choice. Golder (2016) analyzes selected votes with high and low voting participation. He concludes that more than 80% generally voted congruent to their argument preferences. Thus, I am confident in stating that direct-democratic campaigns enlighten voters to a good extent, even more so when they are intensely debated. In fact, most voters in Swiss direct democracy understand policy-related arguments (Colombo 2018) and know about party positions and the issue at stake. Both help them to decide in line with their preferences (Selb et al. 2009).

Evaluation of Dialogue Process and Its Implications for Democracy

As a result of the choices of political actors and journalists, we find a good amount of dialogue in the news media. The comparatively high level of dialogue is plausible if one looks at research investigating similar concepts. For instance, the ideological balance of the press system in regional and national newspapers (balpress[1]) is high in Switzerland:

---

[1] http://www.democracybarometer.org/Data/Codebook_all%20countries_1990-2007.pdf, March 2019.

On average, for this measurement Switzerland ranked among the top five countries of all established democracies between 1995 and 2005, and would rank even higher if direct-democratic campaigns were taken into consideration. Furthermore, Marquis et al. (2011: 146) investigated 24 Swiss referendum campaigns on welfare state issues and found that "[m]edia coverage appears to be relatively balanced, autonomous and substantive". Their findings concur with a study by Tresch (2012), who showed that Swiss newspapers give similar visibility to the pro and contra camps in direct-democratic campaigns.

We started the book by claiming that dialogue in the news media is good for democracy because it offers alternative perspectives on an issue, which allows the public to participate in the decision-making process. But can we be satisfied? Facing severe unsolved problems like migration, inequality, or climate change, it is worth asking how citizens and societies can make competent choices (Lupia 2016: 46). In order for this to happen, how the flow of information works is significant. This book develops a template model for such a process and identifies key actors and mechanisms. I show that, in these campaigns where citizens are most likely to form competent opinions, political communication is elite-driven, that mediation by classical news media increases the quality of information, that arguments are important for opinion formation and do make a difference, but that even in information-rich circumstances some citizens rely more on their partisan identities than on arguments. Thus, to answer the question, let me discuss the implications of each key characteristic individually.

IMPLICATIONS OF ELITE-DRIVEN CAMPAIGNS

My book speaks to literature on democratic theory in general and on redistribution and research such as that triggered by the Task Force on Inequality and American Democracy[2] in particular. I show that citizens are not in a leading position in any phase of the information flow. In ordinary times, we cannot rely on the hope that a representation feedback loop will bring into power those people who reduce inequality (or who solve any other serious problem). Even in an information-rich context like Swiss direct democracy, citizens who have an interest in the

[2] https://www.apsanet.org/portals/54/Files/Task%20Force%20Reports/taskforcereport.pdf, March 2019.

topic rely on the intellectual work and the arguments of the policy makers. In this way, the quality of the debate and of the decision made at the end is dependent on who participates in the debate and which interests are organized. The context here is comparatively advantageous for inclusive debate. NGOs or other less powerful actors, even single actors, can speak up and group together with powerful ones and in such a way bring in their perspectives. In the case of the death penalty in the USA (Baumgartner et al. 2008), it was an innocence movement (driven especially by legal and journalism clinics) that decisively contributed to changing the policy debate. In general, policy shifts need mutually reinforcing elements, and organizational efforts are among the most crucial. However, as is the case in Swiss direct democracy, the long-term and global perspective is more difficult to incorporate or even lacking. Furthermore, in times of globalization and digitalization, complex and technical aspects play a central role and might challenge or overstrain policy makers.

In other words, the developed solutions are only as good as the input of the elites, and in the case of bad solutions, we can say it is the blind leading the blind (see Fig 9.1[3]). From this, it is arguable that we should care less about representation and more for competent leadership. We know—and the book gives strongest support to this perspective—that public opinion emerges endogenously in the political process (Disch 2011). This means that issue-specific preferences are formed dependent on what is communicated during campaigns. Therefore, perhaps we should not ask how we can increase the likelihood that representation works but rather how political decision-makers are able to address the relevant issues, perspectives, or ethical points of view and develop options for the benefit of society and in accordance with democratic values. "The role of political elites in structuring politically relevant cleavages needs to be understood better" (Achen and Bartels 2016: 230), and my book makes a contribution to a greater understanding of how political elites structure the debate. As a society, we should ask which relevant perspectives (i.e., the perspectives of all "those who are affected [or potentially affected] by collective decisions" [Warren 2017: 44]) are missing in a national debate and make sure we can add them and enrich the debate accordingly.

---

[3]https://en.wikipedia.org/wiki/The_Blind_Leading_the_Blind, March 2019.

Fig. 9.1   The blind leading the blind (by Lis Steiner)

By understanding that the elites introduce the key perspectives in the opinion formation process, it is crucial that minorities or oppositional forces can become part of the elites and in this way bring in their perspectives. Scharpf (1970) showed that the short-term oriented and particular interests of the "haves" are more likely to be represented by organizations, whereas the long-term oriented and general interests of the "have-nots" are more difficult to organize. Furthermore, the idea of democratic optimization could challenge this principle that diverse and minority perspectives should be taken into consideration. For instance, Khanna (2017) promotes *technocracy* as an efficient solution to the issue of governing a country. In his vision, freedom is *not* an absolute value to which everything else must be subordinated. To increase the quality of the lead of policy makers, we should provide incentives that make it worth bringing in these relevant but neglected perspectives (such as global or long-term perspectives), discussing and evaluating them in the classical news media, and taking actions based on them. For instance, a committee for the future could be built to bring in long-term perspectives.[4] Such a committee could have the task (among others) of considering long-term perspectives, contributing to the discussion accordingly or evaluating the promoted perspectives based on a long-term orientation. Greta Thunberg or other climate activists can also be helpful to increase the importance of these perspectives. In addition, computer modelling is now so advanced that virtual reality could be employed to simulate the consequences of a vote decision (as in a computer game) and to enable leaders to take on otherwise neglected but relevant perspectives in a playful way. For instance, leaders could virtually meet a person (a child of today thirty years later or a person from Africa) and in such a way adopt a global or long-term perspective.

IMPLICATIONS OF IMPORTANCE OF MEDIATION

My work also speaks to media research. Switzerland has been characterized by a rather large distance between political and media actors (Hallin and Mancini 2004) and a somewhat weak consumer-orientated political communication culture (Pfetsch 2003). Therefore, the media reflect pro and contra viewpoints and provide a rather balanced view. This way of mediating information matters and increases the quality of debates. Policy makers—by anticipating the media logic—offer dialogue in their press releases. They counter-argue and in this way check the arguments of the other side. Journalists continue this quality control and additionally check whether there are other relevant arguments. My study suggests that such an additional actor (journalist) who is not involved in the production of arguments but is concerned with the exchange of arguments is very helpful to achieve contestation. This insight can be applied also to the process of democratic representation in general. Thus, such an independent actor could help to guarantee that both "express and implicit objections from the represented" are mobilized (Disch 2011: 111). It is important we make sure that this mechanism continues. In Switzerland (Puppis et al. 2014; Hofstetter and Schönhagen 2017) as elsewhere, journalistic working conditions have come under pressure. Especially in times of media crisis, misinformation, disinformation, and

---

[4] https://www.eduskunta.fi/EN/lakiensaataminen/valiokunnat/tulevaisuusvaliokunta/Pages/default.aspx, March 2019.

filter bubbles, we need quality news media, which are economically independent so that they can afford not to rely on clicks, sensation, and speed or have their journalistic integrity compromised by financial imperatives.

Since we have a good proportion of people (in our cases approximately a third, in other debate types probably the same or more) who rely on partisan cues, we must also devote our energies to ensuring people can assess the credibility of politicians (i.e., their expertise and whether they have a common interest or not, see Lupia 2016: 88). For this, we should ensure that we publicly discuss the most important decisions of leaders and their societal and environmental consequences. We need journalists who also evaluate the leadership qualities of our politicians, policy makers, and leaders in general (such as CEOs of global companies), their capabilities in addressing and solving relevant problems, bringing in the long-term perspective, etc., and to report not only on societally irrelevant things like a Green politician buying an electric lawnmower, etc. To achieve this aim, we also need to have transparency of financial flows in campaigns (e.g., Facebook ads, or ads generally in Switzerland). Mettler (2018: 19, 148, 153) argues that (business) organizations, groups, and institutions have lost their capacity to translate the role of the state to citizens and to connect citizens in this way back to the state. Business has abandoned its role as partner of government and in this way abandoned the social contract. In other words, news media is of heightened importance in helping citizens understand the role of government.

The content in news media is still vital for opinion formation. Newspapers and TV news are the most important channel for getting information in Switzerland, and social and new media have thus far been of minor importance. If people do get informed *online*, only about 19% (media use index 2017) get their news from social media in Switzerland (as opposed to information from an internet portal of a news provider or via push message from media portal to smartphone). If people do get informed via social media, they still rely to a large extent on shared information *coming from news media* (Puppis et al. 2017: 77). Thus, even if these figures grow, the process does not necessarily change significantly because articles from the classical media will still be shared. Or formulated differently, the importance of finding dialogue in the news media will remain. Thus, I argue that social media or advertising revenue-based media do not or should not really matter in the information flow. In other words, we need to make sure that classic quality journalism standards continue to operate and count in a new media environment. As citizens, we need to be able to rely on it. This means that we must also educate people so that they see the value of traditional news work (which can also mean that its content is accessed electronically). These suggestions are in the sense of a culture of responsibility (Jarren 2018) and also in the spirit of swarm intelligence and co-evolution. Political leaders should not be left alone in their leadership role.

Dialogue in the news media offers the chance to get to know other perspectives: Those who do participate are exposed to all the arguments. This indicates that the process currently works in such a way that arguments can also reach people in filter bubbles (Pariser 2011) or echo chambers (Sunstein 2001). Direct-democratic votes lead to dialogue in the news media, to exposure of diverse perspectives, and to discussion in the everyday life of politically interested people. However, I would like to add a thought on algorithms here. In our everyday life, algorithms play an important role in information processing. We search for and receive information through Google, Facebook, Amazon, Twitter, and others. All of these platforms, social and new media, apply algorithms. Taking into account the insight of this book that journalistic norms drive dialogue to a good extent, I am highly concerned. These algorithms function non-transparently, do not aim to maintain or better the welfare of society, and are legitimated only by their suggested usability for customers. As a society, we should discuss the norms associated with these algorithms and be informed about the consequences of the algorithms.

Implications of Insight That Partisan Identities Help in the Opinion Formation Process

The insights on the opinion formation process are applicable to democratic theory in general. The book shows that frames that mainly come from the input of elites are relevant for opinion formation, but that even in ideal conditions (routine process, two-sided, substantive and salient campaigns, dialogue in press releases and the news media), citizens rely also on partisan cues and do not form their opinions based purely on arguments. In particular, voters who attribute no importance to an issue or cross-pressured voters—that is, voters who experience ambivalence between their issue-specific attitudes and their partisan identity—more often than not resolve such conflicts in favor of their partisan identity (Selb et al. 2009). However, the debate is prepared in a way that potentially allows citizens to digest the information and to link it to their preferences. Among those who participate, information is prevalent and makes a difference particularly for non-ambivalent or interested citizens. Only rarely do we discuss the legitimacy of decisions.

Generalizing to elections or other situations with a lower level of dialogue in the news media, the book gives empirical support to the realistic theory of democracy (Achen and Bartels 2016) in so far as here too, social identities (partisan identities in our cases) are relevant for voters' choices alongside arguments. In the crucial case of ambivalence or low level of issue importance, social identities are even more important than policy preferences or ideology. Furthermore, issue complexity and polarization increase the importance of social identities. Voter participation is relatively low in Swiss referendums and initiatives, with an average voter turnout of 45%. Educated people or those with political knowledge participate more often, while citizens from lower social classes abstain more often (Möckli 1994). Non-Swiss inhabitants are excluded anyway. In this regard, the process can be improved through better education at school, through facilitating the participation of lower status voters or through letting foreigners participate in politics at the local level, for instance.

References

Achen, C. H., & Bartels, L. M. (2016). *Democracy for Realists: Why Elections do not Produce Responsive Government*. Oxford: Oxford University Press.

Baumgartner, F. R., De Boef, S., & Boydstund, A. E. (2008). *The Decline of the Death Penalty and the Discovery of Innocence*. Cambridge: University Press.

Bennett, W. L., Pickard, V. W., Iozzi, D. P., Schroeder, C. L., Lagos, T., & Caswell, E. C. (2004). Managing the Public Sphere: Journalistic Construction of the Great Globalization Debate. *International Communication Association, 54*(3), 437–455.

Bütschi, D. (1993). Compétence pratique. In H. Kriesi (Ed.), *Citoyenneté et démocratie directe* (pp. 99–119). Zürich: Seismo.

Colombo, C. (2016). *Partisan, Not Ignorant—Citizens' Use of Arguments and Justifications in Direct Democracy* (PhD thesis). European University Institute, Florence.

Colombo, C. (2018). Justifications and Citizen Competence in Direct Democracy – A Multilevel Analysis. *British Journal of Political Science, 48*(3), 787–806.

Disch, L. (2011). Toward a Mobilization Conception of Democratic Representation. *American Political Science Review, 105*(1), 100–114.

Golder, L. (2016). *Keine Angst vor Emotionen: in der direkten Demokratie überwiegen Argumente.* Bern: Gfs Bern. http://www.gfsbern.ch/de-ch/Detail/keine-angst-vor-emotionen-in-der-direkten-demokratie-ueberwiegen-argumente. September 2017.

Gruner, E., & Hertig, H. P. (1983). *Der Stimmbürger und die «neue» Politik.* Bern: Haupt.

Hallin, D. C., & Mancini, P. (2004). *Comparing Media Systems Three Models of Media and Politics.* Cambridge: Cambridge University Press.

Hofstetter, B., & Schönhagen, P. (2017). When Creative Potentials are Being Undermined by Commercial Imperatives: Change and Resistance in Six Cases of Newsroom Reorganization. *Digital Journalism, 5*(1), 44–60.

Jarren, O. (2018). Kommunikationspolitik für die Kommunikationsgesellschaft. Verantwortungskultur durch Regulierung. *Aus Politik und Zeitgeschichte, 68,* H. 40–41, S. 23–28.

Khanna, P. (2017). *Technocracy in America: Rise of the Info-State.* CreateSpace.

Kriesi, H. (2005). *Direct Democratic Choice: The Swiss Experience.* Lanham, MD: Lexington Books.

Kühne, R., Schemer, C., Matthes, J., & Wirth, W. (2011). Affective Priming in Political Campaigns: How Campaign-Induced Emotions Prime Political Opinions. *International Journal of Public Opinion Research, 23*(4), 485–507.

Linder, W., Zürcher, R., & Bolliger, C. (2008). *Gespaltene Schweiz- geeinte Schweiz. Gesellschaftliche Spaltungen und Konkordanz bei den Volksabstimmungen seit 1874.* Baden: hier + jetzt.

Lippmann, W. (1947 [1922]). *Public Opinion.* New York: Macmillan.

Lupia, Arthur. (2016). *Uninformed.* Cambridge: Cambridge University Press.

Marquis, L., Schaub, H.-P., & Gerber, M. (2011). The Fairness of Media Coverage in Question: An Analysis of Referendum Campaigns on Welfare State Issues in Switzerland. *Swiss Political Science Review, 17*(2), 128–163.

Mettler, S. (2018). *The Government-Citizen Disconnect.* Russell Sage Foundation.

Milic, T., Rousselot, B., & Vatter, A. (2014). *Handbuch der Abstimmungsforschung.* Zurich: NZZ Libro.

Möckli, S. (1994). *Direkte Demokratie. Ein Vergleich der Einrichtungen und Verfahren in der Schweiz und Kalifornien, unter Berücksichtigung von Frankreich, Italien, Dänemark, Irland, Österreich, Liechtenstein und Australien.* Bern: Paul Haupt.

Nelson, T. E., Clawson, R. A., & Oxley, Z. M. (1997a). Media Framing of a Civil Liberties Conflict and Its Effect on Tolerance. *American Political Science Review, 91*(3), 567–583.

Nelson, T. E., Oxley, Z. M., & Clawson, R. A. (1997b). Toward a Psychology of Framing Effects. *Political Behavior, 19*(3), 221–246.

Pariser, E. (2011). *The Filter Bubble: What the Internet Is Hiding from You.* New York: Penguin Press.

Pfetsch, B. (2003). Politische Kommunikationskultur; ein theoretisches Konzept zur vergleichenden Analyse politischer Kommunikationssysteme. In F. Esser & B. Pfetsch (Eds.), *Politische Kommunikation im internationalen Vergleich; Grundlagen, Anwendungen, Perspektiven* (pp. 393–418). Wiesbaden: Westdeutscher Verlag.

Puppis, M., Schenk, M., & Hofstetter, B. (Eds.). (2017, December). *Medien und Meinungsmacht* (TA-SWISS, Vol. 65). Zürich: vdf. https://www.research-collection.ethz.ch/bitstream/handle/20.500.11850/125191/eth-50273-01.pdf.

Puppis, M., Schönhagen, P., Fürst, S., Hofstetter, B., & Meissner, M. (2014). Arbeitsbedingungen und Berichterstattungsfreiheit in journalistischen Organisationen. *Beiträge und Studien Medienforschung.* Bundesamt für Kommunikation (BAKOM).

Scharpf, F. W. (1970). *Demokratietheorie zwischen Utopie und Anpassung.* Konstanzer Universitätsreden 25. Konstanz: Universitätsverlag.

Schattschneider, E. E. (1988 [1960]). *The Semisovereign People: Realist's View of Democracy in America.* South Melbourne: Wadsworth Thomson Learning.

Scheufele, D. A. (1999). Framing as a Theory of Media Effects. *Journal of Communication, 49*(1), 103–122.

Selb, P., Kriesi, H., Hänggli, R., & Marr, M. (2009). Partisan Choices in a Direct-Democratic Campaign. *European Political Science Review, 1*(1), 155–172.

Sunstein, C. R. (2001). *Republic.com.* Princeton: Princeton University Press.

Tresch, A. (2012). The (Partisan) Role of the Press in Direct Democratic Campaigns: Evidence from a Swiss Vote on European Integration. *Swiss Political Science Review, 18*(3), 287–304.

Warren, M. (2017). A Problem-Based Approach to Democratic Theory. *American Political Science Review, 111*(1), 39–53.

WEMF. (2017). *MA Strategy.* Zürich: WEMF. https://wemf.ch/de/downloads/studien/ma-strategy/broschuere-ma-strategy.pdf.

Wirth, W., Schemer, C., Kühne, R., & Matthes, J. (2010). The Impact of Positive and Negative Affects in Direct-Democratic Campaigns. In H. Kriesi (Ed.), *Manipulation or Deliberation.* Zurich: Unpublished Manuscript.

Appendix

CONTENT ANALYSIS OF CAMPAIGN MATERIAL AND MEDIA CONTENT

The content analysis is most important for my study. In all three campaigns, we conducted a content analysis of the media input (=press releases and documents written for media conferences), political advertisements, letters to the editor, and of the media's news reporting. Additionally, direct mails and information for members were coded in the asylum law campaign. All material was coded in the same manner,[1] with three levels of analysis—the level of the article, the political actor, and the argument.

The first level refers to the *article*, by which we mean a document such as a press release or an article in a newspaper. At the article level, we coded formal information such as the date, name of the newspaper, title, position, length, section, article type, the use of an image, and information about the content such as the cause of the report, inter-media agenda-setting, relevance, source, number of points of view, difficulty of terminology, presence or absence of a lead, and degree of objectivity and emotionality.

---

[1]The codebook is available upon request.

© The Editor(s) (if applicable) and The Author(s), under exclusive license to Springer Nature Switzerland AG 2020
R. Hänggli, *The Origin of Dialogue in the News Media*,
Challenges to Democracy in the 21st Century,
https://doi.org/10.1007/978-3-030-26582-3

The second level refers to a *political actor* who is presented in the news or uses an argument in a campaign document such as a press release. At this level, we coded information such as organization, institution or party with which the political actor is associated, his/her name or regional provenance, and his/her position.

The third level refers to the *argument*. An argument is defined as an expression of a specific point of view. In each document—press release, newspaper article, TV news program, etc.—we coded in great detail *all* of the arguments provided by/reported for each of the relevant actors (organizations or their individual representatives) in our study. Note that, for each argument, we introduce two different codes, one for the pro and one for the contraposition on the issue (see codebook). The arguments allow for the linking together of the different actors—politicians and journalists—and constitute almost exclusively the unit of analysis in this study. I will make clear when the article or speaker level is the relevant level of analysis.

The *arguments* that the two camps produced to support their own position or to undermine the position of their adversaries were used for the operationalization of the *substantive* frames. After coding the arguments, we summarized them in a limited number (<10) of abstract categories (=frames), which we created on the basis of our reading of the points of dispute in a given campaign. The arguments focus mainly on the aspect of the problem definition. While this procedure does not address all of the possible aspects of a frame (Entman 1993), it does at least deal with the most important one. After grouping the arguments according to frames, we defined the main frames (=most important frames) for each side on the basis of their relative frequency in the media input. The camp which used a main frame more frequently than the other camp in the media input is said to own the frame. The use of a main frame by an opponent is called "offensive" (=trespassing), if the opponent uses the frame approvingly. By contrast, if the opponent rejects the frame, it is called "defensive" (=counter-framing) use. Beside the substantive frames, there is another frame type: *Contest frames* are frames which do not address the issue(s) at stake, but focus on the actors involved or on the contest per se—on politics. They consist of personal attacks, or conflicts. A conflict refers to a dispute without a specific substantive content. For instance, a general statement of the type "our organization rejects the accusation of our adversaries" is a conflict. If a speaker is directly attacked, or the legitimacy of the speaker is challenged, it is a personal attack. It is possible that the contest frames put forward by parties to the media differ from the contest frames that the media themselves introduce. For instance, partisans in their media input might use a personal attack rather than substantive, issue-based argument and journalists might introduce contest frames by talking about the horse race rather than substantive, issue-based arguments.

Coding Procedures for Arguments

For the interviews with the political actors, we needed to know the important arguments in advance. On the one hand, we used the parliamentary debate and newspaper articles on previous debates about the same issue to find these arguments. On the other hand, we relied on interviews with experts, such as the person responsible for the ballot pamphlet that is sent to every citizen (Oswald Sigg), a researcher who is very experienced with direct-democratic campaigns and has an astonishing memory (Hans Hirter), a lawyer with excellent knowledge about the asylum law (Maja Gehrig), and experts from the governmental administration (Brigitte Hauser-Süss, Niklaus Sommerer). In such a way, we developed a list of 12 arguments ahead of time and used them in the interviews (see Table A.4). For the content analysis, we used the same arguments but extended the list by complementing it with arguments from the media input and the news media. For this step, we also had the five generic frames (conflict, human interest, economic consequences, morality, and responsibility [Semetko and Valkenburg 2000]) in mind and were looking for arguments representing these generic frames. In this way, we combined an inductive approach (manual holistic approach, see Matthes and Kohring 2008) with a deductive procedure of coding (Matthes 2009; Matthes and Kohring 2008).

Let me illustrate the coding with one example, the abuse frame. We coded the following pro arguments (in favor of the new law): "the abuse of asylum policy must be stopped", "there are already too many (bogus) asylum seekers in Switzerland", and "Switzerland is too attractive for asylum seekers". The contra arguments (against the new law) were the following: "preventing abuse is impossible", "the new law is not needed, since the number of asylum seekers is low/declining", and "tightening the asylum law hits the wrong/real refugees". As already pointed out, we summarized these (and other) related arguments in a single frame, the abuse frame. Since the pro camp used the abuse frame most often in the media input, it was said to own this frame, and its position on this frame was defined as the offensive use. Thus, if the contra camp uses *pro* arguments of the abuse frame, they are called offensive arguments, and their *contra* arguments on this frame are the defensive arguments.

It is important to note that frames and arguments are not the same. Framing is the process by which political actors define the issue for their audience (e.g., Nelson et al. 1997a, b). A frame highlights some aspects of a perceived reality and enhances a certain interpretation or evaluation of reality (Entman 1993). In this respect, a frame is more than an argument because it also provides a specific understanding of the world. When I am referring to this defining function of a frame, I will use the term "frame". By contrast, I will rely on the term "argument" when I am concerned with a specific statement or with the number of arguments an article contains. In the other cases, I use the terms interchangeably.

Reliability

In the asylum law campaign, eight different students coded the material. In the other two campaigns, the coding was carried out by ten students. At the argument level, Cohen's Kappa for intercoder *reliability* is 0.61 in the asylum law, 0.65 in the corporate tax reform, and 0.67 in the naturalization initiative, which although not high, is acceptable. We consider it acceptable because we checked all of the arguments after the coding and corrected for coding errors. In addition, for the analysis, we summarized the detailed codes for arguments into broader categories (frames), which are less error-prone.

Details on Expert Interviews with Political Actors

Our research team deliberately did not focus on the leaders of the organizations. Rather, the campaign managers—i.e., the people acting in the background and responsible for the direct-democratic campaign—were better suited to answer our questions about the campaign strategies. The Swiss campaign managers were very cooperative. With one exception, we had no problem obtaining interview partners. In the one exception, the campaign manager was one of the most powerful politicians at the time, and he did not give a reason for refusing the interview. However, we were still able to interview another key campaign manager of the same party and obtained all of the necessary information. Thus, we can conclude that in Switzerland conducting interviews with the campaign managers is unproblematic. It was, however, difficult to garner information about the campaign budgets. In Switzerland, people tend to only speak about money confidentially. We did receive some honest answers relating to the monetary aspect of the campaigns, but some campaign managers refused to mention any amount at all, some spoke only in vague terms about the budget, and several even lied about the amounts they spent, as indicated by our checks based on secondary material. In order to gain some more reliable information about the financial aspect, we measured the size and number of political advertisements—one of the key budgetary items in a Swiss direct-democratic campaign. Based on the total size of political advertisements, we calculated estimates for the money the political actors spent on advertisements.

Immediately after recording the interviews and taking notes, we wrote minutes, in which we summarized the main statements. The detailed record was used only for clarification. We did not transcribe the interviews and accepted that the minutes already included a degree of interpretation by the two interviewers (Laurent Bernhard and the author). This pragmatic way of using the minutes is sufficient to answer our research questions and allowed us to conduct and analyze a total of no less than 218 interviews. The modal duration of an interview was about 60 minutes. The interviews relied on two structured questionnaires containing more than 200 closed-ended and open-ended questions (see Hänggli et al. 2012 for a more detailed description).

Details on Expert Interviews with Journalists

For information on the resources available to and operating norms of journalists (Chapter 5), I also relied to a very limited extent on data collected in interviews with journalists. The conversations were conducted with journalists of *all* relevant newspapers and TV programs during and after the campaigns (25 in the asylum law, 29 in the naturalization initiative, 37 in the corporate tax reform).

Details on Panel Study (Chapter 8)

Although our samples are representative in terms of participants' sex, age, and residence, three aspects impair the representativeness of our results. First and most problematic is the bias in terms of education, as the lowest educational levels are underrepresented in our data. Second, there is also systematic panel attrition. For instance, less-educated and younger people are more likely to drop out of our samples. These biases, along with a leniency bias, may have produced over-reporting in voting turnout (see Table A.1). This bias is not problematic for the study at hand because participation as a dependent variable is not analyzed. The panel studies come close to the official outcomes of the vote. Apart from parameter estimates at the population level, there are no hints that would prevent us from drawing conclusions about structural relations between variables even if these are affected by panel non-random missingness or panel mortality attrition.

Most of the constructs in the questionnaire were assessed repeatedly. The first part of the questionnaire captured participants' interest in the campaign, interpersonal communication, and information processing strategies. Subsequently, we asked for the knowledge or salience and the approval of the arguments. The knowledge and approval of arguments are of pivotal interest in the present study. For each panel wave in the three studies, respondents were asked whether they knew the specific arguments and the extent to which they agreed or disagreed with the arguments. After the argument block in the questionnaire, respondents were asked to report their emotional reactions toward asylum seekers in the first study, toward foreigners in general in the second study, and their affective reactions in the context of the corporate tax debate in the third study. Subsequently, the attitudes about the specific issue, people's voting intentions and the intended (or actual) participation were gauged. In all three surveys, issue-specific predictors were assessed, such as values, authoritarianism, and threat perceptions. A next measure was the use of different communication channels and news media and the reliance on other sources (e.g., radio, web sites, or campaign advertising). Finally, we asked for general political interest, party identification, ideological left-right self-positioning, trust in government, and demographics (e.g., religion, occupation). Questions about sex, age, education, and residence were asked right at the beginning of the interview. These questions ensured that our quota would be completed. The time to complete the CATI interviews was approximately 20–30 minutes.

DIALOGUE

For the operationalization of dialogue (convergence), I use a formula developed by Sigelman and Buell (2004):

$$100 - \left(\Sigma \left| P_{\mathrm{pf}} - P_{\mathrm{cf}} \right| / 2 \right)$$

P_{pf} and P_{cf} are the percentage of total emphasis that the pro and contra camps, respectively, put on a certain frame, f. This measure is derived from the total of the absolute differences between the two camps in the share of attention each camp devotes to a certain frame. For example, assume that there were four frames for the two camps to address, and that the sides distributed their attention as follows:

	Contra camp (%)	Pro camp (%)
Frame 1	100	0
Frame 2	0	0
Frame 3	0	100
Frame 4	0	0

In this example, the pro camp concentrated exclusively on one frame, the contra camp focused exclusively on a different frame, and both sides ignored the other two frames. Obviously, no dialogue occurred during this campaign. The sum of the absolute differences between the camps would be 200. The differences add up to 200 rather than 100 because two actors are involved, meaning that we are dealing with twice 100%. Thus, we need to divide the sum by 2 in order to calibrate the measure to the range between 0 and 100. In addition, by using the difference, we have a measure of dissimilarity. We need to convert the measure to one of similarity by subtracting the calibrated number from 100. The closer the measure is to 100, the more dialogue we have. A score of, say, 80 for a campaign would indicate an 80% overlap in the two camps' attention profiles. In the example above, we would divide 200 by 2 = 100. Subtracting this from 100 = a zero measure of similarity, i.e., there was no dialogue in this example. I call this measure campaign dialogue because it measures dialogue at the campaign level.

Table A.2 shows the percentage for each frame's presentation in the news media in the asylum law. They differ from each other because on the left hand side, I exclude other and contest frames. For campaign dialogue (illustrated in Chapter 1), I rely on the shares presented at the left hand of Table A.2 (without other arguments and contest frames). I am interested in substantive dialogue. Thus, it does not make sense to include contest frames representing attacks or conflict. Furthermore, the category "other arguments" includes different frames. It does not make sense to include this category because it is unclear which of the other

Table A.1   Results and participation rates: comparison of official outcomes with outcomes of our study

	Results (percent in favor)		Participation rate	
	Official	Our study	Official	Our study
Asylum	67.8	61.3	49.2	87.5
Naturalization	36.0	27.7	45.1	79.9
Corporation tax	50.4	52.6	39.0	86.2

Note Official results without Ticino (Italian-speaking part of the country), which was not covered by our surveys

frames the political actors talk about. In other words, if actor A uses an argument of the "other" frames, we do not know whether actor B replies to the same argument or to a different "other" frame. For campaign dialogue, the sum of all main frames equals 100%. For the remaining analysis (Chapter 7), I also present the percentage of other arguments and the contest frames.

FRAME DIALOGUE

To determine the extent of *frame dialogue* (frame-level convergence), we use the following measure proposed by Kaplan et al. (2006), where P_{pf} and P_{cf} again represent the percentages of emphasis that the pro and contra camps put on a certain frame, *f*.

$$\left(1 - \left|\left(P_{pf} - P_{cf}\right)/\left(P_{pf} + P_{cf}\right)\right|\right) * 100$$

DETAILS ON CAMPAIGN SELECTION CRITERIA (CHAPTER 3)

Complexity: Complexity is measured by the share of voters who had difficulties in making a decision on a given proposal (Kriesi and Bernhard 2010).

Unfamiliarity: Voters who were still undecided at the beginning of the campaign (Kriesi and Bernhard 2010).

Imbalance in Financial Resources of the Campaigns: Difference in pro and contra advertisements in six selected major newspapers—three each in German- and French-speaking Switzerland—over the final four weeks preceding the vote. This indicator is a proxy of campaign budgets, but given that the campaigners mainly use newspaper ads to sway the public, it provides a rather good idea of the balance in monetary terms of a given campaign (Kriesi 2005).

Closeness of Vote Outcome: As far as the expected closeness of a vote outcome is concerned, I draw on the evaluation of the key campaign managers. In the interviews before the vote took place, they were asked to predict the vote outcome. Expected outcomes between 45 and 55% of yes votes were coded as signifying a close race (Tables A.3, A.4, and A.5).

POWER

Power is operationalized by a reputational indicator and is based on a set of questions referring to the list of all organizations involved (Kriesi et al. 2006; Bernhard 2012). In the second interviews, the campaigners were first asked to name the organizations on the list which, from their point of view, had been particularly influential during the campaign. Next, they were asked to name the three most influential organizations, and, finally, the most influential one. For each organization, a summary indicator reflects the number of times it was mentioned by the other respondents in reaction to these questions: mentions as "most influential" are coded as "3", mentions among the "three most influential" as "2", and mentions as "influential" as "1". The values of the indicator range from 0, for an organization that was never mentioned as influential, to 3 times the number of respondents, for an organization that would have been considered to be the most influential actor by all of them.

FRAME STRENGTH

The strength of the frames in communication is operationalized by opponents' defensive reactions with respect to a given frame, i.e., by the share of the opponents' counter-arguments, averaged across the frames in the media input and the media frames (Hänggli and Kriesi 2010). This means that trespassing (=offensive use of opponents' substantive frames) is not part of my measure of strength. I believe that trespassing is an attempt to "steal" an opponent's frame by using the same argument and taking the same position as that opponent. I consider that a frame which can be stolen is not a strong frame. To provide an example for the calculation: The pro camp counter-framed (=defensive use of

Table A.2   Frame shares (shares without other and contest frames form the basis for calculation of campaign dialogue)

	Asylum law (news media) (Table 1.1)		Asylum law (news media) (Table 6.1)	
	Contra camp	Pro camp	Contra camp	Pro camp
Human. trad.	48	25	30	15
Rule-of-law	15	8	9	5
Abuse	26	46	16	28
Efficacy	12	21	8	13
Other arguments	–	–	24	23
Contest frames	–	–	13	16
Total (%)	101	100	100	100
Dialogue	70[a]			

[a]Dialogue = 70, resulting from $100 - ((|48 - 25| + |15 - 8| + |26 - 46| + |12 - 21|)/2)$

the argument) the humanitarian tradition frame in 20.3% of the media input and attained a news media share of 12.6% with it (Table 6.1). The average of the two numbers is 16.5%, i.e., the strength of this frame (Table 7.2). I take the average because it is more intuitive. In such a way, the maximum is 100%, which would indicate that the actor defensively speaks only about his or her opponents' frame. The minimum is 0%.

ZERO-INFLATED NEGATIVE BINOMIAL MODEL
(METHOD DETAILS CHAPTER 7)

Given that we are dealing with count data, the Poisson model is appropriate; however, given the overdispersion found in the data, we use the negative binomial, a special version of the Poisson model that is adapted to this particular type of problem.[2] When interpreting zero-inflated

[2]Overdispersion implies the presence of greater variability (statistical dispersion) in the predicted counts for a given value of x than would be expected based on the Poisson regression model. Stata provides a likelihood-ratio test for overdispersion. In addition, due to the excess zeros in the data, also called zero inflation, a zero-inflated count model is necessary. Greene (2000) proposed the Vuong (1989) test for non-nested models in order to establish whether a zero-inflated model is necessary. Zero-inflated count models assume that there are two latent (i.e., unobserved) groups: an "Always Zero" and a "Not Always Zero" group and that zero counts are generated by two independently operating processes.

Table A.3 Complexity, familiarity, imbalance in financial resources, and expected closeness of the three proposals

	Complexity	Familiarity	Imbalance in finan-cial resources (pro advantage in number of ads)	Expected closeness of vote outcome (percentage of campaigners who expect a close race)
Asylum	38.0	14.3	−2	60
Naturalization	27.0	35.7	73	80
Corporation tax	61.1	28.7	362	40

Note Indicators based on VOX surveys

models, it is easy to be confused by the meaning of the effect parameters (the incidence-rate ratios). Such models have two parts—an inflation model and a count model. The inflation model estimates the effects (incidence-rate ratios) of factors under investigation (e.g., power) on the possibility that an argument will not make it into the media, i.e., on the possibility of its absence from the media. The count model estimates the effects (incidence-rate ratios) of factors under investigation (e.g., input by political actors, minister dummy indicator) on the frequency of an argument's presence in the media. When the same independent variables are included in the equation for both models, the effects from the two models often point in opposite directions, i.e., one is smaller, the other larger than one. This makes sense from a substantive point of view. In the inflation model, a ratio smaller than one implies a higher probability that the frame will make it into the media; correspondingly, in the count model, a ratio larger than one increases the frequency in the media.

In other words, this model allows a distinction to be drawn between frame presence/absence in the media on the one hand and frame frequency in the media on the other hand. Accordingly, frame building can be conceived of as being composed of two processes—the daily frame

In the first process (Inflation Model), the zeros belonging to the "Always Zero" group are generated. An argument in this group has an outcome of zero with a probability of one. This process is binary; it generates zeros or ones. If this first process results in one, the second process is assumed to come into play: a negative binomial regression process (count model) which generates zeros of the "Not Always" group. An argument in this group might have a zero count, but there is a non-zero probability that it has a positive count.

Table A.4   Arguments used in interviews with political actors

---

Asylum

Pro arguments	Frame
The abuse of asylum policy must be stopped	Abuse
Switzerland is too attractive for asylum seekers	
There are already too many foreigners in Switzerland	
The social welfare benefits for asylum seekers are too generous	
The execution of asylum politics must be more efficient	Efficacy
The shifting of costs in the asylum system to the cities must be prevented	Others (cost)
The asylum seekers are placing the fatherland in danger	Others (soc. factor)
Contra arguments	
The humanitarian tradition of Switzerland must be maintained	Human. trad.
Foreign people contribute to the social and cultural quality of Switzerland	
The rights of asylum seekers have to be protected	Rule-of-law
International law and international agreements need to be complied with	
Taking a harder line on tackling the problems in the asylum system is ineffective	Abuse

---

Naturalization

Pro arguments	Frame
Mass naturalization has to be stopped	Mass naturalization
There are too many foreigners in Switzerland	
Each municipality should decide by itself which authority is responsible for naturalization	People final say
Civil servants should not be allowed to decide about naturalizations	
The people should decide about naturalizations	
Court appeals against naturalization decisions should be forbidden	Rule-of-law
We need to make a gesture against the criminality of foreigners.	Others
Contra arguments	
This initiative brings discriminatory and arbitrary naturalization decisions	Rule-of-law
Naturalizations have to be in accordance with the rule of law	
The rights of foreigners have to be protected	
The initiative contradicts the Federal system of Switzerland	
Naturalization candidates are well integrated in general	Mass naturalization (defensive use)
This poll damages the image of Switzerland	Others

(continued)

Table A.4 (continued)

Corporate tax reform

Pro arguments	Frame
This tax reform advances SMEs	SME
This tax reform advances the competitiveness of the Swiss economy	Competitiveness
This tax reform advances investments and creates new jobs	
Double taxation is unfair	Tax equity
The partial taxation of dividends has proven to work in various cantons	(defensive use)

Contra arguments	
A tax relief for major shareholders is unfair	Tax equity
A clear signal against excessive management salaries is needed	
All shareholders should get a tax discount	
This tax reform harms the basic pension insurance (AHV)	Tax loss
This tax reform brings unacceptable tax loss for the federal government and the cantons	
The fiscal competition is damaging for Switzerland	Competitiveness
This tax reform makes the tax system even more complicated	Others
This reform violates the constitution	

Table A.5 Arguments used in panel survey

Asylum

Pro arguments	Frame
The abuse of asylum policy must be stopped	Abuse
Switzerland is too attractive for asylum seekers	
There are already too many foreigners in Switzerland	
The social welfare benefits for asylum seekers are too generous	
The execution of asylum politics must be more efficient	Efficacy
Asylum applications should only be accepted, if identity papers are available	

Contra arguments	
The humanitarian tradition of Switzerland must be maintained	Human. trad.
Foreign people contribute to the social and cultural quality of Switzerland	
The rights of asylum seekers have to be protected	Rule-of-law
International law and international agreements need to be complied with	
Taking a harder line on tackling the problems in the asylum system is ineffective	Abuse

Table A.5 (continued)

Naturalization

Pro arguments	**Frame**
Mass naturalization has to be stopped There are too many foreigners in Switzerland	Mass naturalization
Each municipality should decide by itself which authority is responsible for naturalization Civil servants should not be allowed to decide about naturalizations	People final say
The people should decide about naturalizations	
Contra arguments	
This initiative brings discriminatory and arbitrary naturalization decisions Naturalizations have to be in accordance with the rule of law	Rule-of-law
The rights of foreigners have to be protected	
Naturalization candidates are well integrated in general	Mass naturalization (defensive use)
This poll damages the image of Switzerland	Others

Corporate tax reform

Pro arguments	**Frame**
This tax reform advances SMEs	SME
This tax reform advances the competitiveness of the Swiss economy	Competitiveness
This tax reform advances investments and creates new jobs	
Double taxation is unfair	Tax equity (defensive use)
Contra arguments	
A tax relief for major shareholders is unfair A clear signal against excessive management salaries is needed	Tax equity
All shareholders should get a tax discount	
This tax reform harms the basic pension insurance (AHV) This tax reform brings unacceptable tax loss for the federal government and the cantons	Tax loss
This tax reform makes the tax system even more complicated	Others

absence/presence and the daily frame *frequency*. In a similar way, Tresch (2009) defines two dimensions of standing: presence (=non-absence) and prominence. Since both absence and frequency are measured on a daily basis, I refer in this context to the daily frame absence/presence and daily frame frequency (Tables A.6 and A.7).

Table A.6 Applicability (=Strength) of the frames in thought—estimates from the random intercept probit models of the vote choice for the three campaigns, unstandardized regression coefficients, standard errors and levels of significance (Chapter 8)

	Asylum			Naturalization			Corporation tax		
	Coef.	s.e.	$P > z$	Coef.	s.e.	$P > z$	Coef.	s.e.	$P > z$
Fixed part									
Overall									
Issue pref	0.422	0.067	***	0.253	0.067	***	0.090	0.067	ns
Partisan pref	0.408	0.063	***	0.118	0.061	ns	0.184	0.067	**
Ambivalence	0.318	0.060	***	0.127	0.053	**	0.083	0.062	ns
t1									
Core frame contra	**−0.034**	**0.053**	ns	**−0.185**	**0.051**	***	**−0.111**	**0.049**	*
2nd frame contra	**−0.269**	**0.057**	***				**−0.235**	**0.053**	***
Core frame pro	**0.231**	**0.059**	***	**0.264**	**0.053**	***	**0.275**	**0.055**	***
2nd frame pro	**0.155**	**0.055**	**	**0.220**	**0.057**	***	**0.382**	**0.061**	***
t2−t1	0.001	0.174	ns						
Issue pref t2−t1	0.125	0.091	ns						
Partisan pref t2−t1	0.405	0.090	***						
Ambivalence t2−t1	−0.086	0.092	ns						
t2									
Core frame contra t2	**−0.331**	**0.078**	***	−0.515	0.106	***	0.360	0.132	**
2nd frame contra t2	**−0.140**	**0.076**	*	0.035	0.106	ns	0.039	0.108	ns
Core frame pro t2	**0.397**	**0.077**	***	0.425	0.106	***	0.102	0.106	ns
2nd frame pro t2	**0.367**	**0.073**	***	-0.134	0.091	ns	0.302	0.105	**
t3−t1	0.431	0.193	*						
Issue pref t3−t1	−0.009	0.111	ns						
Partisan pref t3−t1	0.342	0.109	**						
Ambivalence t3−t1	−0.021	0.108	ns						
t3									
Core frame contra t3	**−0.451**	**0.100**	***	−0.232	0.066	***	−0.229	0.057	***

(continued)

Table A.6 (continued)

	Asylum			Naturalization			Corporation tax		
	Coef.	s.e.	P > z	Coef.	s.e.	P > z	Coef.	s.e.	P > z
2nd frame contra t3	−0.353	0.103	**				−0.331	0.057	***
Core frame pro t3	0.521	0.095	***	0.351	0.068	***	0.465	0.066	***
2nd frame pro t3	0.511	0.095	***	0.233	0.068	***	0.507	0.073	***
Undecided				−1.431	0.147	***	−1.175	0.119	***
un_issue pref t3−1				0.686	0.209	***	−0.177	0.152	ns
un_party pref t3−1				0.955	0.207	***	0.031	0.142	ns
un_ambivalence t3−1				0.579	0.196	**	−0.616	0.147	***
Constant	0.284	0.115	*	−0.321	0.067	***	0.028	0.094	
Random part									
/lnsig2u	−0.14	0.17		−1.74	0.67		−1.36	0.49	
sigma_u	0.93	0.08		0.41	0.14		0.51	0.12	
rho	0.46	0.04		0.15	0.09		0.20	0.08	
Chibar2	113.4		***	3.0		*	6.4		**
Rho null model	0.78	0.02		0.51	0.04		0.56	0.04	

$*p < 0.05$, $**p < 0.01$, $***p < 0.001$

Asylum: n observations = 3262, respondents = 1323

Naturalization: n observations = 1859, respondents = 997

Corporation tax: n observations = 1669, respondents = 853

Notes: For the asylum law, the model is estimated without the coefficient for the initially undecided voters, since in this familiar case, indecision did not influence the vote. Only 14.3% of the voters were undecided and all of the effects for the undecided voters turned out to be insignificant. The upper part of the table (most of the table) contains the fixed effects, which are the important effects for the frame strength. In the lower part of the table, information is presented relating to the random effects (random part).[a]

[a]Sigma_u is the variance of the individual error component. Rho is the proportion of variance that is attributable to differences between respondents. It increases when the variance between respondents increases compared to the variance within respondents. The Chibar2 values at the bottom of the table refer to a particular likelihood ratio test, which checks whether or not rho is zero. Since the P-values for these tests are large, the null hypothesis has to be rejected in each case. For purposes of comparison, I have also provided the rho-value for the null model and the corresponding value for the substantive model gives an indication of the explanatory power of the model. Thus, for the asylum case, this difference $(78 − 46)$ is 32. In other words, in this case, the proportion of variance attributable to inter-individual differences has been reduced by 41% $(32/78 = 0.41)$.

Table A.7 Applicability (=Strength) of the frames in thought estimates from the random intercept probit models of the vote choice for the corporation tax campaign, unstandardized regression coefficients, standard errors and levels of significance. Model with interaction terms between undecided voters and frame positions on t2 (Chapter 8)

Corporation tax	Coef.	s.e.	P > z
Fixed part			
Issue pref	0.119	0.079	ns
Partisan pref	0.205	0.080	**
Ambivalence	−0.112	0.073	ns
Core frame contra t1	**−0.137**	**0.059**	*
2nd frame contra t1	−0.264	0.061	***
Core frame pro t1	0.319	0.064	***
2nd frame pro t1	0.431	0.072	***
t2−1			
Issue pref t2−t1			
Partisan pref t2−t1			
Ambivalence t2−t1			
Core frame contra t2			
2nd frame contra t2			
Core frame pro t2			
2nd frame pro t2			
t3−t1	0.427	0.149	**
Issue pref t3−t1	0.014	0.118	ns
Partisan pref t3−t1	0.127	0.116	ns
Ambivalence t3−t1	0.243	0.114	*
Core frame contra t3	**−0.542**	**0.078**	***
2nd frame contra t3	−0.347	0.073	***
Core frame pro t3	0.404	0.086	***
2nd frame pro t3	0.482	0.096	***
Undecided	−2.115	0.204	***
un_issue pref t3−t1	−0.398	0.180	*
un_party pref t3−t1	0.174	0.163	
un_ambivalence t3−t1	0.402	0.162	*
i_undec. core frame contra t3−t1	**0.994**	**0.130**	***
i_undec. 2nd frame contra t3−t1	−0.178	0.140	
i_undec. core frame pro t3−t1	0.294	0.152	
i_undec. 2nd frame pro t3−t1	0.347	0.170	*
Constant	0.202	0.111	
Random part			
/lnsig2u	−0.535	0.329	
sigma_u	0.765	0.126	
rho	0.369	0.077	
chibar2	19.430		***
Rho null model	0.560	0.040	

*$p < 0.05$, **$p < 0.01$, ***$p < 0.001$
Corporation tax: n observations = 1669, respondents = 853
Note Figure 8.3 is based on this model

Bibliography

Achen, C. H., & Bartels, L. M. (2016). *Democracy for Realists: Why Elections do not Produce Responsive Government.* Oxford: Oxford University Press.

Alvarez, R. M., & Brehm, J. (1995). American Ambivalence Towards Abortion Policy: Development of a Heteroscedastic Probit Model of Competing Values. *American Journal of Political Science, 39,* 1055–1082.

Alvarez, R. M., & Brehm, J. (2002). *Hard Choices, Easy Answers.* Princeton, NJ: Princeton University Press.

Ansolabehere, S., & Iyengar, S. (1994). Riding the Wave and Claiming Ownership over Issues: The Joint Effects of Advertising and News Coverage in Campaigns. *Public Opinion Quarterly, 58*(3), 335–357.

Bachrach, P., & Baratz, M. S. (1970). *Power and Poverty.* New York: Oxford University Press.

Bächtiger, A., Niemeyer, S., Neblo, M., Steenbergen, M., & Steiner, J. (2010). Symposium: Toward More Realistic Models of Deliberative Democracy Disentangling Diversity in Deliberative Democracy—Competing Theories, Their Blind Spots and Complementarities. *The Journal of Political Philosophy, 18*(1), 32–63.

Baerns, B. (1979). Öffentlichkeitsarbeit als Determinante journalistischer Informationsleistungen. *Publizistik, 24*(3), 301–316.

Baerns, B. (1991). *Öffentlichkeitsarbeit oder Journalismus: Zum Einfluss im Mediensystem* (2nd ed.). Köln: Wissenschaft und Politik.

Baker, E. C. (2002). *Media, Markets, and Democracy.* Cambridge: Cambridge University Press.

Baker, E. C. (2007). *Media Concentration and Democracy: Why Ownership Matters.* Cambridge: Cambridge University Press.

Basinger, S., & Lavine, H. (2005). Ambivalence, Information, and Electoral Choice. *American Political Science Review, 99*(1), 169–184.

Baumgartner, F. R., De Boef, S., & Boydstund, A. E. (2008). *The Decline of the Death Penalty and the Discovery of Innocence.* Cambridge: University Press.

Banda, K. K. (2015). Competition and the Dynamics of Issue Convergence. *American Politics Research, 43*(5), 821–845.

Bennett, W. L. (1990a). Taking the Public by Storm: Information, Cuing, and the Democratic Process in the Gulf Conflict. *Political Communication, 10,* 331–351.

Bennett, W. L. (1990b). Toward a Theory of Press-State Relations. *Journal of Communication, 40*(2), 103–125.

Bennett, W. L., Lawrence, R., & Livingston, S. (2007). *When the Press Fails: Political Power and the News Media from Iraq to Katrina.* Chicago: University Press.

Bennett, W. L., Pickard, V. W., Iozzi, D. P., Schroeder, C. L., Lagos, T., & Caswell, E. C. (2004). Managing the Public Sphere: Journalistic Construction of the Great Globalization Debate. *International Communication Association, 54*(3), 437–455.

Benson, R. (2009). What Makes News More Multiperspectival? A Field Analysis. *Poetics, 37*(5–6), 402–418.

Benson, R. (2010). What Makes for a Critical Press? A Case Study of French and U.S. Immigration News Coverage. *International Journal of Press/Politics, 15*(1), 3–24.

Bentele, G. (2005). Intereffikationsmodell. In G. Bentele, R. Fröhlich, & P. Szyszka (Eds.), *Handbuch der Public Relations: Wissenschaftliche Grundlagen und berufliches Handeln* (pp. 209–222). Wiesbaden: VS Verlag für Sozialwissenschaften.

Bentele, G., Liebert, T., & Seeling, S. (1997). Von der Determination zur Intereffikation. Ein integriertes Modell zum Verhältnis von Public Relations und Journalismus. In G. Bentele & M. Haller (Eds.), *Aktuelle Entstehung von Öffentlichkeit. Akteure-Strukturen-Veränderungen* (pp. 225–250). Konstanz: UVK.

Benz, M., & Stutzer, A. (2004): Are Voters Better Informed When They Have a Larger Say in Politics? Evidence for the European Union and Switzerland. *Public Choice, 119*(1), 31–59.

Bernhard, L. (2012). *Campaign Strategy in Direct Democracy.* Hampshire: Palgrave Macmillan.

Bernhard, L., & Kriesi, H. (2012). Coalition Formation. In H. Kriesi (Ed.), *Political Communication in Direct-Democratic Campaigns: Enlightening or Manipulating?* (pp. 54–68). Hampshire: Palgrave Macmillan.

Blum, R. (2003). Medienstrukturen der Schweiz. In G. Bentele, H.-B. Brosius, & O. Jarren (Eds.), *Öffentliche Kommunikation* (pp. 366–381). Wiesbaden: Westdeutscher Verlag.

Blum, R. (2005). Politischer Journalismus in der Schweiz. In P. Donges (Ed.), *Politische Kommunikation in der Schweiz* (pp. 115–130). Bern: Haupt.

Blum, R. (2006). Einleitung: Politische Kultur und Medienkultur im Wechselspiel. In R. Blum, P. Meier, & N. Gysin (Eds.), *Wes Land ich bin, des Lied ich sing? Medien und politische Kultur* (pp. 11–23). Bern: Haupt.

Blumer, H. (1948). Public Opinion and Public Opinion Polling. *American Sociological Review, 13*(5), 542–549.

Blumler, J. G., & Gurevitch, M. (1995 [1975]). Towards a Comparative Framework for Political Communication Research. In J. G. Blumler & M. Gurevitch (Eds.), *The Crisis of Public Communication* (pp. 59–72). London: Routledge.

Blumler, J. G., & Kavanagh, D. (1999). The Third Age of Political Communication: Influences and Features. *Political Communication, 16,* 209–230.

Bonfadelli, H. (2000). Schweizerische Aussenpolitik als Medienthema. Eine Inhaltsanalyse der Berichterstattung in der Presse und in den Fernsehnachrichten. In H. Bonfadelli, B. Nyffeler, & R. Blum (Eds.), *Helvetisches Stiefkind. Schweizerische Aussenpolitik als Gegenstand der Medienvermittlung* (pp. 93–234). Zürich, Switzerland: IPMZ.

Boorstin, D. J. (1992 [1961]). *The Image: A Guide to Pseudo-Events in America* (25th Anniversary Edition ed.). New York: First Vintage Book Edition.

Boudreau, C., & MacKenzie, S. A. (2014). Informing the Electorate? How Party Cues and Policy Information Affect Public Opinion About Initiatives. *American Journal of Political Science, 58*(1), 48–62.

Bowler, S. (2015). Information Availability and Information Use in Ballot Proposition Contests: Are Voters Over-Burdened?*. *Electoral Studies, 38,* 183–191.

Bowler, S., & Donovan, T. (2006). Direct Democracy and Political Parties in America. *Party Politics, 12*(5), 649–669.

Boydstun, A. E. (2013). *Making the News.* Chicago: University of Chicago Press.

Brandenburg, H. (2002). Who Follows Whom? The Impact of Parties on Media Agenda Formation in the 1997 British General Election Campaign. *The International Journal of Press/Politics, 7*(34), 34–54.

Brändle, M. (2001). Die finanziellen Mittel der Parteien. In A. Ladner & M. Brändle (Eds.), *Die Schweizer Parteien im Wandel.* Zürich: Seismo.

Breed, W. (1955). Social Control in the Newsroom: A Functional Analysis. *Social Forces, 33*(4), 326–335.

Brewer, P. R., & Gross, K. (2005). Values, Framing, and Citizens' Thoughts About Policy Issues: Effects on Content and Quality. *Political Psychology, 26,* 929–948.

Brody, R. A., & Page, B. I. (1972). Comment-Assessment of Policy Voting. *American Journal of Political Science, 66*(2), 450–458.

Budge, I. (1996). *The New Challenge of Direct Democracy.* Cambridge: Polity Press.

Bullock, J. G. (2011). Elite Influence on Public Opinion in an Informed Electorate. *American Political Science Review, 105*(August), 496–515.

Bütschi, D. (1993). Compétence pratique. In H. Kriesi (Ed.), *Citoyenneté et démocratie directe* (pp. 99–119). Zürich: Seismo.

Campbell, A., Converse, P., Miller, W., & Stokes, D. (1960). *The American Voter.* New York: Wiley.

Carnegie, D. (2010) [1936]. *How to Win Friends and Influence People.* UK: Simon & Schuster.

Carr, N. (2010). *The Shallows: What the Internet Is Doing to Our Brains.* New York: W. W. Norton.

Chaiken, S., & Trop, Y. (1999). *Dual-Process Theories in Social Psychology.* New York: Guildford Press.

Chambers, S. (2009): Rhetoric and the Public Sphere: Has Deliberative Democracy Abandoned Mass Democracy? *Political Theory, 37*(3), 323–350.

Chong, D., & Druckman, J. N. (2007a). Framing Public Opinion in Competitive Democracies. *American Political Science Review, 101*(4), 637–656.

Chong, D., & Druckman, J. N. (2007b). A Theory of Framing and Opinion Formation in Competitive Elite Environments. *Journal of Communication, 57*(1), 99–118.

Chong, D., & Druckman, J. N. (2007c). Framing Theory. *Annual Review of Political Science, 10,* 103–126.

Chong, D., & Druckman, J. N. (2011). Public-Elite Interactions: Puzzles in Search of Researchers, with Dennis Chong. In R. Y. Shapiro & L. R. Jacobs (Eds.), *The Oxford Handbook of the American Public Opinion and the Media* (p. 2011). Oxford: Oxford University Press.

Chong, D., & Druckman, J. N. (2011). Public-Elite Interactions: Puzzles in Search of Researchers. In R. Y. Shapiro & L. R. Jacobs (Eds.), *The Oxford Handbook of the American Public Opinion and the Media.* Oxford: Oxford University Press.

Chong, D., & Druckman, J. N. (2013). Counterframing Effects. *The Journal of Politics, 75,* 1–16.

Ciuk, D. J., & Yost, B. A. (2016). The Effects of Issue Salience, Elite Influence, and Policy Content on Public Opinion. *Political Communication, 33*(2), 328–345.

Cobb, R. W., & Elder, C. D. (1971). *Participation in American Politics: The Dynamics of Agenda-Building.* Baltimore: Johns Hopkins University Press.

Cohen, B. C. (1963). *The Press and Foreign Policy.* Princeton: University Press.

Cohen, G. L. (2003). Party Over Policy: The Dominating Impact of Group Influence on Political Beliefs. *Journal of Personality and Social Psychology*, *85*(5), 808–822.

Colombo, C. (2016). *Partisan, Not Ignorant—Citizens' Use of Arguments and Justifications in Direct Democracy* (PhD thesis). European University Institute, Florence.

Colombo, C. (2018). Justifications and Citizen Competence in Direct Democracy: A Multilevel Analysis. *British Journal of Political Science, 48*(3), 787–806.

Colombo, C., & Kriesi, H. (2017). Party, Policy – or Both? Partisan Biased Processing of Policy Arguments in Direct Democracy. *Journal of Elections, Public Opinion and Parties, 27*(3), 235–253.

Cook, T. (1989). *Making Laws and Making News. Media Strategies in the U.S. House of Representatives*. Washington, DC: Brookings Institution.

Coombs, C. H. (1964). *A Theory of Data*. New York: Wiley.

Cronin, T. E. (1989). *Direct Democracy: The Politics of Initiative, Referendum, and Recall*. Cambridge, MA: Harvard University Press.

Dahinden, U., & Trappel, J. (2005). Mediengattungen, Medienformate. In H. Bonfadelli (Ed.), *Einführung in die Publizistikwissenschaft* (pp. 389–424). Bern: UTB.

Dahl, R. A. (2000). *On Democracy*. New Haven: Yale University Press.

Damore, D. F. (2005). Issue Convergence in Presidential Campaigns. *Political Behavior, 27*(1), 71–97.

Danielian, L. H., & Page, B. I. (1994). The Heavenly Chorus: Interest Group Voices on TV News. *American Journal of Political Science, 38*(4), 1056–1078.

De Vreese, C. H. (2004). The Effects of Frames in Political Television News on Issue Interpretation and Frame Salience. *Journalism & Mass Communication Quarterly, 81*(1), 36–52.

De Vreese, C. (2005). News Framing: Theory and Typology. *Information Design Journal + Document Design, 13*(1), 51–62.

De Vreese, C. H., & Semetko, H. A. (2004). News Matters: Influences on the Vote in a Referendum Campaign. *European Journal of Political Research, 43*(5), 701–724.

De Vries, R., Stanczyk, A., Wall, I. F., Uhlmann, R., Damschroder, L. J., & Kim, S. Y. (2010). Assessing the Quality of Democratic Deliberation: A Case Study of Public Deliberation on the Ethics of Surrogate Consent for Research. *Social Science and Medicine, 70*(12), 1896–1903.

Disch, L. (2011). Toward a Mobilization Conception of Democratic Representation. *American Political Science Review, 105*(1), 100–114.

Druckman, J. N. (2001). The Implications of Framing Effects for Citizen Competence. *Political Behavior, 23*, 225–256.

Druckman, J. N. (2004). Political Preference Formation: Competition, Deliberation, and the (Ir)relevance of Framing Effects. *American Political Science Review, 98*(4), 671–686.

Druckman, J. N. (2009). What's It All About? Framing in Political Science. In G. Keren (Ed.), *Perspectives on Framing*. New York: Psychology Press.

Druckman, J. N. (2014). Pathologies of Studying Public Opinion, Political Communication, and Democratic Responsiveness. *Political Communication, 31*, 467–492.

Druckman, J. N., & Holmes, J. W. (2004). Does Presidential Rhetoric Matter? Priming and Presidential Approval. *Presidential Studies Quarterly, 34*, 755–778.

Druckman, J. N., Peterson, E., & Slothuus, R. (2013). How Elite Partisan Polarization Affects Public Opinion Formation. *American Political Science Review, 107*(1), 57–79.

Druckman, J. N., Kifer, M., & Parkin, M. (2009). *Campaign Communications in U.S. Congressional Elections*. Chicago: Northwestern University.

Druckman, J. N., & Nelson, K. R. (2003). Framing and Deliberation: How Citizens' Conversations Limit Elite Influence. *American Journal of Political Science, 47*(4), 729–745.

Dunaway, J., & Lawrence, R. G. (2015). What Predicts the Game Frame? Media Ownership, Electoral Context, and Campaign News. *Political Communication, 32*(1), 43–60.

Eagly, A. H., & Chaiken, S. (1993). *The Psychology of Attitudes*. New York: Harcourt Brace.

Edelman, M. J. (1993). Contestable Categories and Public Opinion. *Political Communication, 10*, 231–242.

Engeli, I., Anouk, L., & Nai, A. (2008). Analysis of the Federal Votes of June 1, 2008 (Analyse der eidgenössischen Abstimmungen vom 1. Juni 2008). *Vox Analysis*.

Eilders, C. (1997). *Nachrichtenfaktoren und Rezeption: Eine empirische Analyse zur Auswahl und Verarbeitung politischer Information* [News Factors and Reception: An Empirical Analysis of the Audience's Selection and Retention Processes in Political Communication]. Opladen: Westdeutscher Verlag.

Engeli, I., Lloren, A., & Nai, A. (2008): Analyse der eidgenössischen Abstimmungen vom 1. Juni 2008. *Vox-Analyse*. Geneva: University of Geneva.

Entman, R. M. (1989). *Democracy Without Citizens: Media and the Decay of American Politics*. New York: Oxford University Press.

Entman, R. M. (1993). Framing: Toward Clarification of a Fractured Paradigm. *Journal of Communication, 43*, 51–58.

Entman, R. M. (2003). Cascading Activation: Contesting the White House's Frame After 9/11. *Political Communication, 20*, 415–432.

Entman, R. M. (2004). *Projections of Power Framing News, Public Opinion, and U.S. Foreign Policy*. Chicago, IL: University of Chicago Press.

Entman, R. M. (2007). Framing Bias: Media in the Distribution of Power. *Journal of Communication, 57,* 167–176.

Ferree, M Marx, Gamson, W. A., Gerhards, J., & Rucht, D. (2002). *Shaping Abortion Discourse Democracy and the Public Sphere in Germany and the United States.* Cambridge: Cambridge University Press.

Fishkin, J. S. (1991). *Democracy and Deliberation: New Directions for Democratic Reform.* New Haven: Yale University Press.

Fishkin, J. S. (1992). *The Dialogue of Justice: Toward a Self-Reflective Society.* New Haven: Yale University Press.

fög/Universität Zürich. (2013). *Qualität der Medien. Jahrbuch 2013.* Basel: Schwabe.

fög/Universität Zürich. (2014). *Qualität der Medien. Jahrbuch 2014.* Basel: Schwabe.

fög/Universität Zürich. (2015). *Qualität der Medien. Jahrbuch 2015.* Basel: Schwabe.

Franz, M. M. (2014). Interest Group Issue Appeals: Evidence of Issue Convergence in Senate and Presidential Elections, 2008–2014. *Forum, 12*(4), 685–712.

Galtung, J., & Ruge, M. H. (1965). The Structure of Foreign News. *Journal of Peace Research, 2*(1), 64–91.

Gamson, W. A. (1992). *Talking Politics.* Cambridge: University Press.

Gamson, W. A. (2004). Bystanders, Public Opinion, and the Media. In D. A. Snow, S. A. Soule, & H. Kriesi (Eds.), *The Blackwell Companion to Social Movements* (pp. 242–261). Oxford: Blackwell.

Gamson, W. A., Croteau, D., Hones, W., & Sasson, T. (1992). Media Images and the Social Construction of Reality. *Annual Review of Sociology, 18,* 373–393.

Gamson, W. A., & Modigliani, A. (1989). Media Discourse and Public Opinion on Nuclear Power: A Constructionist Approach. *The American Journal of Sociology, 95*(1), 1–37.

Gamson, W. A., & Modigliani, A. (1987). The Changing Culture of Affirmative Action. In R. D. Braungart (Ed.), *Research in Political Sociology* (pp. 137–177). Greenwich: JAI.

Gans, H. J. (1979). *Deciding What's News: A Study of CBS Evening News, NBC Nightly News, Newsweek, and Time.* New York: Pantheon Books.

Gans, H. J. (2003). *Democracy and the News.* New York: Oxford University Press.

Gerth, M., Dahinden, U., & Siegert, G. (2012). Coverage of the Campaigns in the Media. In H. Kriesi (Ed.), *Political Communication in Direct-Democratic Campaigns: Enlightening or Manipulating?* (pp. 108–124). Hampshire: Palgrave Macmillan.

Gerth, M., Rademacher, P., Pühringer, K., Dahinden, U., & Siegert, G. (2009). Challenges to Political Campaigns in the Media: Commercialization, Framing, and Personalization. *Studies in Communication Studies, 9*(1), 69–89.

Gilland, K., & Marquis, L. (2006). Campaigning in a Direct Democracy: Three Case Studies. *Swiss Political Science Review, 12*(3), 63–81.

Gitlin, T. (2003 [1980]). *The Whole World Is Watching: Mass Media in the Making and Unmaking of the New Left.* Berkeley: University of California Press.

Goffman, E. (1974). *Frame Analysis.* Cambridge: Harvard University Press.

Golder, L. (2016). *Keine Angst vor Emotionen: in der direkten Demokratie überwiegen Argumente.* Bern: Gfs Bern. http://www.gfsbern.ch/de-ch/Detail/keine-angst-vor-emotionen-in-der-direkten-demokratie-ueberwiegen-argumente. September 2017.

Graber, D. A. (2001). *Processing Politics: Learning from Television in the Internet Age.* Chicago: University of Chicago Press.

Greene, W. H. (2000). *Econometric Analysis.* Upper Saddle River, NJ: Prentice-Hall.

Groseclose, T. (2001). A Model of Candidate Location When One Candidate Has a Valence Advantage. *American Journal of Political Science, 45*(4), 862–886.

Gruner, E., & Hertig, H. P. (1983). *Der Stimmbürger und die «neue» Politik.* Bern: Haupt.

Habermas, J. (1996). *Between Facts and Norms: Contributions to a Discourse Theory of Law and Democracy.* New Baskerville: MIT Press.

Hackett, R. A. (1985). A Hierarchy of Access: Aspects of Source Bias on Canadian TV News. *Journalism Quarterly, 62,* 256–265.

Hall, Stuart. (1973). *Encoding and Decoding in the Television Discourse.* Birmingham: Centre of Contemporary Cultural Studies, University of Birmingham.

Hallin, D. C., & Mancini, P. (2004). *Comparing Media Systems Three Models of Media and Politics.* Cambridge: Cambridge University Press.

Hänggli, R. (2012a). Key Factors in Frame Building—Model Specification. *American Behavioral Scientist* (Special Issue), 300–317.

Hänggli, R. (2012b). Key Factors in Frame-Building. In H. Kriesi (Ed.), *Political Communication in Direct Democratic Campaigns: Enlightening or Manipulating?* (pp. 125–142). Hampshire: Palgrave Macmillan.

Hänggli, R. (2019). Framing Strategies-Important Messages in Public Debates. In L. Bernhard, F. Fossati, R. Hänggli, & H. Kriesi (Eds.), *Debating Unemployment Policy: Political Communication and the Labour Market in Western Europe.* Cambridge: Cambridge University Press.

Hänggli, R., Bernhard, L., & Kriesi, H. (2012b). Construction of the Frames. In H. Kriesi (Ed.), *Political Communication in Direct Democratic Campaigns: Enlightening or Manipulating?* (pp. 69–81). Hampshire: Palgrave Macmillan.

Hänggli, R., & Fossati, F. (2019). Theoretical Framework: Production of Policy-Specific Political Communication. In L. Bernhard, F. Fossati, R. Hänggli, & H. Kriesi (Eds.), *Debating Unemployment Policy: Political Communication and the Labour Market in Western Europe.* Cambridge: Cambridge University Press.

Hänggli, R., & Kriesi, H. (2010). Political Framing Strategies and Their Impact on Media Framing in a Swiss Direct-Democratic Campaign. *Political Communication, 27*(2), 141–157.

Hänggli, R., & Kriesi, H. (2012). Frame Construction and Frame Promotion (Strategic Framing Choices). *American Behavioral Scientist* (Special Issue), 260–278.

Hänggli, R., Schemer, C., & Rademacher, P. (2012a). Toward a Methodological Integration in the Study of Political Campaign Communication. In H. Kriesi (Ed.), *Political Communication in Direct Democratic Campaigns: Enlightening or Manipulating?* (pp. 39–53). Hampshire: Palgrave Macmillan.

Hänggli, R., & van der Wurff, R. (2019). Quality of Public Debates. In L. Bernhard, F. Fossati, R. Hänggli, & H. Kriesi (Eds.), *Debating Unemployment Policy: Political Communication and the Labour Market in Western Europe.* Cambridge: Cambridge University Press.

Hardmeier, S. (2003). Amerikanisierung der Wahlkampfkommunikation: Einem Schlagwort auf der Spur. In P. Sciarini, S. Hardmeier, & A. Vatter (Eds.), *Schweizer Wahlen 1999* (pp. 219–255). Bern: Haupt.

Harmel, R., & Janda, K. (1994). An Integrated Theory of Party Goals and Party Change. *Jounral of Theoretical Politics, 6*(3), 259–287.

Helbing, D. (2016). Why We Need Democracy 2.0 and Capitalism 2.0 to Survive. *Jusletter IT, 2016,* 65–74.

Helbing, D., Frey, B. S., Gerd, H., Ernst, H., Michael, H., van den Yvonne, H., et al. (2017). Will Democracy Survive Big Data and Artificial Intelligence? *Scientific   American.*   https://www.scientificamerican.com/article/will-democracy-survive-big-data-and-artificial-intelligence/.

Helbing, D., & Poumaras, E. (2015): Build Digital Democracy. *Nature, 527,* 33–34. http://www.nature.com/news/society-build-digital-democracy-1.18690.

Helbling, M. (2008). *Practicing Citizenship and Heterogeneous Nationhood: Naturalizations in Swiss Municipalities.* Amsterdam: Amsterdam University Press.

Helbling, M., Höglinger, D., & Wüest, B. (2009). Public Debates Over Globalization. In H. Kriesi, E. Grande, M. Dolezal, M. Helbling, S. Hutter, D. Höglinger, & B. Wüest (Eds.), *Restructuring Political Conflict in the Age of Globalization.* Zurich: Unpublished Manuscript.

Helbling, M., & Kriesi, H. (2004). Staatsbürgerverständnis und politische Mobilisierung: Einbürgerungen in Schweizer Gemeinden, Schweiz. *Zeitschrift für Politikwissenschaft, 10*(4), 33–58.

Hirter, H., & Linder, W. (2008). Analysis of the Federal Votes of February 24, 2008 (Analyse der eidgenössischen Abstimmungen vom 24. Februar 2008). *Vox Analysis.* Berne: University of Berne.

Hobolt, S. B. (2016). The Brexit Vote: A Divided Nation, a Divided Continent. *Journal of European Public Policy, 23*(9), 1259–1277.

Hobolt, S., & Brouard, S. (2011). Contesting the European Union? Why the Dutch and the French Rejected the European Constitution. *Political Research Quarterly, 64*(2), 309–322.

Hofstetter, B., & Schönhagen, P. (2017). When Creative Potentials are Being Undermined by Commercial Imperatives: Change and Resistance in Six Cases of Newsroom Reorganization. *Digital Journalism, 5*(1), 44–60.

Höglinger, D. (2008). Verschafft die direkte Demokratie den Benachteiligten mehr Gehör? Der Einfluss institutioneller Rahmenbedingungen auf die mediale Präsenz politsicher Akteure. *Swiss Political Science Review, 14*(2), 207–243.

Imhof, K., Lucht, J., Udris, L., Rohner, A., & Vetsch, A. (2008). *Democracy in the Media Society: Changing Media Structures—Changing Political Communication?.* Zurich: NCCR-Democracy.

Iyengar, S. (1991). *Is Anyone Responsible? How Television Frames Political Issues.* Chicago: The University of Chicago Press.

Iyengar, S., & Kinder, D. R. (1987). *News That Matters: Television and American Opinion.* Chicago: University of Chicago Press.

Iyengar, S., & McGrady, J. A. (2007). *Media Politics: A Citizen's Guide.* New York: W. W. Norton.

Iyengar, S., & Valentino, N. A. (2000). Who Says What? Source Credibility as a Mediator of Campaign Advertising. In A. Lupia, M. D. McCubbins, & S. L. Popkin (Eds.), *Elements of Reason: Cognition, Choice, and the Bounds of Rationality* (pp. 108–129). Cambridge, MA: Cambridge University Press.

Jackson, D. (2011). Strategic News Frames and Public Policy Debates: Press and Television News Coverage of the Euro in the UK. *Communications, 36*(2), 169–193.

Jacoby, W. G. (1988). The Impact of Party Identification on Issue Attitudes. *American Journal of Political Science, 32*(3), 643–661.

Jacobs, L. R., & Shapiro, R. Y. (2000). *Politicians Don't Pander.* Chicago: University of Chicago Press.

Jarren, O. (2018). Kommunikationspolitik für die Kommunikationsgesellschaft. Verantwortungskultur durch Regulierung. *Aus Politik und Zeitgeschichte, 68*, H. 40–41, S. 23–28.

Jarren, O., & Donges, P. (2002). *Politische Kommunikation in der Mediengesellschaft: Eine Einführung. Band 1: Verständnis, Rahmen und Strukturen. Band 2: Akteure, Prozesse und Inhalte.* Wiesbaden: Verlag für Sozialwissenschaften.

Jasper, J. M. (2006). *Getting Your Way: Strategic Dilemmas in the Real World* (Vol. 9). Chicago: University of Chicago Press.

Jerit, J. (2008). Issue Framing and Engagement: Rhetorical Strategy in Public Policy Debates. *Political Behaviour, 30,* 1–24.

Jerit, J. (2009). How Predictive Appeals Shape Policy Opinions. *American Journal of Political Science, 53*(2), 411–426.

Johnson, J. B., & Joslyn, R. A. (1991). *Political Science Research Methods.* Washington, DC: Congressional Quarterly.

Kahn, K. F., & Kenney, P. (1999). *The Spectacle of U.S. Senate Campaigns.* Princeton, NJ: Princeton University Press.

Kaid, L. L., & Strömbäck, J. (2008). Election News Coverage Around the World: A Comparative Perspective. In J. Strömbäck & L. L. Kaid (Eds.), *The Handbook of Election News Coverage Around the World.* New York: Routledge.

Kaplan, N., Park, D. K., & Ridout, T. N. (2006). Dialogue in American Campaigns? An Examination of Issue Convergence in Candidate Television Advertising. *American Journal of Political Science, 50*(3), 724–736.

Keele, L., & Wolak, J. (2008). Contextual Sources of Ambivalence. *Political Psychology, 29*(5), 653–673.

Kepplinger, H. M. (1998). Inszenierung. In O. Jarren, U. Sarcinelli, & U. Saxer (Eds.), *Politische Kommunikation in der demokratischen Gesellschaft. Ein Handbuch mit Lexikonteil* (pp. 662–663). Wiesbaden: Opladen.

Kepplinger, H. M., & Habermeier, J. (1995). The Impact of Key Events on the Presentation of Reality. *European Journal of Communication, 10*(3), 371–390.

Khanna, P. (2017). *Technocracy in America: Rise of the Info-State.* CreateSpace.

Kinder, D. R. (1998). Communication and Opinion. *Annual Review of Political Science, 1,* 167–197.

Kinder, D. R. (2003). Communication and Politics in the Age of Information. In D. O. Sears, L. Huddy, & R. Jervis (Eds.), *Oxford Handbook of Political Psychology* (pp. 357–393). Oxford: Oxford University Press.

Kinder, D. R., & Sanders, L. M. (1990). Mimicking Political Debate with Survey Questions: The Case of White Opinion on Affirmative Action for Blacks. *Social Cognition, 8,* 73–103.

King, G., & Zeng, L. (2001). Logistic Regression in Rare Events Data. *Political Analysis, 9*(2), 137–163.

King, G., Keohane, R. O., & Verba, S. (1994). *Designing Social Inquiry: Scientific Infer-Ence in Qualitative Research.* Princeton, NJ: Princeton University Press.

Kiousis, S., Mitrook, M., Wu, X., & Seltzer, T. (2006). First- and Second-Level Agenda-Building and Agenda-Setting Effects: Exploring the Linkages Among Candidate News Releases, Media Coverage, and Public Opinion During the 2002 Florida Gubernatorial Election. *Journal of Public Relations Research, 18*(3), 265–285.

Klinger, U. (2013). Mastering the Art of Social Media. *Information, Communication & Society, 16*(5), 717–736.

Koopmans, R. (2004). Movements and Media: Selection Processes and Evolutionary Dynamics in the Public Sphere. *Theory and Society, 33*(3/4), 367–391.

Koopmans, R., Statham, P., Giugni, M., & Passy, F. (2005). *Contested Citizenship. Immigration and Cultural Diversity in Europe*. Minneapolis: University of Minnesota Press.

Kriesi, H. (1998). Einleitung. In H. Kriesi, W. Linder, & U. Klöti (Eds.), *Schweizer Wahlen 1995* (pp. 1–16). Bern: Haupt.

Kriesi, H. (2005). *Direct Democratic Choice: The Swiss Experience*. Lanham, MD: Lexington Books.

Kriesi, H. (2009). The Role of the Federal Government in Direct-Democratic Campaigns. In N. Stéphane & V. Frédéric (Eds.), *Rediscovering Public Law and Public Administration in Comparative Policy Analysis: A Tribute to Peter Knoepfel* (pp. 79–96). Bern: Verlag Haupt.

Kriesi, H. (2010a). The Role of Predispositions. In H. Kriesi (Ed.), *Enlightening or Manipulating?* (pp. 143–167). Hampshire: Palgrave Macmillan.

Kriesi, H. (2010b). Conclusion. In H. Kriesi (Ed.), *Enlightening or Manipulating?* (pp. 225–240). Hampshire: Palgrave Macmillan.

Kriesi, H., Adam, S., & Jochum, M. (2006). Comparative Analysis of Policy Networks in Western Europe. *Journal of European Public Policy, 13*(3), 341–361.

Kriesi, H., & Bernhard, L. (2012). The Context of the Campaigns. In H. Kriesi (Ed.), *Political Communication in Direct-Democratic Campaigns: Enlightening or Manipulating?* (pp. 17–38). Hampshire: Palgrave Macmillan.

Kriesi, H., Bernhard, L., & Hänggli, R. (2009). The Politics of Campaigning— Dimensions of Strategic Action. In F. Marcinkowski & B. Pfetsch (Eds.), *Politik in der Mediendemokratie*. Wiesbaden: VS Verlag für Sozialwissenschaften.

Kriesi, H., Fossati, F., & Bernhard, L. (2019). The Political Contexts of the National Policy Debates. In L. Bernhard, F. Fossati, R. Hänggli, & Hp. Kriesi (Eds.), *Debating Unemployment Policy: Political Communication and the Labour Market in Western Europe* (pp. 43–70). Cambridge: Cambridge University Press.

Kriesi, H., Grande, E., Lachat, R., Dolezal, M., Bornschier, S., & Frey, T. (2008). *West European Politics in the Age of Globalization*. Cambridge University Press.

Kriesi, H., & Hänggli, R. (2019). The Positioning of the Actors in the Public Debates. In L. Bernhard, F. Fossati, R. Hänggli, & H. Kriesi (Eds.), *Debating Unemployment Policy: Political Communication and the Labour Market in Western Europe*. Cambridge: Cambridge University Press.

Kriesi, H., & Trechsel, A. H. (2008). *The Politics of Switzerland*. Cambridge: Cambridge University Press.

Kühne, R., Schemer, C., Matthes, J., & Wirth, W. (2011). Affective Priming in Political Campaigns: How Campaign-Induced Emotions Prime Political Opinions. *International Journal of Public Opinion Research, 23*(4), 485–507.

Künzler, M. (2005). *Das schweizerische Mediensystem im Wandel: Herausforderungen, Chancen, Zukunftsperspektiven.* Bern: Haupt.

Lang, G. E., & Lang, K. (1981). Watergate: An Exploration of the Agenda-Building Process. In M. E. McCombs & D. L. Protess (Eds.), *Agenda Setting: Readings on Media, Public Opinion and Policymaking* (pp. 277–289). Hillsdale, NJ: Erlbaum.

Lawrence, R. (2000). *The Politics of Force: Media and the Construction of Police Brutality.* Berkeley: University of California Press.

Lenz, G. S. (2009). Learning and Opinion Change, Not Priming: Reconsidering the Priming Hypothesis. *American Journal of Political Science, 53*(4), 821–837.

Lenz, G. (2012). *Follow the Leader?* Cambridge: Cambridge University Press.

Lijphart, A. (1971). Comparative Politics and the Comparative Method. *The American Political Science Review, 65,* 682–693.

Linder, W. (1999). *Schweizerische Demokratie - Institutionen, Prozesse, Perspektiven.* Bern.

Linder, W., Zürcher, R., & Bolliger, C. (2008). *Gespaltene Schweiz- geeinte Schweiz. Gesellschaftliche Spaltungen und Konkordanz bei den Volksabstimmungen seit 1874.* Baden: hier + jetzt.

Lippmann, W. (1947 [1922]). *Public Opinion.* New York: Macmillan.

Livingston, S., & Bennett, L. W. (2003). Gatekeeping, Indexing, and Live-Event News: Is Technology Altering the Construction of News? *Political Communication, 20,* 363–380.

Lodge, M., & Hamill, R. (1986). A Partisan Schema for Political Information Processing. *The American Political Science Review, 80*(2), 505–520.

Long, S. J., & Freese, J. (2006). *Regression Models for Categorical Dependent Variables Using Stata.* College Station, TX: Stata Press.

Longchamp, C., Bucher, M., Ratelband-Pally, S., & Imfeld, M. (2008). Meinungsumschwung bei Gesundheitsartikel und Einbürgerungsinitiative. Stabile Mehrheit gegen die Initiative „Volkssouveränität statt Behördenpropaganda". *Medienbericht* zur 2. Welle der Trendstudie „Abstimmungen vom 1. Juni 2008" im Auftrag der SRG SSR idée suisse. Gfs. bern.

Lucht, J., & Udris, L. (2008). *Democracy in the Media Society: Changing Media Structures—Changing Political Communication?* Zurich: University of Zurich, Forschungsbereiche Öffentlichkeit und Gesellschaft (fög).

Lupia, A. (2016). *Uninformed.* Cambridge: Cambridge University Press.

Maatsch, S. (2007). The Struggle to Control Meanings: The French Debate on the European Constitution in the Mass Media. *Perspectives on European Politics and Society, 8*(3), 261–280.

Marcinkowski, F. (2006). Mediensystem und politische Kommunikation. In U. Klöti, P. Knöpfel, H. Kriesi, W. Linder, Y. Papadopoulos, & P. Sciarini (Eds.), *Handbuch der Schweizer Politik* (4th ed., pp. 394–424). Zürich: NZZ-Verlag.

Marr, M., Wyss, V., Blum, R., & Bonfadelli, H. (2000). Die Berufsrealität der Medienschaffenden in der Schweiz In M. Marr, V. Wyss, R. Blum, & H. Bonfadelli (Eds.), *Journalisten in der Schweiz. Eigenschaften, Einstellungen, Einflüsse* (Vol. Forschungsfeld Kommunikation Bd. 13). Konstanz: UVK Medien.

Marquis, L., Schaub, H.-P., & Gerber, M. (2011). The Fairness of Media Coverage in Question: An Analysis of Referendum Campaigns on Welfare State Issues in Switzerland. *Swiss Political Science Review, 17*(2), 128–163.

Matthes, J. (2009). What's in a Frame? A Content Analysis of Media Framing Studies in the World's Leading Communication Journals 1990–2005. *Journalism & Mass Communication Quarterly, 86*(2), 349–367.

Matthes, J., & Kohring, M. (2008). The Content Analysis of Media Frames: Toward Improving Reliability and Validity. *Journal of Communication, 58*, 258–279.

Mazzoleni, G. (1987). Media Logic and Party Logic in Campaign Coverage: The Italian General Election of 1983. *European Journal of Communication, 2*, 81–103.

Mazzoleni, G., & Schulz, W. (1999). "Mediatization" of Politics: A Challenge for Democracy? *Political Communication, 16*(3), 247–261.

McClosky, H., & Chong, D. (1985). Similarities and Differences Between Left-Wing and Right-Wing Radicals. *British Journal of Political Science, 15*(3), 329–363.

McCombs, M. E., & Shaw, D. L. (1972). The Agenda-Setting Function of Mass Media. *Public Opinion Quarterly, 36*(2), 176–187.

McQuail, D. (1992). *Media Performance: Mass Communication and the Public Interest.* London: Sage.

Media Use Index. (2017, November). https://www.yr-group.ch/mui/yr-group-switzerland-publiziert-media-use-index-2017.

Meier, W. A. (2004). Switzerland. In M. Kelly, G. Mazzoleni, & D. McQuail (Eds.), *The Media in Europe* (pp. 248–260). London: Sage.

Mermin, J. (1999). *Debating War and Peace: Media Coverage of U.S. Intervention in the Post-Vietnam Era.* Princeton, NJ: Princeton University Press.

Mettler, S. (2018). *The Government-Citizen Disconnect.* Russell Sage Foundation.

Milic, T., & Scheuss, U. (2006). Analysis of the Federal Votes of September 24, 2006 (Analyse der eidgenössischen Abstimmungen vom 24. September 2006). *Vox Analysis.* Zurich: University of Zurich.

Milic, T., Rousselot, B., & Vatter, A. (2014). *Handbuch der Abstimmungsforschung.* Zurich: NZZ Libro.

Möckli, S. (1994). *Direkte Demokratie. Ein Vergleich der Einrichtungen und Verfahren in der Schweiz und Kalifornien, unter Berücksichtigung von Frankreich, Italien, Dänemark, Irland, Österreich, Liechtenstein und Australien.* Bern: Paul Haupt.

Mutz, D. (2006). *Hearing the Other Side: Deliberative Versus Participatory Democracy.* New York: Cambridge University Press.

Nassmacher, K.-H. (2002). Die Kosten der Parteitätigkeit in westlichen Demokratien. *Österreichische Zeitschrift für Politikwissenschaft, 31*, 7–20.

Neidhardt, F. (1994). Öffentlichkeit, öffentliche Meinung, soziale Bewegungen. In F. Neidhardt (Ed.), *Kölner Zeitschrift für Soziologie und Sozialpsychologie* (Vol. Sonderheft 34, pp. 7–41). Opladen and Wiesbaden: Westdeutscher Verlag.

Neidhart, L. (1970). *Plebiszit und pluralitäre Demokratie: eine Analyse der Funktion des schweizerischen Gesetzesreferendum.* Bern: Francke.

Nelson, T. E. (2004). Policy Goals, Public Rhetoric, and Political Attitudes. *The Journal of Politics, 66*(2), 581–605.

Nelson, T. E., Clawson, R. A., & Oxley, Z. M. (1997a). Media Framing of a Civil Liberties Conflict and Its Effect on Tolerance. *American Political Science Review, 91*(3), 567–583.

Nelson, T. E., Oxley, Z. M., & Clawson, R. A. (1997b). Toward a Psychology of Framing Effects. *Political Behavior, 19*(3), 221–246.

Norris, P., Curtice, J., Sanders, D., Scammell, M., & Semetko, H. A. (1999). *On Message: Communicating the Campaign.* London: Sage.

Olson, M. (1971 [1965]). *The Logic of Collective Action: Public Goods and the Theory of Groups* (Rev. ed.). Cambridge, MA: Harvard University Press.

O'Keefe, D. J. (2002). *Persuasion* (2nd ed.). Thousand Oaks, CA: Sage.

Page, S. E. (2008): *The Difference: How the Power of Diversity Creates Better Groups, Firms, Schools, and Societies.* Princeton, NJ: Princeton University Press.

Pan, Z., & Kosicki, G. M. (1993). Framing Analysis: An Approach to News Discourse. *Political Communication, 10*(1), 55–75.

Pariser, E. (2011). *The Filter Bubble: What the Internet Is Hiding from You.* New York: Penguin Press.

Perloff, R. M. (2010). *The Dynamics of Persuasion. Communication and Attitudes in the 21st Century.* Routledge.

Perron, L. (2007). *How to Overcome the Power of Incumbency in Election Campaigns?.* Zürich: Institute of Political Science.

Petrocik, J. R. (1996). Issue Ownership in Presidential Elections, with a 1980 Case Study. *American Journal of Political Science, 40*(3), 825–850.

Pfetsch, B. (2003). Politische Kommunikationskultur; ein theoretisches Konzept zur vergleichenden Analyse politischer Kommunikationssysteme. In F. Esser & B. Pfetsch (Eds.), *Politische Kommunikation im internationalen Vergleich; Grundlagen, Anwendungen, Perspektiven* (pp. 393–418). Wiesbaden: Westdeutscher Verlag.

Puppis, M., Schönhagen, P., Fürst, S., Hofstetter, B., & Meissner, M. (2014). Arbeitsbedingungen und Berichterstattungsfreiheit in journalistischen Organisationen. *Beiträge und Studien Medienforschung*. Bundesamt für Kommunikation (BAKOM).

Puppis, M., Schenk, M., & Hofstetter, B. (Eds.). (2017, December). *Medien und Meinungsmacht* (TA-SWISS, Vol. 65). Zürich: vdf. https://www.research-collection.ethz.ch/bitstream/handle/20.500.11850/125191/eth-50273-01.pdf.

Price, V., & Tewksbury, D. (1997). News Values and Public Opinion: A Theoretical Account of Media Priming and Framing. In G. A. Barnett & F. J. Boster (Eds.), *Progress in Communication Sciences: Advances in Persuasion* (Vol. 13, pp. 173–212). Greenwich, CT: Ablex.

Putnam, R. (2000). *Bowling Alone: On the Internet's Social Capital*. New York: Simon & Schuster.

Rabe-Hesketh, S., & Skrondal, A. (2005). *Multilevel and Longitudinal Modeling Using Stata* (2nd ed.). College Station, TX: Stata Press.

Rahn, W. M. (1993). The Role of Partisan Stereotypes in Information Processing About Political Candidates. *American Journal of Political Science, 37*, 472–496.

Reinemann, C., Fawzi, N., & Röder, P. (2012). Mehr Beteiligung = bessere Berichterstattung? Ein Vergleich der Presseberichterstattung überdie parlamentarische Entscheidung und den Volksentscheid zum Nichtraucherschutzgesetz in Bayern. *Studies in Communication/Media, 1*(3–4), S. 351–380.

Riker, W. H. (1996). *The Strategy of Rhetoric: Campaigning for the American Constitution*. New Haven, CT: Yale University Press.

Rohrschneider, R. (2002). Mobilizing Versus Chasing: How Do Parties Target Voters in Election Campaigns? *Electoral Studies, 21*, 367–382.

Rudolph, T. J. (2005). Group Attachment and the Reduction of Value-Driven Ambivalence. *Political Psychology, 26*, 905–928.

Scammell, M. (1999). Political Marketing: Lessons for Political Science. *Political Studies, 47*(4), 718–739.

Scharpf, F. W. (1970). *Demokratietheorie zwischen Utopie und Anpassung*. Konstanzer Universitätsreden 25. Konstanz: Universitätsverlag.

Scharpf, F. W. (1999). *Governing in Europe: Effective and Democratic?* Oxford and New York: Oxford University Press.

Scharpf, F. W. (1998). *Interdependence and Democratic Legitimation* (MPIfG Working Paper, 98/2).

Schattschneider, E. E. (1988 [1960]). *The Semisovereign People: Realist's View of Democracy in America*. South Melbourne: Wadsworth Thomson Learning.

Scheufele, D. A. (1999). Framing as a Theory of Media Effects. *Journal of Communication, 49*(1), 103–122.

Scheufele, D. A. (2000). Agenda-Setting, Priming, and Framing Revisited: Another Look at Cognitive Effects of Political Communication. *Mass Communication and Society, 2&3*(3), 297–316.

Schmitt-Beck, R., & Pfetsch, B. (1994). Politische Akteure und die Medien der Massenkommunikation. Zur Generierung von Öffentlichkeit in Wahlkämpfen. In F. Neidhardt (Ed.), *Öffentlichkeit, öffentliche Meinung, soziale Bewegungen. Kölner Zeitschrift für Soziologie und Sozialpsychologie, Sonderheft 34* (pp. 106–138). Opladen and Wiesbaden: Westdeutscher Verlag.

Schneider, W. (1972). *Electoral Behavior and Political Development.* Harvard: Center for International Affairs, Harvard University.

Schudson, M. (1998). *The Good Citizen: A History of American Civic Life.* Cambridge: Harvard University Press.

Schudson, M. (2000, Spring). Overcoming Voter Isolation: Citizenship Beyond the Polls. *The Responsive Community*, 38–45.

Schulz, W. (1976). *Die Konstruktion von Realität in den Nachrichtenmedien.* Freiburg and München: Verlag Karl Alber.

Schulz, W. (1989). Massenmedien und Realität. *Kölner Zeitschrift für Soziologie und Sozialpsychologie, Sonderheft, 30,* 135–149.

Schulz, W. (1997). *Politische Kommunikation theoretische Ansätze und Ergebnisse empirischer Forschung zur Rolle der Massenmedien in der Politik.* Opladen: Westdeutscher Verlag.

Schumpeter, J. A. (1976 [1942]). *Capitalism, Socialism and Democracy.* London: Allen & Unwin.

Schwarz, N., & Clore, G. L. (1983). Mood, Misattribution, and Judgments of Well-Being: Informative and Directive Functions of Affective States. *Journal of Personality and Social Psychology, 45,* 513–523.

Seeberg, H. B., Slothuus, R., & Stubager, R. (2017). Do Voters Learn? Evidence that Voters Respond Accurately to Changes in Political Parties' Policy Positions. *West European Politics, 40*(2), 336–356.

Selb, P. (2003). *Agenda-Setting Prozesse im Wahlkampf.* Bern: Haupt.

Selb, P., Kriesi, H., Hänggli, R., & Marr, M. (2009). Partisan Choices in a Direct-Democratic Campaign. *European Political Science Review, 1*(1), 155–172.

Semetko, H. A., & Valkenburg, P. M. (2000). Framing European Politics: A Content Analysis of Press and Television News. *Journal of Communication, 50,* 93–109.

Seymour-Ure, C. (1974). *The Political Impact of Mass Media.* London: Constable.

Shen, F., & Edwards, H. H. (2005). Economic Individualism, Humanitarianism, and Welfare Reform: A Value-Based Account of Framing Effects. *Journal of Communication, 55*(4), 795–809.

Shoemaker, P. J., & Reese, S. D. (1996). *Mediating the Message: Theories of Influences on Mass Media Content* (2nd ed.). White Plains, NY: Longman.

Sides, J. (2006). The Origins of Campaign Agendas. *British Journal of Political Science, 36*(3), 407–436.

Sides, J. (2007). The Consequences of Campaign Agendas. *American Politics Research, 35*(4), 465–488.

Siegfried, C. (2009, December). Switzerland. *Press in Switzerland.* http://www.pressreference.com/Sw-Ur/Switzerland.html.

Sigal, L. (1973). *Reporters and Officials.* Lexington, MA: D.C. Heath.

Sigelman, L., & Buell, E. H. (2004). Avoidance or Engagement? Issue Convergence in U.S. Presidential Campaigns, 1960–2000. *American Journal of Political Science, 48*(4), 650–661.

Simanowski, R. (2016). *Data Love: The Seduction and Betrayal of Digital Technologies.* New York: Columbia University Press.

Simon, A. (2002). *The Winning Message: Candidate Behavior, Campaign Discourse, and Democracy.* New York: Cambridge University Press.

Skowronski, J. J., & Carlston, D. E. (1989). Negativity and Extremity Biases Inv Impression Formation: A Review of Explanations. *Psychological Bulletin, 105*(1), 131–142.

Slothuus, R. (2008). More Than Weighting Cognitive Importance: A Dual-Process Model of Issue Framing Effects. *Political Psychology, 29*(1), 1–28.

Slothuus, R. (2010). When Can Political Parties Lead Public Opinion? Evidence from a Natural Experiment. *Political Communication, 27*(2), 158–177.

Smith, G. (1976). The Functional Properties of the Referendum. *European Journal of Political Research, 4*(1), 1–23.

Smith, D. A., & Tolbert, C. (2001). The Initiative to Party: Partisanship and Ballot Initiatives in California. *Party Politics, 7,* 738–757.

Smith, D. A., & Tolbert, C. (2004). *Educated by Initiative: The Effects of Direct Democracy on Citizens and Political Organizations in the American States.* Ann Arbor: University of Michigan Press.

Sniderman, P. A. (2000). Taking Sides: A Fixed Choice Theory of Political Reasoning In A. Lupia, M. D. McCubbins, & S. P. Popkin (Eds.), *Elements of Reason: Cognition, Choice, and the Bounds of Rationality* (pp. 67–84). Cambridge, UK: Cambridge University Press.

Sniderman, P. M., & Theriault, S. M. (2004). The Structure of Political Argument and the Logic of Issue Framing. In P. M. Sniderman & S. M. Theriault (Eds.), *Studies in Public Opinion: Attitudes, Nonattitudes, Measurement Error and Change* (pp. 133–165). Princeton, NJ: Princeton University Press.

Snow, D. A., & Benford, R. D. (1988). Ideology, Frame Resonance and Participant Mobilization. In B. Klandermans, H. Kriesi, & S. Tarrow (Eds.), *From Structure to Action: Social Movement Participation Across Cultures.* Greenwich, CT: JAI Press.

Steenbergen, M. (2008). *Count Models*. Bern: University Bern (Unpublished document).

Steenbergen, M., & Brewer, P. R. (2004). The Not-So-Ambivalent Public: Policy Attitudes in the Political Culture of Ambivalence. In W. E. Saris & P. M. Sniderman (Eds.), *Studies in Public Opinion. Attitudes, Nonattitudes, Measurement Errors, and Change* (pp. 93–132). Princeton, NJ: Princeton University Press.

Strömbäck, J., & Kaid, L. L. (2008). *The Handbook of Election News Coverage Around the World*. New York: Routledge.

Strömbäck, J., & Nord, L. W. (2006). Do Politicians Lead the Tango? A Study of the Relationship Between Swedish Journalists and Their Political Sources in the Context of Election Campaigns. *European Journal of Communication, 21*(2), 147–164.

Sunstein, C. R. (2001). *Republic.com*. Princeton, NJ: Princeton University Press.

Sunstein, C. R. (2017). *#Republic: Divided Democracy in the Age of Social Media*. Princeton, NJ: Princeton University Press.

Tillie, J. (1995). *Party Utility and Voting Behavior*. Amsterdam: Het Spinhuis.

Tilly, C. (1978). *From Mobilization to Revolution*. Boston, MA: Addison-Wesley.

Tilly, C. (1986). *The Contentious French*. Cambridge: Cambridge University Press.

Tilly, C. (1995). *Popular Contention in Great Britain, 1758–1834*. Cambridge: Cambridge University Press.

Tresch, A. (2007). *Öffentlichkeit und Sprachenvielfalt. Medienvermittelte Kommunikation zur Europapolitik in der Deutsch- und Westschweiz* (Doctoral thesis). Zurich: University of Zurich.

Tresch, A. (2009). Politicians in the Media: Determinants of Legislators' Prominence in Swiss Newspaper. *The International Journal of Press/Politics, 14*(1), 67–90.

Tresch, A. (2012). The (Partisan) Role of the Press in Direct Democratic Campaigns: Evidence from a Swiss Vote on European Integration. *Swiss Political Science Review, 18*(3), 287–304.

Tuchman, G. (1978). *Making News a Study in the Construction of Reality*. New York: The Free Press.

Van der Eijk, C., Van der Brug, W. W., Kroh, M., & Franklin, M. (2006). Rethinking the Dependent Variable in Voting Behavior: On the Measurement and Analysis of Electoral Utilities. *Electoral Studies, 25*(3), 424–447.

van der Wurff, R., De Swert, K., & Lecheler, S. (2016). News Quality and Public Opinion: The Impact of Deliberative Quality of News Media on Citizens' Argument Repertoire. *International Journal of Public Opinion Research, 30*(2), 233–256.

Van Schuur, W. H. (1993). Nonparametric Unfolding Models for Multicategory Data. *Political Analysis, 4*, 41–74.

Van Schuur, W. H., & Post, W. J. (1998). *MUDFOLD: A Program for Multiple Unidimensional Unfolding*. Version 4.0 [Software manual]. Groningen: ProGAMMA.

Vuong, Q. H. (1989). Likelihood Ratio Tests for Model Selection and Non-Nested Hypotheses. *Econometrica, 57*, 307–333.

Wahl-Jorgensen, K. (2007). *Journalists and the Public: Newsroom Culture, Letters to the Editor and Democracy*. Cresskill: Hampton Press.

Warren, M. (2017). A Problem-Based Approach to Democratic Theory. *American Political Science Review, 111*(1), 39–53.

Wassermann, S., & Faust, K. (1999). *Social Network Analysis: Methods and Applications*. Cambridge: Cambridge University Press.

Weaver, D. H., & Wilhoit, C. G. (1991). *The American Journalist: A Portrait of U.S. News People and Their Work* (2nd ed.). Bloomington: Indiana University Press.

WEMF. (2015). *MA Strategy 2014*. Zürich: WEMF.

WEMF. (2017). *MA Strategy*. Zürich: WEMF. https://wemf.ch/de/downloads/studien/ma-strategy/broschuere-ma-strategy.pdf.

Wessler, H. (2008). Investigating Deliberativeness Comparatively. *Political Communication, 25*(1), 1–22.

White, D. M. (1950). The "Gate Keeper": A Case Study in the Selection of News. *Journalism Quarterly, 27*, 383–390.

Wirth, W., Matthes, J., & Schemer, C. (2011). When Campaign Messages Meet Ideology: The Role of Arguments for Voting Behaviour. In H. Kriesi (Ed.), *Political Communication in Direct Democratic Campaigns: Enlightening or Manipulating?* (pp. 188–204). New York: Palgrave Macmillan.

Wirth, W., Schemer, C., Kühne, R., & Matthes, J. (2010). The Impact of Positive and Negative Affects in Direct-Democratic Campaigns. In H. Kriesi (Ed.), *Manipulation or Deliberation*. Zurich: Unpublished Manuscript.

Wolfsfeld, G. (1997). *Media and Political Conflict: News from the Middle East* (Reprint ed.). Cambridge, MA: Cambridge University Press.

Zaller, J. R. (2003). A New Standard of News Quality: Burglar Alarms for the Monitorial Citizen. *Political Communication, 20*, 109–130.

Zaller, J. R. (2005 [1992]). *The Nature and Origin of Public Opinion*. Cambridge: Cambridge University Press.

Zhang, W., Cao, X., & Tram, M. N. (2013). The Structural Features and the Deliberative Quality of Online Discussions. *Telematics and Informatics, 30*(2), 74–86.

INDEX

CPI Antony Rowe
Eastbourne, UK
November 27, 2019